Matthew Saad Muhammad

ALSO BY WILLIAM DETTLOFF
AND FROM MCFARLAND

Ezzard Charles: A Boxing Life (2015)

Matthew Saad Muhammad
Boxing's Miracle Man

WILLIAM DETTLOFF

McFarland & Company, Inc., Publishers
Jefferson, North Carolina

LIBRARY OF CONGRESS CATALOGUING-IN-PUBLICATION DATA

Names: Dettloff, William, author.
Title: Matthew Saad Muhammad : boxing's miracle man / William Dettloff.
Description: Jefferson, North Carolina : McFarland & Company, Inc., Publishers, 2023 | Includes bibliographical references and index.
Identifiers: LCCN 2023015417 | ISBN 9781476685250 (paperback : acid free paper) ∞
ISBN 9781476648767 (ebook)
Subjects: LCSH: Saad Muhammad, Matthew, 1954-2014. | African American boxers—Pennsylvania—Philadelphia—Biography.
Classification: LCC GV1132.S33 D48 2023 | DDC 796.83092 [B]—dc23/eng/20230414
LC record available at https://lccn.loc.gov/2023015417

BRITISH LIBRARY CATALOGUING DATA ARE AVAILABLE

ISBN (print) 978-1-4766-8525-0
ISBN (ebook) 978-1-4766-4876-7

© 2023 William Dettloff. All rights reserved

No part of this book may be reproduced or transmitted in any form or by any means, electronic or mechanical, including photocopying or recording, or by any information storage and retrieval system, without permission in writing from the publisher.

Front cover: Matthew Saad Muhammad (formerly Matthew Franklin) stands over David Lee Royster during their match at the Spectrum in Philadelphia in November 1977. (Photograph courtesy of John DiSanto) Cover design by Michael Kronenberg

Printed in the United States of America

*McFarland & Company, Inc., Publishers
Box 611, Jefferson, North Carolina 28640
www.mcfarlandpub.com*

To the forgotten pugs

Table of Contents

Acknowledgments   ix
Preface   1
Introduction   3

1. James City   5
2. The Juniper   15
3. From Paris to Missoula   24
4. Do You Want Me to Stop It?   40
5. Neanderthals Throwing Rocks   56
6. Tightrope   72
7. Thicker Than Water   83
8. Guns and Switchblades   96
9. MAPS   111
10. Roots   122
11. The End of Miracles   139
12. The Big Lie   149
13. What Goes Around   161
14. He's a Fighter   168
15. A Reckoning   181

Chapter Notes   193
Bibliography   203
Index   205

Acknowledgments

This work draws on the labor of a generation of newspaper boxing columnists, an occupation that no longer exists. My sympathies lie with future would-be biographers who sit down to write long-form profiles of today's prizefighters using internet articles and interviews as their primary sources. The good work done by guys on the boxing beat, specifically in and around Philadelphia and New York, served as a snapshot of events and reactions and points of view particular to Matthew Saad Muhammad's world and are thus untainted by the passage of time, which often brings with it new prejudices or spin or some contrivance born of ego.

This is not to say every column and fight report penned during Saad Muhammad's career is a perfect example of journalistic integrity; everything we write carries the imprint of its cultural and personal context and bias and is vulnerable to error. But they are time stamps applied by men whose job it was to supply their readership with compelling, accurate, informative copy on deadline. They were professionals, and without them, this work and others like it would have little or no protection from the vagaries of modernity.

So I am thankful for and praise the work of Tom Cushman, Jack McKinney, Michael Katz, and Lewis Freedman. I thank Rich Hofmann, Gene Courtney, and Bernard Fernandez. Same for Thom Greer, Bill Verigan, and Dick Young. So it goes too for Dick Weiss, Gary Smith, Stan Hochman, Chuck Newman, Skip Myslenski, and the dozens of other newspaper men who scribbled quotes onto little notepads and pounded out copy at ringside in the dead of night under a fog of cigarette smoke and adrenaline—on deadline—so that I could sit here, decades later, and at my leisure, more or less, peck away at a rate of, sometimes if I was lucky, a page or two a week. Gods among men.

Almost no biography can be all it is possible of without the participation of those to whom the subject was close, so I must acknowledge the help I received in this regard from two men—Mustafa Ameen,

Matt's right-hand man during his championship run and his closest friend, and Shawn Darling, who employed Matt for several years during the bad times and worked to restore in him the dignity and sense of self-worth he deserved but frequently found elusive. Both Ameen and Darling answered every email, every call, every text with generosity and patience with no expectation beyond helping me share Matt's story. Matt was fortunate to have them in his life, as was I when it came time to write about it. They have my unending gratitude, as does Larry Tornambe, another tireless and valuable resource, and John Disanto too.

My thanks also to Zakiyyah Mitchell, Matthew Jr., and Michael, three of Matt's children who were instrumental in providing detail I couldn't have obtained anywhere else. Ditto for his ex-wives, Michelle LeViege-Cortija and Elaine Austin, and his buddy and main sparring partner, Tony Green. My gratitude also to Nick (Sonny) Belfiore, Jr., Seiyid Bilal Muhammad, and dozens of fight game characters, roustabouts, and no-goodniks who provided detail large and small, some in interviews, some in stories that captured them living their lives, impossibly almost, in the insane whirlwind that is the fight game. What a business this is.

My thanks also to my sister and faithful cheerleader Mary Dettloff-Reilly; my agent, Richard Henshaw; my editor, Charlie Perdue; and my children, Kayla, Angelina, and Billy Boy, who endured, with mostly good cheer, the mood swings, absent-mindedness, and bleakness of mind that inevitably accompany my writing a book. Ditto for my wife, Kim, who one would think by this time would have come to her senses and abandoned me for one not so enamored of the morose study of long-gone men revered for knocking loose another's brain stem. Her love for and dedication to our family makes what I do possible. Put another way, I couldn't do what I do if she didn't do what she does.

Preface

In 2004, I was writing a series of "Where Are They Now?" features for HBO's boxing website when my editor suggested Matthew Saad Muhammad. I contacted him through Shawn Darling and Matthew was polite, upbeat, and cooperative. When the formal interview concluded, we chatted a bit and he asked me if I'd be interested in working with him to write a book about his life and career.

I had just worked on a biography with another ex-fighter, and after 18 months we abandoned it when we couldn't find a publisher. And the subject of that book was more famous than Matt (if less accomplished). If we couldn't get that guy's story published, what were the chances with a book about Matt? It didn't help that Matt had been fully retired at that time for only 12 years, thus precluding the "nostalgia" hook. There was just no reason to think it would get published.

I passed.

I felt embarrassed for Matt for asking and then too for getting turned down. I had watched him fight on television during my teens and knew all about his heroics in the ring and also what he'd gone through as a child. For years, I rooted against Dwight Muhammad Qawi solely because he dominated Matt in their two fights and seemed to so enjoy doing it. Matt wasn't my favorite fighter while I was growing up—that was George Foreman—but he was one of them. Seriously, who could root against him?

So it is not without some regret that I sat down to start writing Matt's story 16 years after he asked me to and six years after his death. I still think we'd have struggled to find a publisher, but maybe we'd have gotten lucky and Matt could have made a few dollars out of it. He sorely needed it, and I would have been happy to help him. He deserved that and more.

While researching this book, I found that Matt started talking about book deals and screenplays as early as the 1980s, before he'd even lost the championship. Paul Trace, his photographer, told me he accompanied Matt and Bilal Muhammad, his manager, to a pair of meetings in California with a couple of so-called movie producers who told Matt they were going to make a film about his life. "These guys were bullshitting him and Bilal like you would never believe," Trace told me.

I discovered too that over the years, Matt had asked at least three other people to help him write his story. For various reasons, those plans never worked out either. It would be a happier story for everyone involved if Matt had lived long enough to see a book about his life come together no matter who wrote it. He had to know it would happen eventually. That's why he kept asking, kept trying. He knew a good story when he saw one, even if no one else did.

So why now?

The generation of fight fans who grew up watching Matt go to war on free television on Saturday afternoons is now made up of men in their 50s, and I am included in their numbers. Like every generation before ours (and certainly the generations that come after too), we believe the markers of our youth represent if not a pinnacle, then something of a quality markedly superior to what exists today. Our music was better. Our cars were better. The way we were raised was better. Boxing was better. Everything was better—not because we were young, mind you, but because they were just, well, better. For men of a certain age, this habit of reminiscence becomes chronic. We fill our days with "If only things were now the way they were when I was young."

The older we get, the more we look back. Everyone who was around to see Matthew Saad Muhammad taking care of business would like to go back to that time, to relive it, especially those of us who did so with adulthood still an unfathomable state to be navigated somewhere in the distant fuzzy future, where everything was still possible.

Introduction

The only story more common to prizefighters than rags to riches is rags to rags. So in that respect, Matthew Saad Muhammad was better off than most. For every fighter who makes it to the top, earns a fortune, and squanders it, there are hundreds who never make more than a few hundred a fight and carry on anyway for the thrill it gives them and the demons it quiets, temporarily or otherwise. Prizefighting is a niche sport in America these days and true fight gyms disappear at a depressing rate, but there are few things better for the souls and futures of young, forlorn boys than the company of other boys in a gym dedicated to honing savage instincts into a skill requiring discipline and a bit of courage.

Of course, it is rare that boys (and girls) who come from families of means find themselves in a fight gym in the heart of a ghetto (because that's where all the real gyms are). So the ability to imagine oneself fighting out of a life of poverty and into a Bentley is, for a certain type of very serious and desperate boy, part of the allure of the fight game. The odds are against him, but they were also against the comparatively few who made it and were able to live large until the money ran out. The odds are greater still against him living within his means and dying before the money is completely gone, and you can count probably on one hand in the whole modern history of prizefighting those who were able to pull it off and also escape cognitive degradation.

But no man fights solely for the money. Certainly, there are easier ways to make a living, and as George Foreman once observed, once you answer the bell for the opening round, you're getting your purse almost no matter what happens next. It was always "what happened next" that made Matthew Saad Muhammad the prizefighter and champion he was. Money makes the world go 'round, but there's not enough of it in the world to pull a man off the canvas when he's fallen face first or to make him keep punching through a waterfall of blood and bone-deep exhaustion. That comes from somewhere else, some place deep and feral, where money has no meaning.

It was always going to end up the way it did for Matthew Saad Muhammad (or, if you prefer, Matthew Franklin, and we'll get to that shortly). Like most prizefighters who make millions, he didn't have the type of personality or guidance he needed to make his fortune last, and even if he did, there is also the requirement that he constantly be on guard against those trying to steal it from him. Such is business. But it wasn't just that he wasn't protective of what he earned; he was the opposite.

"He was always childlike. People took advantage of him everywhere he went," one source who knew Matt well told me. "If anyone needed a full-time body guard, it was him; he was always a child. He never was really an adult." The same source said, and this is no coincidence, that everyone loved Matt, that his smile lit up the room, and wherever he went, people wanted to be around him.

Promoter J Russell Peltz used similar language to describe the Matt he knew before his championship reign. "He was a friendly kid. Just like a big kid." Matt went with Peltz to New Orleans for Marvin Johnson's title-winning fight against Víctor Galíndez in 1979. "He was starting to make money and carried around this little checkbook with him, and whenever he would go into a store, he would whip out his checkbook and write checks. I mean he was like a kid; it's just the way he was."

It's easy to blame boxing for how things turned out, but it must be remembered that for a time, Matt lived a princely life, traveling the world, bedding beautiful women, making millions, hearing crowds chant his name. Considering his origin, it's miraculous he made it out of South Philly at all. He might have lived an unremarkable life if not for what he was able to do in a prize ring. The graveyards are full of men who would have given anything to live for one day the way he did from, say, 1978 to early '81. Yes, it ended badly and too soon, but doesn't it for everyone?

* * *

My affection for form made me want to refer to this work's subject by his surname almost exclusively in the text and his first name when appropriate. His conversion to Islam—and consequent name change from Matthew Franklin to Matthew Saad Muhammad—made this tricky but not unmanageable. However, complicating things further was that some people in his life called him Matt or Matthew, even after his conversion, and others Saad. Moreover, after his conversion, there were too many "Muhammads" in play to simply refer to him by that surname without confusing the reader. Last, several sources told me that later in his life, he renounced Islam, though he never formally or legally changed his name back to Matthew Franklin. For all these reasons, I refer to him throughout the text as Matt or Matthew, form be damned.

Chapter 1

James City

Interval between Onset of Symptoms and Death: "Years"

It was a nothing punch, really, the one that put him down. He'd taken harder ones than that all night, dozens of them. He'd taken harder ones than that for 28 years. They'd warned him not to fight this guy, that he didn't need him to get the big-money fight next. It was the suits who pushed for it. He could've refused, but he needed the money. He always needed the money. Hell, he'd been up against it so many times that he'd lost count, and he'd always survived. But he was tired, so tired,[1] and when he went down, he did it slowly, letting go little by little and then all at once.

* * *

The clerk at the registrar's office had misspelled Matilda Murphey's surname. The top part was all right, but he'd typed "Muprhey" on the lower part, right above where she had to sign. She could have asked him to correct it, but it was already typed up. He'd probably charge her to do it over. She signed it and slid it back over to him so he could sign where he had to, it would be official, and she could be on her way.

Earlier that morning, December 6, 1917, a munitions ship had exploded in Halifax, Nova Scotia, in Canada, killing almost 2,000 people. It was a big story in Canada, but to the folks in James City, it may as well have been a million miles away. And to Matilda in particular, there was nothing more important in the world than the event that brought her that morning to the registrar's office. Her daughter, Roberta Gunner, was getting married. It was time. She was 23 years old, as was the boy she was marrying, Nathaniel Loach. They both had been born and raised in James City, and their families knew each other, as most of the families did. The boy's parents, Willie and Henrietta Loach, had been born and raised there too, as had his grandparents, Shade and Rosa Loach.

All the families still in James City in 1917 were holdouts, the hard cases that refused to be driven off the land. And why should they? They'd built houses and churches and had babies there and raised them to be God-fearing people. Even if sharecropping wasn't far from being a slave, James City was home. It wasn't what they'd hoped it would be back when it all started, but is anything ever?

A lot of the holdouts remembered what it had been like in the beginning in James City, and those who were too young to remember had parents and grandparents who were there and told them the stories. They told them what it was like in 1862 when the rumors started spreading through the slave plantations in northeast North Carolina that Union soldiers had taken Roanoke Island and were headed to nearby New Bern. There had been rumors before; there were always rumors because people had to have a reason to live. But this time, the rumors were true.

In New Bern, the Neuse and Trent Rivers came together, and the Union army wanted the port there for moving supplies and men. On March 14, they ran off the Confederates defending New Bern and took the city. It wasn't long before the news reached the plantations, and men and women who knew no other life than a slave's life heard that Union soldiers were treating all escaped slaves as freedmen. Soon, runaway slaves by the hundreds from all over eastern North Carolina poured into New Bern, eager to start their lives as free people. For some, that meant joining the Union army to fight the Confederates; for others, it meant a chance to build a home and work the land—*their* land.

And they kept coming. So many former slaves arrived in New Bern that Union army officials had to establish a settlement along the Trent River. The land had belonged to Peter G. Evans, a Confederate colonel, but as far as the Union soldiers were concerned, it was theirs now, the spoils of war, and they needed every bit of it to accommodate all the men and women who found freedom there and had nowhere else to go. It got so big that the generals had to get someone to manage it, so they brought in the Rev. Horace James, a Union army chaplain and longtime abolitionist, and put him in charge of turning the overcrowded encampment into a town. James brought in medicine and decent food and solicited donations of clothes and other living supplies from his well-to-do congregations in Massachusetts.

Under James's supervision, residents of the settlement built Fort Totten, where the Union army later fought off two Confederate attempts to retake New Bern. Others loaded and unloaded supply ships or rebuilt the railroad bridge across the Trent River that the Confederates had destroyed during their retreat. They built churches and attended classes in the evenings at a makeshift schoolhouse. Soon, the settlement was named "James City" and contained 800 houses, mostly occupied by men and women who months before had been slaves.

By the end of 1865, almost 3,000 former slaves and other refugees lived in the camp, and in the years immediately following the war, James City became if not the Promised Land then a place where the men and women could live their lives as free people. The town was theirs. The land they farmed was theirs, the crops they planted and harvested were theirs, the houses were theirs, and they could raise their babies and dream of giving them lives that were better by magnitudes than the lives their parents and grandparents had been born into. They could make their destiny in James City. They established a local government and built more businesses. They strived. They lived. Imagine that, a town filled with former slaves and the kin of former slaves, governing themselves, working for themselves, bettering their lives.

Then the bad times came. For several consecutive years in the late 1860s, bad weather killed crops. A boll weevil infestation followed. The government cut back on the assistance they gave James City and other towns like it. If that wasn't bad enough, James Bryan, a relative of Peter Evans, the Confederate general who, prior to the war, had owned the land on which James City was built, sued to get the land back in the family. In 1867, he won. He started charging rent. Some refused to pay. It was their land; the Union army had said so. Others became sharecroppers, working the land for Bryan rather than for themselves.

Come the 1880s, just 1,100 remained in James City. By the time Nathaniel Loach and Roberta Gunner married, it was down to 700. Seven hundred from 3,000. The Murphys and the Loaches were among them but not for much longer. Willie, Nathan's father, heard there were jobs at factories in the north that paid three times what a man could make sharecropping in the south, and there were jobs for women too, who wanted them. Everywhere you looked up north, there were jobs in factories, foundries, and slaughterhouses and not enough men to fill them.

When America entered World War I, eight months after Nathan and Roberta were married, demand for industrial workers in the big cities grew even more, as the war all but killed immigration from Europe. The Loach family joined roughly one million other blacks and headed up north. Later in schools, they would call this the "Great Migration," but to the Loaches and to everyone else who went by train, bus, boat, or even horse-drawn wagon, it wasn't anything but trying to make a better life.

By 1920, the Loaches were living in the Francisville section of North

Philadelphia. Philadelphia's black population had increased by 500 percent over the last decade, and like most of the new residents, the Loaches lived in an overcrowded ghetto—in their case, a row home at 1719 Olive Street. Later, they moved to Folsom Street in the same neighborhood. It was a full house, consisting of Willie and Henrietta, aged 46 and 42, respectively; the relative newlyweds, Nathan and Roberta, both 26; Nathan's younger brother, Thomas, 22, and his wife, Louise, also 22; and a 19-year-old named Lorena Watson, who rented a room. The stories they'd heard about jobs being plentiful were true. Nathan was a laborer for a streetcar company, while Roberta worked as a stacker in a factory. Thomas found work as a laborer at the nearby naval yards, Louise as a machine operator in a sweatshop. Watson, the lodger, was an ironer. None of these jobs was glamorous; they were dirty, tedious, and dangerous, but they beat sharecropping.

In 1924, Nathan and Roberta started having kids of their own and moved to a different row home at 1618 Swain Street, a block away from Folsom. First came a son, Daniel. Then, three years later, a girl, Bessie. Four years later, Helen arrived, and then, three years after that, in 1934, twins, Henrietta (named after her grandmother) and Henry.

The Loaches did the best they could. Philadelphia during the 1920s and '30s was corrupt and dangerous, run by crooked politicians, bootleggers, organized crime, and dirty cops. It was strictly segregated, not only in terms of housing but also in education, access to community services, and religion. Although the mass influx of black southerners resulted in more black doctors, homeowners, and shop owners, blacks were prohibited from patronizing restaurants, bars, hotels, lunch counters, and theaters in and around the city center. This resulted in dense pockets of neighborhoods throughout the city where black working people filled every square inch. By 1940, a three-quarter-square-mile area from 7th to Broad, Fairmount to Susquehanna, was home to 15,000 families, or more than 60,000 people.[2]

Complicating matters was tension between the European immigrants—particularly the Irish, who had arrived before the start of World War I and established communities in Philadelphia—and the incoming blacks. Rioting between blacks and whites in major U.S. cities, including Philadelphia, peaked during the "Red Summer" of 1919, in most cases instigated by whites trying to evict black newcomers from white neighborhoods. Although America's entrance into World War II in 1941 created even more need for labor—the Philadelphia naval shipyard went from employing a few thousand to 58,000 at its peak—blacks remained trapped in ghettos and frozen out from all but the most menial and back-breaking jobs.

Chapter 1. James City

By the mid–'40s, Nathan and Roberta's children, the first Loaches to be born in Philadelphia, had grown up. Daniel was in the military. Bessie, at 18 years old, married a man named John Harold White and moved to Delaware in 1942. Henrietta would eventually marry a man named Ansley and move to a home on nearby Merion Avenue. Helen met a man, and when she was 17, she had a baby girl. The following year, she had another girl, then a boy. She met another man, had another girl, then another boy. Two children died in infancy. When all was said and done, there were eight children. That's hard on any woman, but Helen was a drinker. She drank every day until she couldn't drink anymore. When she woke, she started drinking again and kept at it until the night came. The next day, she'd start anew.

Helen's love of drink was greater than her love of mothering, and she couldn't do both. The children's fathers, to whom she was not married, disappeared to wherever it is that men go who can feel neither shame nor the tug of responsibility or conscience, regardless of how heavy another might judge them to be. Whatever they had done when the opportunity was present, they did without questioning, apparently, their role in damaging lives already injured by drink, poverty, and insanity, and thus they were free to go about their lives unburdened, anonymity shielding them from consequence and history.

The task of raising Helen's children fell to her family, primarily her younger sister, Henrietta, and to a lesser extent, the children's grandparents, Nathan and Roberta. As a family, they did the best they could while Helen slowly drank herself to death. Several of the children lived full time with Henrietta. This arrangement was doomed from the start. She had enough problems and mouths of her own to feed. Something had to give, and years later when everyone found out how it went down, they clucked and shook their heads and wondered how she could have done such a thing with nary a thought to the men who had abandoned all of them to lives of deprivation and poverty.

* * *

"C'mon, get dressed," the boy said to his brother. "We're going out." Older by almost four years, he knew his little brother would obey.

"Where we goin'?" the little one asked.

"Grandma's," came the reply, and the little one was happy. He loved going to Grandma's house.

It was June 16, 1959. A Tuesday. Sunny out. Clear. The boys began to walk. After a while, the older one said, "Hey, let's race!" And he took off running. The little one, being only four, quickly fell behind and soon lost sight of his brother. He couldn't keep up. He kept running, hoping he would catch sight of him. He didn't. When he couldn't run anymore, he walked.

The boy was frightened. He'd never been this far from home alone. He didn't know how to get to his grandmother's house. He didn't know where his brother was. He walked for a long time, hoping his brother would show up behind him to let him know everything was all right. He never did. By early afternoon, the boy had walked all the way to the Ben Franklin Parkway. He sat on a bench and cried. Shortly, a woman approached him. She asked him his name, if he was lost. He couldn't get it out. Where did he live? Where were his parents? He couldn't get anything out. He didn't know. He didn't know anything. He was four.

She took him to the ninth district police station on North 21st Street. They asked him the same questions. He didn't know. The next day, one of the Philadelphia papers ran a photo of the boy. The caption read: "Found on highway."

No one responded.

The police took him to the Catholic Social Services office on North 17th Street and turned him over to the nuns.

"What's the child's name?" one of the nuns asked.

"We're not sure. When he was picked up, he said something that kind of sounded like 'Matthew,' but who knows?"

It was up to the nuns. They went with "Matthew" after the saint and chose as his surname "Franklin" after the parkway on which he was found. It became the job of his caseworker, a young nun named Sister Bernadine, to find him a home. The boy lived mostly at the church's orphanage over the next several years before being placed in the home of John and Bertha Santos at 1025 Catharine Street in South Philadelphia.

Santos was from Cabo Verde Island, Portugal, and had moved to the United States in his teens. He and Bertha Lorraine Johnson met in Atlantic City, married, and moved to Philadelphia, where they raised six children who were biologically theirs. Already in their mid–60s, they took in five more from the Catholic Social Services, including Matthew.

Santos supported the brood as a longshoreman at the docks, a cook, and a part-timer at the Singer Optical Company. Bertha minded the family and took quickly to young Matthew. She said he had a sadness in his eyes. He didn't say a word to anyone in the house for the first two weeks he was there. Then, one night, out of nowhere, "I want something to eat."[3]

Despite their disparate roots, the brood got along as well as most large families can, owed largely to the Santoses' simple love of family. There was no favoritism or jealousy among the children of the type that rots families and can create resentments and complexes for generations.

Chapter 1. James City

From Matthew's perspective, all the children were treated equally.[4] "I probably couldn't love this family more if I'd been born into it," he said years later.

"Pop" Santos enrolled Matthew in the local Catholic school. To get to school, he had to walk to Broad Street by way of 13th Street—the domain of the 13th and South Street gang, which specialized in robberies and assaults. Philadelphia was busting with street gangs in the 1960s. A report published by the city counted 83,000 gang members, and those were just the ones in the system.[5]

The gangs would ask Matthew what street he was from, and when he told them, it was open season. Young Matthew took beating upon beating before subscribing to the age-old wisdom that advises us to join those whom we cannot beat. He did so and found, as the terrorized sometimes do, that terrorizing is not merely more fun than being terrorized; it carries an allure all its own.

"I had to walk through some pretty tough neighborhoods. I was always getting into fights, mostly because I didn't want to join a gang," he said years later. "But I finally did. Then I was getting into fights because I just wanted to fight."[6]

"I remember when I first got in a gang I was scared. But once I got on the right road toward being a really bad kid, I lost my fear. I was an extra bad kid growing up, a gang kid, one of the worst, and I was into everything that goes along with gangs."[7]

Matthew soon became such a proficient street fighter that he took over as leader of the 13th and South Street gang and was given the nickname "Iceman" for his ability to knock other boys unconscious. One of the members of his gang was neighborhood boy Alfonso Evans, whose friendship would later yield significant dividends. Of their gang life, Evans once said, "We were all into the street scene. It seemed impossible to me even then but either you fought or you were labeled a punk. There wasn't much of a choice. I lost some really close friends in gang wars."[8]

No civilized society tolerates such lawlessness and mayhem among its youth, irrespective of its role in having created it, so at about the age of 13, young Matthew was arrested and remanded to the Youth Study Center, the initial detention point for kids waiting to be transferred to a reform school or to have their cases otherwise adjudicated. Undeterred by this effort to corral his need to bash others with his fists—"I liked the attention," he admitted later—he got into fights whenever possible with other boys, with staff, with guards. For his insolence, he spent a full year there before being sent off to Saint Gabriel's Hall, a reform school, in Phoenixville, about 20 miles northwest of Philadelphia. A priest there,

Father Brown, frequently tried to help Matthew and keep him out of trouble, but he was a poor match for Matthew's aggression.

While young Matthew was fighting for his life on 13th and South and then padding his files in Philadelphia's various juvenile delinquent facilities, the Loach family was coming apart, as all families do sooner or later. Willie, the family patriarch who brought his wife, his sons, and their wives to Philadelphia from James City, died at Saint Luke's Hospital from heart disease in 1955 at 72 years old. Nathan, his son, was working as a messenger when he died in 1963 from asphyxia and carbon monoxide poisoning following a fire at his home on Sydenham Street in Francisville. He was 62. His daughter Henrietta was with him when he died. His wife, Roberta, died 26 days later, also at 62, from causes that were presumed by the attending physician to be natural.

Nathan's son Daniel died in 1957 at age 33 from heart failure and secondarily from cirrhosis of the liver. And on Saint Patrick's Day in 1966, Helen Loach died from the effects of alcoholic cirrhosis at 4:25 p.m. at Hahnemann Hospital. She was 35 years old. A second-year intern named David Major signed Helen's death certificate. In the field where the attending physician is required to indicate the interval between onset of symptoms and death, Major wrote, "Years."

In the fall of 1968, Matthew was again arrested for fighting and gang activity and was sent to the Daniel Boone School at Hancock and Wiley Streets in North Philly, a "remedial and disciplinary educational facility." He was 14. Nothing changed much for him there. He was quiet and kept to himself but was always ready to fight if the opportunity presented itself, which it frequently did. An English teacher there, Edgar Carlis, exasperated at the repeated failures to curb Matthew's fighting using conventional methods, encouraged him but told him to get something out of it.

"Matthew, since you fight all the time anyway, why don't you make some money out of it?"[9]

Even the fight business has rules against 14-year-old kids fighting professionally, but the seed had been planted.

"He told me to get myself together. He said since I was a young strong kid who liked to fight, I should try to do something for myself."[10]

Things were always the same in these places. Wherever Matt went, he fought. He fought other kids. He fought instructors and guards, one time knocking one of them cold with unfortunate results; nine other guards came running. Years later, Matt would say, not without pride, that he gave them pretty good action for a while, but they eventually "did a number" on him. They put him away by himself for that one, "quarantine" they called it, locked him in a room that had no lights, and at night he would pull the blankets over his head in the dark in hopes that the rats and mice he could hear running around couldn't get to him. He did his time, was released, and in 1972, was again arrested in South Philadelphia when police found him carrying a knife that measured seven inches.

This time, he wasn't going to reform school.

Matthew was sent to Camp Hill, the state prison just outside Harrisburg. It housed both adults and minors, a point of contention between prison officials and youth advocates that was settled by the state supreme court in the latter's favor, in 1977, after which minors were moved to a different facility. Matthew was 17 years old, and as always, he was quiet, but in prison especially, it's the quiet ones who are most dangerous.

After the first couple of skirmishes, they moved him from the general population to the more restrictive E Ward; when he continued to get into fights, he was moved to H Ward, which was reserved for the apparently incorrigible. There, a couple of guards named Stover and Egan had free rein and exploited it to their satisfaction, such that years later when he visited the prison as a free man to counsel newer versions of himself, Matt was reminded of the worst of it, and he shoved his hands into his pockets the way a man does when bracing himself against something suddenly remembered and mumbled, "Egan ... he was something."[11]

Sometimes, Matthew wrapped his hands in towels and punched the cinderblock walls in his cell or propped up his mattress and punched away. One of his friends inside was Saleem El-Amin, another South Philly kid who couldn't stay out of trouble. He and Matthew had met in the Daniel Boone School, and now, years later, here they were in what the guards liked to remind them all was the "last stop." El-Amin was a peacemaker, breaking up fights where he could.

"We shouldn't be stabbing and killing each other because we'll never get out of here," he warned the others. Sometimes it helped; sometimes it didn't. He got no credit for it from the screws. "The guards were crazy; why did they keep me under lock and key when I'm stopping these guys from fighting?"[12]

El-Amin had converted to Islam in his late teens. Guys on the inside found out that sometimes, violent criminals who converted and took the tenets of the religion seriously became gentlemen, or at least something closer to the ideal than they had been before. Matthew was attracted to Islam too, later saying it contained none of the hypocrisy and contradictions he found in the teachings of Christianity. He joined the American Muslim Mission. He also started attending electrician workshops and avoiding fights. And he had a kind of epiphany.

"One day, while I was looking in the mirror, I actually slapped myself. I said 'Matthew, the way you're going you have a great chance of spending the rest of your life in places like this.'"[13] Around that time, he asked El-Amin to show him how to box. He knew how to fight. He wanted to learn boxing and El-Amin was as good a teacher as he'd find in Camp Hill. Before getting locked up, he'd been trained on and off by Jimmy Arthur, who coached fighters at the Passyunk Gym in Philly and was considered a local legend. The Passyunk, owned by Jimmy Riggio and run by Eddie Aliano, was at one time or another the training headquarters for virtually every well-known fighter on the East Coast.

Gaining entry was a workout in itself. To enter, one had to open a heavy steel door, climb 17 steps, turn a corner, pass by the pool hall and the private social club, open another door, and climb 19 more steps. The gym was at the top of the stairs. Lockers lined the rear wall, along with fight posters, a full-length mirror on another wall, a padded table (for sit-ups), two speed bags, two heavy bags, and, of course, a ring.

Joe Frazier trained there early on, and it wasn't unusual in the late 1960s to find him asleep in a corner waiting for Yank Durham to arrive and put him through his paces. Sonny Liston trained there when he lived in Philly. Ernie Terrell, Johnny Saxton, Rubin Carter, and Kid Gavilan all trained there at one time or another. Joey Giardello was known to dump buckets of water from the third-floor window onto the heads of passing policemen.

El-Amin had learned well at Passyunk, and he showed Matt what he knew. Matt decided then that when he got out, he'd be straight and he'd be a fighter, like Mr. Carlis had suggested. That's how he would stay out of hellholes like Camp Hill. That's how he would survive. On the day he walked out, he told himself he'd never see Camp Hill again. They gave him a suit, and he went back home to Catharine Street in South Philly and told Pop Santos that he wouldn't get into trouble anymore and he shouldn't worry about him because from now on, he would do his fighting in a ring, not in the streets. Pop smiled, and if he didn't believe a word of it, you couldn't blame him. Matthew looked up his friend from his gang-war days, Alfonso Evans. Evans was training to be a fighter at the Juniper Gym at 1326 South Juniper Street.

Chapter 2

The Juniper

They just want to make some eatin' money.
—Tony Morgano

The Juniper Gym was a tiny hollow on the second floor of one of those old buildings that were everywhere in South Philly. A visitor would find a roll-top desk, two heavy bags, a speed bag, a ring in the center, and a small locker room shielded by a curtain. The walls were decorated with fight posters and photos as all gyms are, many of them autographed and made out to the gym's proprietor, Nick Belfiore. An astute observer might notice that all the signatures were made in exactly the same handwriting and bore an uncanny similarity to Belfiore's, but then, no one went there to look at autographs.[1]

Belfiore was born Nicholas Montefiore in the old country, Gessopalena, in the Abruzzo region of central Italy in 1910. His father, Joseph, brought his wife, Mary, and their children to America in 1913 and changed the family name to Belfiore. Almost as soon as they arrived, the whole family, including the kids—Nick, his sister, Elizabeth, and brother, Joe—went to work in the fields, picking vegetables at a farm in South Jersey. While there, the family slept in a chicken coop, the usual tenants temporarily relocated. They worked barefoot in the dirt. They had just one pair of good shoes each, if that, and they weren't going to ruin them in the fields.

"I worked on a farm as a kid," Belfiore told a reporter in 1981. "Not just summer months. Nowadays, you keep a kid out of school, they send a truant officer. Then, you'd leave the city in April and you wouldn't come back until October. Picked tomatoes, peppers, string beans, lettuce. Not for a whole lot of money. But livin' was cheaper then."[2]

Belfiore made it as far as the fourth grade before it was decided survival was more important than learning fractions and cursive. He worked and worked and never looked back, even when, later in life, he became an important man, a man who was quoted in newspapers, and some looked down on him for his lack of formal education.

"I can read all right. I come to a word I don't know, I skip it," he said. "But I can't write good at all. People said night school, how come you never went to night school. A year goes by, another year goes by, what am I gonna do, go to school when I'm 71?"[3]

In 1930, Belfiore married Jennie Negro, whose family had also emigrated from Italy. Jennie was three years old when her family arrived in America, and she and Nick knew each other for most of their lives, having grown up picking vegetables in the same fields year after year. Shortly after they married, Nick became a butcher on Ninth Street in the Italian Market in South Philadelphia and did odd jobs on the side: carpentry, masonry, whatever would bring a few more bucks into the house. He was always hustling. A plaster job here, a roof repair there, a weekend on the highway behind the wheel of a big rig, home on Mountain Street to sleep a few hours, back to work Monday morning. He and Jennie had four kids—Dolores, Marie, Nick Jr., and Joseph—and Nick wouldn't have them busting their humps in the fields like he did. His kids would be educated.

Eventually, Nick landed a job with the City of Philadelphia. "I used to drive a truck. Big tractor trailer, cross country. I'd see city truck drivers sittin' there, readin' papers," he said. "Hey, I figured, let me get a city job, sit down. So I went to the ward leader. He said the only thing open was laborer. I took it."[4]

Within a year, he was running the paver and bulldozers and other heavy equipment, and he did that until he retired 30 years later. At the same time that he was busting his ass for his family, Belfiore was indulging his obsession with the fight game, which began when his brother Joey started boxing as a teenager.

"My brother Joe wanted to be a fighter. He was 15. I told him he was too young. The next summer, he came back from the farm, went to the South Side Boys Club. He took to fightin,' I took to trainin'."[5]

Belfiore studied the trainers and fighters at South Side Boys Club, a second-floor gym at 1111 South Broad Street in South Philly. Jimmy Costi and Jack Stanley trained kids there, but the head coach and owner was the revered Tony Morgano. Morgano fought as a high-level pro lightweight throughout the late 1920s and '30s against a lot of the bigger names of the era. He quit fighting in 1937 and was enjoying the retired life hanging around with buddies on street corners. Local cops kept busting up their get-togethers, so Tony and his buddies decided to run a dance, pool the money they made from it, and get a clubroom where they could hang out without getting hassled by the cops.

Eventually, that clubroom became the South Side Boys Club, which they divided into three rooms: a reading room, a playroom, and a gym.

Chapter 2. The Juniper

Before he knew what hit him, Morgano had 30 kids in the club every day, and he figured the only thing he knew was how to box, so that's what he taught them. He got into such good shape boxing with the kids every day that he made a comeback. But he wasn't fighting for himself. He was fighting for the ghetto kids for whom his gym was a second home.

"They come into my little boys' club, some with no soles on their shoes, some without no shirts and mostly all without no underwear," Morgano said in 1941.[6]

"They want to learn to box, some can box, others never will. But they'll take a beating no matter, 'cause it's a short cut to some money. These kids ain't spenders or tough guys at heart—they just want to make some eatin' money, maybe for the folks at home, too."[7]

Nick and Joey Belfiore were among them. And with the knowledge he picked up at South Side, Nick trained Joe to a 35-fight amateur career while opening up a gym of his own. In 1940, he turned an abandoned machine shop at 3033 Salmon Street into the Lambast Athletic Club, and he, Tony Martini, and Nick Ferriola trained dozens of neighborhood fighters and entered them in tournaments in Pennsylvania and New Jersey. Nick turned Joey pro a year later. His career peaked with a points loss to popular TV fighter and perennial contender Joe Miceli in '49.

Nick convinced his brother to retire in 1950. And when Nick and business partner Sonny Leek opened the Juniper in 1967, Nick brought in Joey to help him train the kids. Nick was still working for the city at the time and Joey was an iron worker. They'd work all day and then head to the gym at night. A couple of years later, Belfiore retired from the city and ran the gym and trained fighters full time.

Belfiore dreamed of what every trainer dreams of—getting himself a champion. And these were the real heroes of the slums and the alleyways in the cities. The men, usually middle-aged or older but not always, who spent their days sweeping hand wraps off the floor, emptying buckets of water, saliva, blood, and sometimes teeth into the toilets; teaching a wild kid off the street how to tuck his chin behind his shoulder when he jabbed and how to step with the left foot forward, move on the balls of his feet, and for Chrissake move his head after punching.

A lot of these kids didn't listen, they weren't the smartest, after all, but Belfiore and guys like him all over the city and in slums all over the country burned hours, days, lifetimes in gyms just like Juniper drilling the fundamentals over and over and over even when it seemed the lessons would never take. (Indeed, Belfiore kept a plastic Wiffle ball bat in the corner of the Juniper ring apron where he stationed himself during sparring sessions and on occasion would use it to "knock some sense" into a fighter who just wasn't getting it. "Bring the left back straight after you jab!" Bop!)[8]

And when there was a show, the trainers would fill up their cars with the kids they thought were ready and some who they knew were not and drive them all over kingdom come to match them with other slum kids whose trainers filled their own cars with kids in hopes that they too might find a champion. Most of them never would, of course, and that was the hell of it. Grown men spent their whole lives on these kids knowing maybe one in a hundred might stick around long enough to become even a decent pro, and when they didn't, it wouldn't be because they weren't good enough or tough or talented enough but because they got distracted by a broken heart, booze, or the streets.

The guys who had been at it a long time, like Belfiore, knew that it wasn't the guy with the perfect left hook they were looking for or the fastest but the one who would do what he was told, all the time, every time, for as long as it took. That was 90 percent of winning in the fight business. But most of the kids couldn't do it. They could for a little while but not over the long haul. Not for as long as it took to be a champion.

Nick Belfiore and his brother Joe in the gym, ca. 1940s (photo courtesy of Nick Belfiore, Jr.).

Even worse was the chance that the fighter would dump his trainer just when he was getting into the money. It happened all the time, an occupational hazard. That was the gamble. Even if you were lucky enough to catch lightning in a bottle and make a kid into a champion, you had to hope he didn't turn on you just when all the sacrifice was about the pay off. All it took was for some wise guy to get in your fighter's ear and fill his head with a bunch of fairy tales about how much money

Chapter 2. The Juniper

he could be making and all the sweet tail he could be getting and how he was getting ripped off. The fighters fell for it all the time; who could blame them? They weren't businessmen. They were slum kids who had learned early on that the people who were supposed to be looking out for them weren't, that they really couldn't trust anyone. The first teacher was usually the kid's old man, who had either disappeared or, worse, hung around and tortured everyone into wishing he'd taken off before making a mess of everything.

The gyms were full of kids who were there in the first place because their fathers had failed as men, so they went looking for ways to show them how they had failed. They also were looking for men who could give them the things their fathers couldn't or wouldn't. The kids didn't know this, but the trainers did, the older ones, anyway, and they used it. That's why it was so important that the trainers weren't just good fight men but also good men. They had power. They were all stand-ins for shitty fathers. There were some, the perverts and weirdos, who got into it because it put them around these vulnerable kids and because no one talked about it, so they could do as much damage to the kids as any punches to the head. But they were the exception.

Belfiore? A fight guy through and through. A lifer. You couldn't have a conversation with him without it turning into a boxing lecture. Ask him how he was doing and he'd tell you how his fighters were doing. Ask him about the weather and he'd talk about how his guys better do their roadwork whatever the weather was like. If his kids had friends over and they were talking about DiMaggio, Unitas, or Jayne Mansfield, he'd jump in and soon it would be all about boxing.

When his son Nick Jr. was about 12, Belfiore talked him into joining the Police Athletic League (PAL) and boxing. The kid won his first two bouts, but when he lost the third, he decided he'd stick with Pop Warner football and played all the way through high school. The old man attended just one game in all that time. He was always over at the gym. He'd bust his kid's balls: "Be a fighter! In the ring you only have one guy chasing you. In football it's 11!"[9]

The thing guys would remember about Nick Belfiore years later was that to him, it didn't matter if you were a 15-year-old kid entering the novice class in the local Golden Gloves tournament or a 30-fight pro. He treated all his fighters the same. He hollered a lot, he took no shit, and he didn't baby anyone. When you were in the Juniper you knew it was his house. He was in charge. And after his guys had fought on a card or in a tournament, he'd shamble into the house on Mountain Street at midnight, wake up Jennie, and have her cook all the kids a big spaghetti dinner. Some of them he'd drive home after, and the next day, he'd be in the gym bright and early.

Belfiore was as tough outside the gym as he was in it. There were stories of him striding into the most dangerous bars and neighborhoods in South Philly like he owned them, staring down thugs and criminals like he was laying down the law to a 12-year-old kid in the gym. One had him getting into a fight with three guys following a near collision on the Ben Franklin Bridge and laying them all out with a tire iron he kept under the front seat. When his kids came to the Juniper to visit, he made it clear to everyone in the gym that if anyone got out of line with his kids, they'd have to deal with him. Nobody ever did.

Belfiore was 63 years old the night Matthew Franklin, broad-shouldered, with a slim waist and skinny legs, walked into the Juniper in 1972. Since getting out of Camp Hill, he'd been working as a longshoreman down at the docks, slinging 60-pound crates of meat into trailers. He'd also run a jackhammer on a construction crew. A little later, he'd be slicing up chickens for a poultry company. He was 18 years old, about 165 pounds, and when he walked into the Juniper that night, Belfiore couldn't have known that his champion had arrived.

He put Matthew to work like he did any other new kid, and that alone was enough to make a lot of kids leave that first day and never come back. Shadowboxing, skipping rope, calisthenics. Right away, Belfiore could see the kid was dirt poor, maybe the poorest kid in the gym, but he worked like hell and was cut from marble. Matthew kept showing up, so Belfiore showed him how to stay on balance, how to keep his chin down, how to move forward and back. Matthew picked it up quickly, quicker than Belfiore would have expected, but that could be explained. As Matthew said years later, he'd been practicing fighting all his life. He just needed a style.

Belfiore worked him. Speed bag, heavy bag, more shadowboxing, more drills, more calisthenics—the harder he worked Matthew, the more the kid responded. Soon, he was sparring, and everyone could see right away that he had balls in the ring and you couldn't hurt him. He was made from iron. And he'd train all night if Belfiore let him. If there was a problem, it was that he fought in the style that boxing guys called a "cutie," a hit-and-hold kind of style that wasn't especially pleasing to watch, but for a kid as raw as Matthew was, it worked well enough. Belfiore found that the hardest part sometimes was just getting through to him.

"At times he wouldn't listen [and was] a little thick-headed, but I knew he had something all along because he was always a good puncher," Belfiore said years later. "And he took a good punch."[10]

Still, Matt was just another hungry kid banging the heavy bag every night and doing push-ups in the corner. The Juniper was full of fighters

Chapter 2. The Juniper

when Matt showed up. There was Danny Parker, Mike Everett, Robert Adams, and Matthew's buddy Alfonso Evans. There were heavyweights Virgil Kid and Mike Montgomery and featherweight Luke Robinson. Belfiore's nephew, Joe's son Joey, fought out of the Juniper for a while. James Williams, Gino Graziano, and a hundred other kids who came and went for reasons of their own who no one ever heard of again, who never got their names in the paper or their hand raised after a fight, who maybe gave up after the first bloody nose or after the first time Belfiore raised his voice or smacked them with the plastic bat.

Maybe they lost their stomach for it the first time a hook to the ribs knocked the wind out of them or when they went home with a black eye or bloody nose. Whatever the case, guys came in and then were gone, back to the streets without so much as a "so long," and you couldn't blame them; there is shame in giving up. And the ones who stayed, well, they were the ones who had no good choices.

A few months later when Belfiore felt that Matt gotten his legs under him, he started looking to match him at tournaments and smokers. It wouldn't be hard. Boxing was so big in Philly that you could throw a rock in any direction and hit a club full of kids just like Matthew. There was the Hennelly Boys Club, Ballard PAL, Cobbs Creek PAL, and Upper Darby Police Youth Association (PYA). There was Cloverlay Gym and the Passyunk. There was Frankford PAL, Bucceroni Gym, Ocean City Boxing Club, and Rizzo PAL. There was the 23rd PAL, the Beresin, and the Mid-Atlantic representing North Philly, the Southside and Eastside gyms, the Arcadia, the Olympia, and the Annunciation Boys Club.

Over the bridge in Jersey was the Seven Champs Gym, the Millville Athletic Club, the Ocean City Boys Club, and the Laurel Athletic Club. They were all busting with hard kids just like Matt who were also trying to turn something ugly inside them into something beautiful in the ring, though none of them would have said it like that if you asked them. They didn't know it. They would have said they did it because it was fun or gave them something to do so they wouldn't run the streets or that they were learning to someday be a champion so they could have nice cars and clothes and pretty women. But they were all there for the same reason when it came down to it.

Pretty soon, Belfiore got Matthew a match against 21-year-old Chuck Davis, a petty officer at the local naval hospital. They fought on a smoker at the Hennelly Boys Club. Davis trained out of the Frankford PAL and was good beyond his years—fast and smooth. Willie Reddish, Jr.—the son of Willie Reddish, who trained Sonny Liston, Gil Turner, and others—had been coaching Davis and watched from the corner as Davis dropped Matt with a hook on the way to winning on points. Matthew was back in the gym right away, which would become his habit, win or lose. Belfiore got him several more fights quickly to get him ready for the *Daily News* Golden Gloves tournament, which started on February 12, 1973. How Matt did in the Golden Gloves would tell Belfiore a lot about his new kid.

Matt's division, novice light heavyweight, kicked off the second week of the tourney, February 17, at Upper Darby Junior High. On that night, he won a decision over James Moncrief, an unattached fighter. After getting a bye in the next round, he drew Ed Weichers, a former backup quarterback and free safety on the Westchester State College football team. Weichers had switched to boxing after getting kicked off the team for failing grades and entered the tournament out of the Upper Darby PYA. He'd won his first two bouts by first-round knockout and was getting positive press from the local scribes.

On March 16, at the Blue Horizon in the tournament quarter finals, Matthew stopped him in the first round. That set up a rematch with Davis in the semifinal on March 23 at John F. Kennedy High School in Willingboro, New Jersey. Davis was sailing through the tournament, winning all of his bouts by knockout. He probably would have knocked out Matt, too, if Matt hadn't clinched throughout, drawing boos from the crowd. Davis took a clear decision.

"Franklin wasn't in there to fight. He was just in there to go three rounds," said Reddish, Davis's trainer. Davis agreed. "I guess he was determined not to let it happen again," said Davis, referring to the knockdown he scored the first time they'd fought. "It was frustrating as hell. All he did was hold. I was afraid he was going to steal the fight."[11]

In the third, referee Leon Robinson told the fighters he'd call the fight a no-contest if they didn't stop wrestling, though by all accounts, Matt initiated the clinches. Davis ended up winning the tourney, and Matt went back to the Juniper. He fought again a couple of weeks later. Then again a couple of weeks after that. He got better. He sparred with everyone. He learned how to use his strength and improved his balance and fought again and again in South Philly, over the bridge in Jersey, in Millville, in North Philly, then out in the boonies in western Pennsylvania, then in Philly again, then back out to Jersey. Belfiore racked up the miles on his car. Jennie made a lot of midnight spaghetti dinners.

At Juniper, Montgomery and Everett were the stars, the guys everyone looked up to and the guys Belfiore spent the most time with. But quietly, Matt was making progress. Another night in North Philly, another loss to Chuck Davis but closer this time, back to the Juniper, a win, a loss to future heavyweight contender Jimmy Clark but learning all the while, getting better. And before you knew it, a year had passed and Matt had around 20 fights, almost all of them wins and a stockpile of trophies in his room at the Santos house on Catharine Street.

Belfiore believed he had something with Matt, that the kid could be something. He took a special interest in him. At home, he asked his sons Nick and Joe to go through their closets and give him any clothes they didn't want so he could give them to Matt. Later, Belfiore cosigned on a loan so Matt could buy his first car. Everything was "Matt this and Matt that." Nick Jr. got so used to hearing about Matt that he said to his father, "Why don't you just adopt him?"[12]

Two events conspired to change Matthew's course in 1973. The first was that he became a father to twin girls that he and the girls' mother, to whom he was not married, named Sheena and Rashidah. And in October, Belfiore got word that Pete Mangone, the athletic director at the state prison out in Woods Run, near Pittsburgh, was putting together a show and looking for area fighters to come out and face kids from Willow Club, the local gym, and their inmates, who either were fighters before getting locked up or who learned to be while inside. It was over 300 miles from Philly out there to the prison—five hours by car—but Nick and Joe decided to head out with a couple of guys to see if they could get a fight.

Harry Savage from the 23rd PAL went and also Marvin Edwards, Johnny Barr, and Steve Temple, all from the Mid-Atlantic gym in North Philly. Matthew got matched up with Larry Chisholm, an experienced fighter out of the Daniels Athletic Club in Pittsburgh. Chisholm stopped him in the second round. Not long after, Matt and Belfiore had a frank conversation about the futility of getting punched in the head for free. That is, if one is going to get punched in the head, then the least one should expect is to get paid for it. Or as Belfiore put it, "Matthew, you can't eat them trophies."[13]

Chapter 3

From Paris to Missoula

*"It doesn't make sense to fight
in your own town and get robbed."*
—Matt Franklin[1]

Pat Duffy lived boxing. Born and raised in South Philadelphia, the son of a fireman, he was hanging around Harry "Kid" Brown's gym on South Broad Street sometime in the 1930s when he saw Chris Dundee and two of his fighters exit a train and head into the gym. One of the fighters was Midget Wolgast, the flyweight world champion. Duffy thought, "Look at these guys, all sunburned and making a living. This is a great business!"[2]

That's how he got the bug. In 1936, he opened the 48th Ward Boys Club at 24th and Wolf, headed there every night after his day job in the research laboratory of Gulf Oil Company, and spent the next 60 years in the business, ostensibly in the amateurs. He was the president of the Middle Atlantic Amateur Boxing Federation and managed the U.S. Olympic boxing teams in 1964 and '68.

In the '68 Olympic Games in Mexico City, it was Duffy who handed George Foreman the miniature American flag which Foreman waved while bowing to ringsiders. Duffy breathed and bled boxing. "My entire life has been wrapped around boxing," he once said. "I think boxing day and night. If I go to church, I'm thinking boxing." Such a man could never be satisfied solely with the amateur game, no matter the degree to which his duties there ran his life. A man like Duffy had to get his hands in the pro game too. The problem was, there were rules against men who held high office in the amateurs involving themselves with professionals. A conflict of interest, the rules makers said. So he did what any man would do in such a situation: he got himself a front man and did whatever the hell he wanted. "Everyone knew it," he said.[3]

Pinny Schafer was Duffy's front man and, from 1960 to 1974, head of the local bartenders' union in Philly. His given name was William, but everyone called him "Pinny" because he was a large man with a booming voice and a disproportionately small head. It started when a South Philly hatmaker who had trouble sizing him would see him coming and announce, "Here comes Pinhead!"[4] Schafer started in construction as a boilermaker's helper in the 1930s, just when a union was being formed. He'd grown up tough in South Philly around 28th and Tasker, and when union busters and scabs came in to break up the strikes, Pinny was one of the guys who sent them back to their bosses with busted noses and jaws.[5]

He became a bartender around 1938 at Smitty's at 23rd and Pearce and later moved to Ray's at 20th and Green, a violent neighborhood where "every day was a fight." He loved to tell the story about the time two brothers who ruled the neighborhood came into the bar and started giving him lip. "How much of this shit do I have to take?" he said to the bar owner. "No more than I do," came the reply. The owner threw all of the other customers out and locked the doors, leaving just himself, Pinny, and the two brothers to settle things. The brothers took a licking. "We put them in the crapper," Pinny said.[6]

Duffy and Schafer started working together in the late '30s, running amateur shows for Diggers AA in South Philly. They put together the show on which Sugar Ray Robinson fought for the last time anywhere as an amateur and for the next 35 years or so managed Philadelphia fighters together. It was an open secret in the trade, but the manager of record was always Schafer, the quotes in the papers always from Schafer. It had to be that way and it fit their personalities; Duffy was soft spoken and precise, Schafer colorful, loud, and charmingly profane. As Duffy put it, "Who ever needed a Pat Duffy quote when Pinny was available?"[7]

Either way, everyone in the bustling universe of Philadelphia boxing knew it was a lie and couldn't have cared less as long as they got to make some money and watch good fights. The pair hit their stride after 1950, guiding the careers of perennial top welterweight contender Gil Turner; middleweight stalwarts Bennie Briscoe, Bobby "Boogaloo" Watts, and Marty Feldman; heavyweights Leotis Martin and Jimmy Young; Olympian and top bantamweight Sammy Goss; and the popular lightweight Jimmy Soo, among others.

In 1972, a fighter showed up to audition for Duffy fresh off winning a bronze medal at the Olympics. His first question: "How much do I get paid for signing?" Duffy told him, "You get your plane ticket back to Indianapolis and here's $10 for your trouble." He had no interest in a fighter who was worrying about how much money he was going to make before he even signed. The fighter was future three-time light heavyweight champion Marvin Johnson.[8]

Nineteen months before Matt and Belfiore had their talk about the economy of amateur fighting, Mike Everett, a junior welterweight, turned pro under Duffy and Schafer. He showed enormous potential. His older brother, Tyrone, trained out of the Passyunk and was on his way to becoming a world-rated junior lightweight. Duffy and Schafer moved Everett smartly and swiftly up the ranks. The only problem was, Schafer the manager and Belfiore the trainer didn't get along. One might imagine it was because they were too similar: both were loud, profane, and fancied themselves, with good reason, tough guys. Nevertheless, when the decision was made for Matt to turn pro, he did so with Schafer and Duffy. They were all South Philly guys, and if there was anything South Philly guys could do, it was put aside differences for the sake of making a buck.

Schafer and Duffy had a good working relationship with a young Philadelphia promoter named J Russell Peltz. Peltz was raised in Bala Cynwyd, the son of the owner of a successful plumbing, heating, and air-conditioning business. The first televised fight he watched was Gene Fullmer's knockout win over Carmen Basilio in August 1959, and that planted the seed. His fascination with the fight game grew. For his 14th birthday, his father took him to Convention Hall in West Philadelphia on December 6, 1960, to see local lightweight contender Len Matthews.

Matthews lost to Doug Vaillant in the main event, but Peltz was hooked and decided boxing would play a big role in his life. He attended Temple University in Philadelphia as a journalism major and later got a job at the *Evening & Sunday Bulletin* in Philadelphia with the intention of becoming the paper's boxing writer. The writer he hoped to replace refused to retire, and rather than wait any longer, Peltz decided to use his savings to start promoting fights. He quickly built a following in Philadelphia and became known for matching fighters tough, which led to exciting fights.

Peltz made the Blue Horizon a household name among boxing fans and four years later was named director of boxing at the 18,000-seat Spectrum in South Philadelphia. He was one of the most successful fight promoters in the world. From 1974 through '78, the Spectrum was one of the hottest venues in the country for fights, rivaling Madison Square Garden in New York and the Olympic Auditorium and the Forum in California. Because of his close relationship with Duffy and Schafer, which was based on a handshake, it only made sense for Peltz to serve as Matt's promoter. On January 14, 1974, Matt, weighing 180 pounds, won his first pro fight, stopping Billy Early at 0:27 of the second round at the Spectrum arena.

Peltz's star fighter, the middleweight Bennie Briscoe, was slated to

Chapter 3. From Paris to Missoula

fight Tony Mundine in Paris a month after Matt made his debut. Since Matt was about as tall as Mundine, Peltz used him as one of Briscoe's sparring partners. Briscoe was a 60-fight pro by this time, and the first time he and Matt sparred, at Cloverlay Gym in Philadelphia, Briscoe dropped him with a straight right hand. This pleased Peltz, as he saw Matt as a talented kid. He knew Briscoe would be ready for Mundine.[9]

They took Matt to Paris with them, and Matt was like a big, overgrown kid, smiling, laughing, taking in the sights. On fight night, Briscoe stopped Mundine in the fifth round. On the second fight on the card, Matt outpointed Mukeba Apolosa over four rounds. Working Matt's corner were Briscoe's guys, Quenzell McCall and Milt Bailey. Belfiore had passed on the trip, and Li'l Abner's trainers, Eddie Goodman and Joe Collins, were afraid of flying.

Three weeks later, it was back to Philadelphia, where Matt, with Nick and Sonny back in his corner, outpointed journeyman Roy Ingram over four rounds at the Spectrum. Two months later, Peltz had Matthew at the Spectrum again, this time against Joe Middleton. Matt stopped him in six rounds.

Schafer, Duffy, and Peltz kept Matthew busy, and the wins kept coming. In July, Matt stopped Joe Jones in three rounds. Seven weeks later, it was Lloyd Richardson's turn, out in four. Then it was Joe

Matt and stablemate Perry Abney in the dressing room minutes before Matt's second pro fight, in February 1974, against France's Mukeba Apolosa (photo from the collection of Arnold Weiss, courtesy of J Russell Peltz).

Matt and gym mates Perry Abney (over Matt's left shoulder), and Bennie Briscoe (far right) take in the sights in Paris in February 1974 (photo from the collection of Arnold Weiss, courtesy of J Russell Peltz).

Matt moves in on Apolosa. He won a four-round decision at the Palais des Sports, his second victory as a pro. He won five more fights before losing a decision to Wayne McGee in Philadelphia the following December (photo from the collection of Arnold Weiss, courtesy of J Russell Peltz).

Middleton again, this time in Alexandria, Virginia, where a cut eye led to a stoppage win in the fifth. The next fight, in December, was a bit of a gamble. The opponent, Wayne McGee, was only 1–0 (1) but was far more experienced than his record implied. Fighting out of the Long Island Volunteers Gym, he'd won the New York Golden Gloves championship in 1967, '68, and '69 (becoming the first Golden Gloves champ ever from Suffolk County) before moving to West Philadelphia and turning pro in 1974. McGee was a tireless puncher who relied on a heavy right hand. In his pro debut, he stopped Bob Bethea, who outweighed him by 31 pounds,[10] and in the weeks before the fight with Matthew, McGee sparred with top middleweight contender Willie "The Worm" Monroe at Joe Frazier's Gym on North Broad Street to help Monroe prepare for his fight with Billy Douglas.[11] He was a good test.

McGee beat Matthew that night at the Blue Horizon in the show's semifinal, winning a unanimous six-round decision. The loss demonstrated that Matthew still had a lot to learn in the gym. McGee was a short, powerfully-built fire hydrant of a fighter, and Matt couldn't do a thing with him.

Peltz had Matt back at the Blue Horizon two months later with a sixth-round knockout of Vandell Woods. That was followed by a five-month layoff during which Schafer and Duffy sold Matthew's contract as part of a multi-fighter deal to a young manager named Frank Gelb. Originally, Matthew wasn't part of the deal. Schafer, and to a lesser degree Duffy, were slowing down—indeed, Schafer would die of a heart attack on Christmas Eve the following year, 1976—and were looking to sell the contracts of Mike Everett and Alfonso Evans. But Schafer still couldn't get along with Belfiore who trained all three. When Duffy told Matthew he'd have to change trainers if they were going to keep working together, Matthew told him he preferred not to. Duffy told Schafer, "Let's throw Franklin in on the deal." So Gelb got Matthew for nothing.[12]

Frank Gelb was born and raised in Philadelphia. His grandfather owned a successful furniture business in West Philadelphia, which Gelb's father inherited. When race riots broke out in North Philadelphia in 1964, Gelb convinced his father to move the family business to Norristown. Gelb worked for his father and his grandfather before starting to manage fighters in the late 1960s. He built a stable of solid, mid-level pugs: Billy Freeman, Leroy Roberts, Lloyd Nelson, and Ray Hall. Later came Tyrone Everett, Ronnie McGarvey, Jimmy Young, and others.

He wanted to expand his stable with high-quality fighters, hence the deal with Duffy and Schafer in 1975. He already had a solid working relationship with Peltz; on the second show Peltz ever did, Gelb supplied him with Leroy "Hurricane" Roberts. Gelb and Peltz trusted each other and collaborations were sealed with a handshake.

Now being managed by Gelb, Matthew stopped Roosevelt Brown in four rounds at the Spectrum in July of 1975. Gelb and Peltz didn't believe in babying their fighters, so signed for a rematch with McGee for October. Since their first fight, McGee had fought just once, losing by decision to Vonzell Johnson. Matthew did better this time, having learned since the first fight how to use the uppercut more on the inside when he had to and to jab more to keep McGee outside when he could. He was still more boxer than puncher, so didn't hurt McGee and still didn't listen to Belfiore as much as he should have, but he got enough good work done to get a draw on the judges' scorecards. Three months later, Matthew stepped in as a late replacement for Jerry Judge and outpointed Harold Carter in Owings Mill, Maryland.

Then it was all the way to Milan, where Matt faced Yugoslavia's undefeated Mate Parlov, winner of more than 200 amateur fights, several amateur world championships, and the gold medal in the light heavyweight division in the 1972 Munich Olympics. Despite the enormous difference in experience, Matthew won an eight-round decision in May 1976. This was important. The *Ring* magazine rated Parlov number 10 in their ratings at light heavyweight; a top-10 rating was the key to getting a fight with the world champion.

Two months after the Parlov fight, Gelb took Matthew to the Civic Auditorium in Stockton, California, to face Montana's Marvin Camel. Camel was a member of the Confederated Salish and Kootenai Tribes of the Flathead Indian Reservation in northwestern Montana and was a popular local figure in Missoula. Born on the Flathead Reservation to a Native American mother and African American father, his background rivaled Matthew's for its poverty and isolation. Like Matthew and others, Camel used the anger and desperation from his childhood to fuel him in the ring, and in the beginning, he fought with rage.

"In my first seven or eight fights, the majority were knockouts," he said in 1976. "I'd just bear in and be all over the man. But a veteran fighter cannot just go in and wail away for seven or eight rounds. He's got to settle down and take the knockout when it comes." The turning point came, his manager said, when Camel, a southpaw, hurt his left hand while sparring California swarmer Karl Vinson. The injury never fully healed.[13]

"But it's made him into a damn fine boxer," Elmer Boyce said. "It took away his power punch and forced him to become a boxer. Before, he used to think about nothing but knocking people out, but he's had to go 10 rounds in his last four fights and it's made him a good boxer." Four years later, in 1980, Camel outboxed Parlov to become the first recognized champion in the new cruiserweight division.[14]

The Camel fight marked two important milestones in Matthew's career: it was his first 10-rounder, and it was the first time he'd be seen on national television. A "technical foul-up," according to promoter Joe Gagliardi,[15] resulted in the card not airing, but landing a fight on TV was a huge step in the career of any up-and-comer. The other fights that were supposed to be televised featured Vinson (the same one whose head injured Camel's hand) against world-rated Rudy Robles (Vinson won in an upset), and Álvaro "Yaqui" López, a top-10 light heavyweight, against Ray Castaneda in a tune-up for López's world title fight three months later against England's John Conteh. Both López and Conteh would figure heavily in Matthew's future.

Camel entered the ring as he always did, in a full eagle-feather headdress, and the two battled for 10 rounds. Camel was most effective with the left uppercut, which snapped Matthew's head back again and again. Matthew was stronger and more aggressive and appeared to land the harder punches. He floored Camel twice (one was ruled a slip by the referee). In the fourth round, Camel returned the favor, flooring Matthew. In a reasonably close fight, Matthew won the decision by scores of 97–94, 97–95, and 91–95.

Camel's manager, Elmer Boyce, made Gelb a good offer for a second meeting. He figured a rematch in October, this time in Missoula, Camel's hometown, would bring out the fans eager to see the local boy avenge the first defeat of his career. He would also promote it. Gelb agreed but wanted Matthew to stay active in the interim, so he signed to face journeyman Bobby Walker at the Catholic Youth Center in Scranton, Pennsylvania, in September.

Walker was no world beater, but he got around. A few months earlier, he'd been hired by light heavyweight champ Víctor Galíndez to help Galíndez prepare for his title defense against Richie Kates in Johannesburg. Galíndez ended up knocking him out in a sparring session.[16] Matthew, now rated the ninth-best light heavyweight in the world at 22 years old, did what he was supposed to do. He hurt Walker with body shots in the second round and floored him with a left to the body in the third. Two more knockdowns followed in the fourth before referee Hank Cisco stopped it at 1:54 of the round.

"I think Bobby Walker was a little scared after he found out I could hit," Matthew said afterward. "I wasn't worried about him after I knew he couldn't take a body shot. I got him with a left uppercut to the stomach and he was hurt. I'd like to fight again in Scranton. I thought I put on an impressive show." Indeed he had. Unfortunately, only 789 fans showed up to watch it.[17]

Gelb, Matthew, and Belfiore flew out to Montana a week before the rematch with Camel. Already, Gelb and Matthew were becoming close. Gelb found Matthew to be an unusually good and likable person, especially among fighters. A few days before the Camel rematch, he and Matt visited the University of Montana and decided to have an impromptu game of one-on-one on the basketball court. Gelb was about 20 years older than Matt but played a lot of basketball in his free time and was about the same height. The problem was, he was wearing dress shoes. Matt had on sneakers. "No problem," Gelb said. "I'll play you barefoot." He did just that, won their game, and for the next 20 years busted Matt about it at every opportunity.[18]

Meanwhile, there was the business of the rematch. Camel had a host of excuses for having lost the first fight, as fighters always do. You can't blame them. No man can continue to fight with any confidence if he admits to himself that when he was at his best, he was beaten by a better man. He has to believe it was an anomaly or he could never truly believe in himself again in the ring. And a fighter with damaged self-belief is a dead man walking.

"To be truthful, that fight was one of my worst. Not only was it the worst as far as how I looked, but it was the worst I felt. I just wasn't there," Camel said. "And I really couldn't tell you what was wrong. I couldn't punch as hard as I usually do. I felt right from the first round that I was dead." According to Camel's handlers, he was in a car crash two weeks before the fight and lost a pint of blood, which affected his training and contributed to his lethargic performance. "Somewhere along the line I lost something," he said. "I don't think I'll really know where. But I'm getting it back. I feel I'm getting my power back."[19]

Matt took a more analytical approach. "Sometimes a fighter can change some of the things he does, but not everything. I've been watching his moves carefully. I learned from the last fight that the only thing he's got going for him is that left uppercut. If I stay in close, stay on him all the time and not give him a chance, he'll get tired. I figure I can always win a fight if I'm in shape," he said.

"Marvin can take a good punch and he hits pretty hard. I dropped him in Stockton and he had me down once, too. I know he's from Missoula, and I hope the people don't rob me, that I can go back to my state and tell them that it's a fair game here. I came to fight. And I hope they give it to the person who is most aggressive and throws the hardest punches—that they give it to the person that wins."[20]

A man can hope all he wants. The local newspaper reported, "Once the fight was underway, it was evident that Franklin found Camel's style anything but confusing. Or at least the style Camel was using Saturday night.... He didn't dictate the tempo of the fight, he didn't move as well as he had before and his punches didn't seem to carry the authority they did against [previous opponents]. He was confronted by a quicker opponent, but one that could still punch hard. But Camel managed to adapt. Since he couldn't control the fight, he did his best to make sure Franklin couldn't either. In the middle rounds Camel would land a lead or a combination and tie up Franklin in a clinch—a tactic that won him no friends in the audience, but that proved effective."[21]

After 10 mostly uneventful rounds, Camel was awarded the decision, and it wasn't so much that Matt lost that was the story, it was the way he lost. The judges, Billy McFarland, Joe Antonetti, and former world light heavyweight champion Bob Foster who refereed and had a vote in the scoring, scored the fight 98–96, 96–96, and an outrageous 100–91, respectively, meaning Foster gave Camel all 10 rounds. The scorecards of McFarland and Antonetti seemed reasonable to many. The local fight reporter observed, "My card had Camel a 97–96 winner, although it was a stand I took without much conviction."[22]

Local official Jimmy Shea, who had judged several of the other bouts on the card, had Matt winning by a narrow margin but conceded it could have gone "either way." Most of the fans—all 854, a disaster for Boyce, as the promoter—"thought Franklin had won. Some were outraged."[23]

Gelb was among them. He demanded to see the scorecards, which was his right. But it seemed the Board of Athletics representatives, Sonny O'Day and Bob Blome, had high-tailed it out of the Adams Fieldhouse before the decision was announced, reportedly to catch bus rides home, a ridiculous proposition even by fight game standards. The only board member on hand was Mary Lou Crawford, the secretary, who was there as an inspector. Gelb, nearly apoplectic, filed an official protest, and the next day Crawford declared the fight a "no contest" pending a ruling by the board. Matt, Gelb, and Belfiore left for Philadelphia expecting to be notified when the hearing would take place. Instead, by the time their plane landed, the Board of Athletics had already ruled that the decision in Camel's favor would stand.

"I knew from the minute we set foot in that place that we were going to get the shaft," Gelb told reporters in Philadelphia. "Franklin won eight of the 10 rounds. Now let me tell you how I know we were going to get robbed. The referee, Bob Foster, voted all 10 rounds to Camel and that stuck in my throat. Now listen to this: Camel's chief second is Billy Edwards, who is also the manager of Foster, the referee. And further, the promoter, Elmer Boyce, is Camel's manager."[24]

It went even deeper than that. Foster had recently fought twice in Missoula, stopping Al Bolden in May in the same arena and Harold Carter in August. Both bouts were promoted by Boyce—again, Camel's manager—and Camel fought on both cards. Having Foster referee and vote in a fight involving Camel and promoted by Boyce was a clear conflict of interest that shouldn't have been permitted for the very reason that was evident when Foster turned in a scorecard giving Camel all 10 rounds. Gelb did all the things a manager is supposed to do in these circumstances—threaten to sue, call for an investigation, and so forth—but strategies useful at righting wrongs in the real world are powerless in boxing, so he, Matt, and Belfiore took the loss and moved on.

Gelb's luck got worse on November 30 when his star fighter, Tyrone Everett, fought Alfredo Escalera in Philadelphia at the Spectrum for the world junior lightweight title and lost an obviously corrupt decision that some called the most blatant robbery in the history of modern boxing. Adding to the suspicion that a payoff determined the result more than what happened in the ring was that it was the 145–143 score of Pennsylvania official Lou Tress that gave Escalera the victory. The *Philadelphia Daily News* reported, "There is no way to explain how this kind of thing happens in Philadelphia. On the way to what should have been his title, Tyrone Everett defeated Alfredo Escalera so decisively that not one person at ringside scored it less than 10–5 in rounds."[25]

On the night Everett was robbed, Matt and Belfiore were in Trieste, the capital city of the Friuli–Venezia Giulia region in northeast Italy for a rematch with Parlov, whom Matt had beaten on points in Milan seven months earlier. Since their first fight, Parlov, now the light heavyweight European champion, had won three straight, two by knockout. As he prepared for his flight to Rome to meet with Matt and Belfiore, Gelb was still steaming over the Everett fight. "The only reason I'm not lying down, screaming, beating my fists on the floor is because of the pride I feel in the way Tyrone handled himself. I was the one running around kicking things afterwards. He was the guy talking quietly to the writers, to people telling him how he'd been robbed. He was the guy with the class."[26]

Gelb arrived in plenty of time to see Matt and Parlov struggle against each other in a close fight similar to their first one. In another fight that could have gone either way, Gelb (and Matt) got a small measure of revenge for what had happened to Everett when the sole Yugoslavian judge scored the bout in Matt's favor, resulting in a draw. Had the judge voted for Parlov, a Yugoslavian, Matt would have lost for the second straight time.

Chapter 3. From Paris to Missoula

The next month, Gelb got a call from local matchmaker and promoter Don Elbaum and Hank Schwartz, an entrepreneur and inventor whose company Video Techniques had over the last several years become one of the leading television distributors of big fights. They were going to start a televised boxing tournament called World Television Champions to compete with a televised tournament Don King was running on ABC. The series would be shown on home television in 39 of the nation's 40 prime markets but would be blacked out in Philadelphia, where the first show would take place at the Arena. (The series was canceled after sponsors backed out about a month after its debut, following the discovery that King's tournament was corrupted with phony ratings and payoffs.) The two televised fights would be Cyclone Hart against Vito Antuofermo and Matt against another young rising light heavyweight contender named Eddie Gregory.

Gregory was born and raised in the Brownsville section of Brooklyn, one of the most dangerous and poorest neighborhoods in New York. An unimposing building at the corner of Saratoga and Livonia Avenues in his neighborhood was once the headquarters of Murder Incorporated, the infamous crime syndicate that served as the enforcement arm of the local Italian and Jewish mobs. He was a teenager in the mid–1960s when riots and arson ravaged a neighborhood already destroyed by crime, unemployment, and poverty. He went to PS 125 in Brownsville, then to Junior High 263 in Brownsville, and then to James Madison High School in Sheepshead Bay. He gave Brooklyn College a try but dropped out after two days. "That's all. I walked out. All those [guys] did was smoke reefer and drink wine. I figured there was no degree for me in that, so I left."[27]

It was around that time that Gregory was handing a guy his ass in a street fight, and Clinton Patrick, a former amateur fighter from Virginia and the boxing coach at the Brownsville Community Center, happened by, liked what he saw, and told Gregory that if he came to the gym and applied himself, he could make some money. Gregory took him up on it. "Boxing kept me away from all of that [crime], it was something I wanted to do ... become a world champion," he said years later.[28]

Boxing kept Gregory out of trouble most of the time, but there were exceptions, like the time police showed up to break up a craps game he was winning on the corner of Demarest Avenue and Rockaway Boulevard. "I was playing a good ol' ghetto game, see low, three dice in the hallway of our apartment building." The cops grabbed the $25 lying on the floor, and when someone said Gregory had the rest of the pot, the cops demanded he hand it over. "I had $325 in my pocket that I had won and wouldn't give it to them. They started to hassle me. I punched out three of them, and the fourth guy hit me on the head with a blackjack." When he woke up, Gregory was being hauled away. His mother came running after them. "That's my son!" she screamed. "He's not a criminal!" The cops laughed. "He is now!"[29]

"Fightin' was mandatory in Brownsville," Gregory said. "If someone makes it in Brownsville, he makes it anywhere. Fly Williams, Lloyd Free, Willie Randolph, they're only a few of the guys I ran with. I remember the time I had to ice a big, white guy back in James Madison High. The police had to take me home and I was out of school for six months. Afterwards I went on a study-work program, going to school one week and working for the police the next week."[30]

Despite his success in street fights, Gregory's amateur career got off to an uneven start. In his first Golden Gloves competition as a sub-novice in 1969, he lost his second bout. After two fights in the open class in 1970, he withdrew from the tournament with the flu. Still, he was establishing himself as a serious threat to other amateur welterweights in New York.

He moved from the Brownsville Club to the PAL gym in Brooklyn and, under Al Fischetti,[31] gained a reputation as a thunderous puncher. "[Gregory] is one of the deadliest punchers in the field," reported one paper previewing the 1971 Gloves competition.[32] Another: "His best punch is his right. Give him an opening and you're likely a goner."[33] He ended up winning the open-class welterweight title in '71 and '72, in the latter knocking out four straight opponents and beating future middleweight world champion Antuofermo on points in the final.[34]

Gregory turned pro in September 1972, under manager Jack Singer and trainer Chickie Ferrera, who was best known for training two-division world champion Dick Tiger in the 1960s. Fighting as a middleweight, he racked up six straight wins before losing a decision against Radames Carbrera at the Felt Forum in New York. He built an early lead, did nothing over the middle rounds, and rallied too late to get the decision. This so infuriated Ferrera that he stormed from the ring before the decision was announced, leaving Gregory's robe hanging on the ring post. Ferrera did not baby his fighters; when they screwed up, he let them know it. Gregory said afterward, "I got no excuses but I did have the sniffs in my nose."[35]

Gregory redeemed himself with a draw against the far more experienced French champion Nessim Cohen and a spectacular knockout of the once-formidable Eugene "Cyclone" Hart. Three months later, he faced underdog Mario Rosa at the Felt Forum. In the audience was Joe Scorcia, who was looking for fighters to sign to a management deal. "He was supposed to win easy but he was getting smeared. He was down

Chapter 3. From Paris to Missoula 37

twice and losing through seven rounds," Scorcia said. "Then, bang, he knocks Rosa out. I said, 'That's the guy for me.' I went to the dressing room and asked if he was for sale. That's how we ended up together."[36]

Scorcia paid $10,000 for the contract and kept Gregory busy; he fought 11 times over the next two years, winning 10, all by knockout, with the only loss a close split decision to Briscoe at the Spectrum. It was true that none of the 10 was a world beater, but Gregory was getting the rounds and the exposure and putting in the work. That's how champions become champions. They fight.

Matt and Gregory met at the Arena on March 11, 1977, in front of an estimated 3,000. Matt had to sweat off a pound and a half to get to the contracted weight of 176,[37] but at 22 years old, he could do that without even trying. During referee Tommy Reid's instructions, Matt and Gregory talked trash and got forehead to forehead, evincing not just the importance of the fight as it concerned their immediate ability to make money and progress in their careers but, more urgently, a kind of primal energy that erupts when two young hard men meet up in the ring to see who is tougher, stronger, better. And in that moment, the fight had nothing whatever to do with the money, the ranking, the next fight, or the new car.

It was more important than that, something the middle-aged mon-eyed men at ringside in their leisure pants and with double chins and bald spots couldn't imagine in even their wildest fits of delusion: that something could possibly be more important than the money. But there *was* something more important; Matt knew it in the moment, Eddie Gregory knew it, and the fighters watching knew it because they had felt it before. And no matter how badly things would end for most of them sooner or later, in those moments they were more alive than most civilians would be if they lived a thousand lifetimes.

Matt came out bouncing and moving around the ring, hands high and tight. This wasn't Parlov or Camel; he couldn't play around like he had with those guys, walking around with his hands down when he felt like it. Eddie Gregory could *motherfucking* punch. Matt could tell already from the jabs Gregory was heaving at him: straight, hard jabs from the shoulder, the kind that knocked you off balance so that you never saw the right hand coming behind it, and before you knew what happened you were in the locker room with an ice pack on your head asking your trainer what happened.

So Matt was on his best behavior, following the game plan, jabbing, moving, staying off the ropes, all nervous energy and adrenaline, and if you'd never seen him before, you'd think maybe he was fighting a little scared. But with a minute left in the first, he jumped in with a right-hand counter straight and true. Gregory was throwing at the same time and never saw it. It dumped him on his ass, and when he jumped up and strutted to a corner to take the standing eight count, Matt smiled a little from the other side of the ring. One round down. Nine to go.

Matt kept it up in the second, bouncing, feinting, never standing still for long, and grabbing Gregory tight when they got inside. He bounced a couple more right hands off Gregory's forehead late in the round and then grabbed him before Gregory could reply. All three judges gave Matt the second round. Two in a row. Gregory's trunks started to sag in the third, a metaphor for his dwindling chances it seemed, as Matt continued to score from outside and tie Gregory up before he could get his fists moving to respond. Three in a row. This was the strategy Belfiore and Matt had worked on. *Box, box, box.*

After the third round, they swapped Gregory's blue trunks for green, and it was as though a switch had been thrown. Early in the fourth, he buzzed Matt with a hook and came alive, haranguing him on the ropes with hooks and right-hand bombs. He paused and Matt waved him in, the cycle repeated and they took turns smiling at each other, Gregory winging bombs, Matt slinging quick counterpunches from the ropes. Matt went to the ropes and waved Gregory in again and Gregory obliged, missing as many as he scored, but a puncher only has to land one so long as it's the right one. He didn't land the one he was looking for, but he'd won his first round of the fight, and when Matt got to his corner, Belfiore told him to stay off the goddamn ropes and go back to boxing.

For the rest of the fight, Matt did what he was told for the most part. He moved. He boxed. He didn't take dumb chances. He stayed away from exchanges most of the time. When he saw Gregory loading up, he got the hell out of there. He didn't worry about landing big punches. He didn't try to punch a hole through Gregory's big smug head. Oh, he wanted to. Man, did he want to. Every instinct told him to get in Gregory's face and punch with him, but he didn't. *Box him*, Nick told him. *Don't punch with him.* He did everything he was told to do, except in the 10th when he figured he had it wrapped up and could have some fun trying to take Gregory's head off. But otherwise he did what he was told. And then the decision came.

Judge Herb Rhodes scored it 47–45 for Matt. Tom Ross liked Gregory by a point, 46–45. Reid, the referee, gave it to Gregory by three points, 47–44. And that was it. The crowd booed. (They were in Philadelphia after all, Matt's hometown. It would have been bad manners if they hadn't.) The Philadelphia fight writers had a field day.

"Franklin used defense and a left jab to completely defuse the well-respected hand grenade Eddie Gregory clinches in his right hand.... Gregory suffered the bout's only knockdown, crumpling like a ball of aluminum foil in the first when Franklin surprised him with a straight right."[38]

Another: "The corruption and rip-off segment was handled by the officials of the second bout, who fleeced Matt Franklin in a 10-round split decision and handed it to Brooklyn's Eddie Gregory instead."[39] Matt, of course, agreed. "I was robbed. I dropped him in the first, outboxed him in each round, and took it to him in the 10th."[40]

The majority of writers felt it was a close fight that could have gone either way. Given the decades-long history of hometown fighters getting the nod in such circumstances, it was a wonder it didn't go to Matt. When his buddy Alfonso Evans lost a controversial 10-round decision to William "Red" Berry at the Blue Horizon a month later, Matt spoke out. "The Philadelphia judges want blood. They don't respect boxers. They gotta learn to respect skill, endurance, and boxing ability. That's why I've been going overseas. It doesn't make sense to fight in your own town and get robbed."[41]

Chapter 4

Do You Want Me to Stop It?

> *"It was the only time in my career that I covered a fight from ringside where I thought both guys might die."*
> —Nigel Collins

Six weeks after the loss to Gregory, Matt was in Wilmington, Delaware. Gelb had arranged for him to fight journeyman "Wild" Bill Hardney, 29–26–1 (14), at the Fournier Hall. Despite the loss to Gregory, Matt retained his top-10 ranking in both governing bodies; the World Boxing Council ranked him at eight and the World Boxing Association at 10, making him the highest-ranked fighter to do business in Wilmington in several years. A couple of days before the fight, the promoter yanked Hardney from the card, claiming he just wasn't good enough. "Hardney won his last two bouts against only mediocre opponents and had been chopped up by fighters of Matt's caliber," Gus Parodi said.[1] He then replaced him with Joe Maye, a heavyweight who had lost 16 fights in a row and would retire in 1980 with a record of 3–45–2 (1). Matt pummeled him without letup and won a wide decision in front of 702 fans.

"He's real tough. I don't think he can hit but he has a good chin," Matt said afterward. "I was trying for a knockout and threw my best punches. I figure going 10 rounds helps my endurance, so I'm not upset. I think I'm ready for anyone in the top 10."[2]

Matt was back on track, but the loss to Gregory stung. It seemed like Gelb's fighters had to knock their man out or win every round to get a victory, even in Philadelphia. Tyrone Everett had his own theory as to why Gelb's fighters weren't getting decisions even in their hometown. And despite what Matt said after the Evans fight, it had nothing to do with the manner in which they fought or how much blood they spilled. According to Tyrone, he was in San Antonio, Texas, to see his brother Mike fight in Don King's tournament on ABC. "A guy walks up to me in the lounge of the motel one day and says, 'Tyrone, you might be the best fighter in the world, but you ain't gonna win the title unless you get help.

Chapter 4. Do You Want Me to Stop It?

If your manager had been smart, you'd have had help in Philadelphia for the Escalera fight. Help is always available"

"I told Frank about that conversation and he froze," Everett told a Philadelphia newspaper columnist. "Frank still thinks it's possible to run around, work hard, and have everything come out the way it does in the movies. I've seen others lose decisions that were almost as bad as the one I lost, Alfonso Evans and Matt Franklin, to name two recently. Frank's fighters. I said, 'Frank, you're a terrific guy but you're gonna have to learn to throw a little dirt in this game to get some respect.' Frank's problem is he's playing it honest and this is a dirty game."[3]

"Hard as he tries, there are things about me and things about this business Frank just doesn't understand," Everett continued. "He came from a furniture store into a world where they don't think nothing of roughing up a person. My contract runs out next year. If Frank can't turn things for me a little faster, I'll have to look in another direction. A lot of Frank's fighters are thinking that way. Frank's working against the grain. He just doesn't realize nice people get run over in boxing."[4]

The day after Everett gave that interview, he was murdered by his girlfriend after she reportedly found him with a transvestite. Carolyn McKendrick, Everett's girlfriend of two years, returned to the South Philadelphia row house she shared with Everett earlier than she was expected to and found the door locked with a chain. After some delay, Everett let her in and she discovered Tyrone Price, a transvestite, hiding in her children's bedroom.

McKendrick grabbed Everett's handgun, which sat atop a chest of drawers, and fired once, striking him in the face. The bullet exited through the back of his head, went through the window behind him, and was later found on the sidewalk across the street. Everett died on the way to the hospital. Prosecutors said she shot Everett in a fit of jealousy. McKendrick claimed Everett moved toward her to strike her and that he beat her at least once every couple of weeks. In December, McKendrick was convicted of third-degree murder and possession of an instrument of crime (the gun). The following June, she was sentenced to 5–10 years in prison.

Everett's murder rocked the Philadelphia boxing scene. Everett was a star, the best chance the city had for a world champion. Gelb had been working on getting him a rematch with Escalera, but Escalera's camp kept delaying and pushing for the fight to take place in San Juan. Gelb heard about the murder on the radio when he was in his car driving to Wilmington to pick up a set of ring ropes to be used in Atlantic City later that summer. He turned the car around and drove back to Philadelphia. He was shocked.

"The thing is [McKendrick and Everett] had been going together for two or three years," he said. "Tyrone wasn't the kind of guy who ran around with a lot of different girls, and this particular one he was really crazy about. The summer before last, they came down and stayed at my house at the shore. She used to come to the gym and watch him train. She was very good for him."[5]

Peltz, ever the realist, was less surprised. "What can I tell you except that I'm not as shocked as the average person on the street who has nothing to do with boxing," he said. "I don't know that much about the circumstances, but more than anything I have to say it's the atmosphere. The lives the fighters lead, where they come from, the people they associate with ... all of it is like walking along a precipice."

"Murder is so senseless," Peltz continued. "If it was a lover's quarrel, then what a stupid thing to do. If it has anything to do with boxing, that makes it even more scary. I do know this much, there is no way a talent like Tyrone Everett should have passed through his career without winning a championship."[6]

It didn't take Gelb long to start putting together a card to establish a memorial in Tyrone's name, with Tyrone's brother Mike headlining. Proceeds would go to the Tyrone Everett Memorial Scholarship Fund at Bok Vocational Technical High School, which Tyrone attended. "The idea for this came from Mike and the other kids in the gym," Gelb said. "There's no way of telling exactly how we'll do because we don't know if we'll get any kind of a tax break, but the local fighters are working strictly on a percentage, and the percentage is about half of what they'd usually get. We'd like to get the scholarship fund off the ground and provide the foundation for it to be perpetuated."[7]

Roughly 1,200 fans attended the show at the Arena and watched Mike Everett outpoint Rocky Ramon over 10 rounds. In the co-feature, Matt stopped Ed "Savage" Turner of Orlando, Florida, in the sixth round. He was all business.

"I tried to get him early, and I didn't, so then I decided to take my time," he said. "I told my fans it would probably be a knockout around the eighth round anyhow, so they're not disappointed. Everybody knows I got screwed on the decision when I fought Eddie Gregory, so I want him back ... *bad*."[8]

The world didn't realize yet that the Matt Franklin who had lost a close decision to Gregory was gone and wouldn't be seen in a ring again almost ever. They couldn't know. But he knew. He'd decided that night that his days as a stick-and-move boxer were gone. All those drills in the gym teaching him over and over to slip punches and counter, to roll under a punch and come up with something, to punch and then grab

Chapter 4. Do You Want Me to Stop It?

and to move out of the way, over and over he and Nick practiced them until they became second nature—what had they gotten him?

In the most important fight so far of his career, he did everything he was supposed to do, that he had trained to do, and three guys with pencils in their hands who probably had never thrown a punch in their lives decided he wasn't good enough. Who were they? What did they know about boxing? Who were they to say he wasn't good enough? And they were in his hometown! He couldn't even get a break at home. How could he hope that next time they'd get it right when they couldn't get it right in Philadelphia?

There were so many things Matt could not control, things over which he had had no say. No one had asked if he wanted to be born to parents who didn't want him. No one had asked him if he wanted to be abandoned on the Ben Franklin Parkway or if he wanted to live in an orphanage. No one had asked him if he wanted to fight off thugs on the way to school every day or if he wanted to live in a neighborhood where gangs were everywhere and fighting was a way of life. He'd had so few choices in his life over important things. Well, no more.

When he walked back to the dressing room after the Gregory fight, he'd decided he was done doing things the way Belfiore and Gelb wanted him to. He had to do it his way from now on. And from now on, he'd be a puncher. He'd knock guys out. They couldn't steal a win from you when the other guy was unconscious. And if he had to take a few punches to give some? That was okay. He'd pay that price.

"The reason I started slugging more is that they took the decision away from me when I fought Gregory," Matt said after his next fight, after the whole world saw what the new Matt Franklin was willing to do in a prize ring. "They'll never take a decision away from me again."[9]

Old habits are hard to break, so it wasn't obvious in the wins immediately after the Gregory fight, over Maye and Turner, two guys who had no business in the ring with him in the first place. But after that, you couldn't miss it. He wasn't the same old Matt Franklin, hit-and-grab boxer puncher out of South Philly. He was something no one had ever seen and that no one would forget.

* * *

"Franklin's style won't bother me. Some guys hold, some wrestle, some come to you. I always train in the gym for different styles. Whatever fight Franklin comes out with, it won't be nothing I didn't see before. So I'll adjust my fight to whatever he does." Marvin Johnson had just finished an outdoor workout at John F. Kennedy Plaza in Philadelphia. It was July 22, 1977, four days before his fight with Matt at the

Spectrum. A few feet away, Matt was trying on the gold-and-red North American Boxing Federation (NABF) championship belt he and Johnson would be fighting for. "Fits real good," he said.[10]

Johnson looked up at him and smiled.

You couldn't blame Johnson for his confidence. He'd gone 65–5 (55) as an amateur, winning three national titles and then the bronze at the '72 games. It took a while for him to get going after Pat Duffy sent him packing in 1972. First he signed with a group of Indianapolis businessmen who had good intentions and gave him a $200 per week salary, a new Cadillac, and a $10,000 signing bonus.[11] But they had no connections in the boxing business and couldn't get him fights. That agreement was dissolved and he aligned himself with another Indianapolis group, a promotional firm. That contact was terminated after two fights. Eventually, he landed with Arnold Weiss, a Philadelphia accountant who managed Briscoe and also happened to be the brother-in-law of Peltz, Matt's promoter and the most powerful man in Philadelphia boxing.

In his first fight with Weiss, Johnson knocked out Wayne McGee—the same man who had beaten and drawn with Matt. Three more knockouts followed, including one over Tom Bethea in Indianapolis. (The Bethea fight was televised on the soon-to-be-canceled World Television Boxing series. Johnson later said he never got paid for the bout. His purse was supposed to be $5,000; he received a check for $3,500. It bounced. Other fighters were stiffed too.[12]) The Bethea fight brought Johnson to 14–0 (11) and led to the matchup with Matt for the NABF title, a regional title that was typically a stepping-stone to a shot at the world championship.

All was going according to plan. Tickets to the fight were selling, Matt and Johnson were peaking in training, and the newspapers were giving the card plenty of promotion. (Briscoe, in his first fight since getting an emergency appendectomy in May, would meet Sammy Barr in the main prelim.) A phone call about a week before the fight put the whole event in jeopardy. A European boxing manager named Rodolfo Sabbatini called Weiss and offered Johnson a shot at WBA champ Víctor Galíndez on September 17 in Copenhagen but with a catch: if he went through with the fight against Matt and lost, the Galíndez fight was off. It was a risk. Weiss and Johnson had to consider whether a fight with Matt was worth maybe losing a title shot for a lot more money. Johnson wasn't concerned.

"I'm looking forward to Galindez," he said. "From day one I had a dream to become the champion. This is the year for me. I see myself in September fighting Galindez and I can see myself champion of the world."[13]

Curiously, he claimed to have never seen Matt fight, and he still

Chapter 4. Do You Want Me to Stop It?

wasn't concerned. "I've had 80 amateur fights and 15 professional ones. In over half of them, I never saw the guy I was fighting—particularly on those amateur tours I took to England, Russia and Germany," he said.[14] "I know I have to win, but I don't expect Franklin to cause me any undue concern. The way I look at it, each of my fights has taken me one step closer to Victor Galindez."[15]

Weiss wasn't so sure. He called Peltz and asked for his advice. Peltz told him to consider the money it would cost him to pull out a week before the fight and also that Johnson needed the work. It had been three months since the Bethea fight.[16] Weiss decided to go ahead with the fight against Matt, who was thrilled at the news. "I'd just like to say this: Johnson fights like an amateur. He's used to going threes and fives. If we get past the fifth on Tuesday, he'll start to tire and then I'll have him. I'll just keep on coming."[17] Matt was sparring big guys, heavyweights, in the gym—Obie English and Joe Gholston, among them—and told the press he was ready to handle anything Johnson could dish out.

A crowd of 6,459 filed into the Arena and watched Briscoe manhandle poor Barr over seven rounds, then settled in probably expecting to see Johnson chase Matt around the ring all night. Johnson, 15–0 (12), fairly flew out of his corner, as was his custom, throwing hard, fast, southpaw punches. He was just 25 years old, but his comically receding hairline made him look at least a decade older, and the incongruity of it all—a seeming old man fighting like a tornado with the echo of the first bell still in his ears—may have surprised the crowd, but it didn't surprise Matthew or rattle him.

He moved judiciously, and when Johnson got inside, he backed him off with short hard uppercuts to the body and right-hand leads. By the middle of the round, they were already engaged in hard, fast, back-and-forth slugging of the type that doesn't occur in even the best fights until the guys have a few rounds under their belts and they're warmed up. But this was Johnson's style; he overwhelmed opponents with a swarming, nonstop attack. And as the hooks and uppercuts ricocheted off Matt's jaw, one wondered how many of those he was prepared to take. Quite a lot, as it turned out.

The Matt from a year earlier might have greeted the arrival of the second round from his bicycle, but that guy was dead and buried. The judges in the Gregory fight had killed him. This Matthew stood right with Johnson and fought him on the inside. Johnson, exuberant, flush with the certainty of a man who had beaten every pro he'd faced, favored a wicked left-uppercut, right-hook combination. The uppercut lifted Matt's chin in the air right into the path of the hook over and over again, and over and over again Matt threw back and refused to retreat. He stayed right there, as close to Johnson as he could while dropping his own bombs. Every time he looked hurt, he rose again and started swinging.

"I wanted to stay real close to him," Matt said later. "You fight southpaws that way, he couldn't hit hard then and really get his stuff off."[18] Already, the crowd was roaring, and there were 10 rounds to go. Right at the bell ending the second round, Matt ate yet another huge uppercut that drew blood from his nose. He responded by raising his hands over his head while walking back to his corner, the blood already streaming down onto his mouth and chin.

The third started the same way, and as Johnson ripped more uppercuts and hooks off Matt's jaw, Nick and Sonny screamed from the corner at Matt to move. He didn't. He relaxed. He stood stock still in front of Johnson and took it all. With the round almost over, he came alive and backed Johnson up with ringing head blows. Then he backed off, waited for Johnson to charge in again and whacked him with a right hand. And if you looked closely at Johnson, you could see just the slightest hint of something no one had seen before on his face: panic. In fighting, this is called breaking a man's will and Matt was breaking Johnson's round by round, punch by punch—not just with his own punches but with his ability to take Johnson's.

In the fourth, it was Matt's turn to come out winging bombs, and he landed a series of terrible right hands that had Johnson flopping all over the ring. Matt relaxed again and then Johnson took over, firing his combinations, but the zip wasn't there like it had been earlier. Matt opened up again at the end of the round and hurt Johnson again, but Johnson wasn't done yet. He started the fifth calm and measured, always throwing, but picking the shots he wanted to put mustard on. At the bell, he landed a pair of huge left hands that might've knocked down a building. He took the sixth too and then the seventh, big. Matt went back to the corner appearing spent.

For the past couple rounds, Belfiore had been considering stopping it. Matt was taking everything flush. He wasn't throwing back as much. He looked beaten. He returned to the corner after the seventh with his head down. Belfiore sat him down on the stool. "Come on Matt, let's call it a day, okay? Let's call it off, you're taking too many shots. Do you want me to stop it?" Matt shook his head and shot Belfiore a look. No one was stopping anything.

The bell rang for the eighth and for the next two and a half minutes, Matt jabbed Johnson silly and shook him with straight right hands. The counter he'd been looking for all night—a right uppercut after Johnson's straight left—finally started landing. He rattled Johnson with straight, hard counterpunches and backed him up. This was death to a swarmer like Johnson; if he wasn't coming forward, the fight was essentially over. But with thirty seconds left, Matt stopped punching and Johnson came to life, ramming home hard power punches of his own. Matt opened the ninth with a big right uppercut and they went to war again, trading bombs inside. And in the middle of this mayhem, both men landing and taking bombs, Matt stepped on Johnson's foot, causing him to stumble. They stopped. Matt extended his left arm in apology. Johnson looked at him, nodded, and accepted the apology with a gentle tap on the glove. Then they went back to trying to dislodge the other's brain stem.

The 10th was barbarism, plain and simple. They stood close enough to each other to hit and to be hit and worked each other like they worked the heavy bag in the gym. The crowd stood, clapped, hollered themselves silly, and why not? This was fighting, broken down to its most base and purest form. The 11th started the same way. Then a right staggered Johnson. He came right back, pushing Matt to the ropes. It was here that Johnson's fight was lost, according to him.

"Really, I got mixed up on my rounds. Normally they'd have someone show a card at the end of each round but they didn't have one. Champ [Johnson's trainer, Colin 'Champ' Chaney] thought the 12th round was coming up when the 11th round began. He told me to throw a lot of punches because my right eye was closed. I threw more punches in the 11th than in the 12th. I was exhausted in the last round and when I was knocked down I was just too exhausted to get back up," he said.[19] "I remember walking back to my corner after the 11th round thinking, 'It was a close fight,' but I believed I'd edged it out. Then I saw the stool sitting there and I knew something was wrong."[20]

With Johnson floundering, Nick and Sonny screamed at Matt from the corner, and Matt turned it around, battering Johnson. With 10 seconds left, Saddler, the referee, leaped between them and waved his arms. It looked like he was stopping it and Matt started celebrating, but no, he thought he'd heard the bell and was breaking them. It made no difference. Johnson started the 12th well enough, but Matt had broken him, finally, as clearly and expertly as a cowboy breaks a horse.

There was nothing Johnson could do to Matt that he hadn't already tried, so when Matt started landing again, Johnson went down on his back, holding on to the ropes with his left glove, the only show of defiance he could still muster. Saddler stopped it without a count. The TV broadcasters were screaming. The crowd was screaming. Nick and Sonny were screaming. Matt, right eye swollen, mouth and nose bleeding, smiled wide and proud and held his arms over his head. Then he collapsed on his stool and stayed there for several minutes while Johnson lay spread-eagled on the canvas.

It had been anyone's fight going into the last round. The judges, Harold Lederman and Paul Harris, and the referee, Saddler, had it 51–48 for Matt, 53–49 for Johnson, and 51–51, respectively. The final round would have determined the winner. But Matt, good to his word, wasn't going to let a fight go to the judges if he could help it. Those days were over, even if he needed a little reminder from Belfiore in the corner. "He had started getting exhausted around the 10th round," Matt said afterward. "But going into the last round, my manager told me I had to knock him out to win. I heard a lot of people saying to throw the right. I was putting out my left hand to size him up and then nailing him," he said. "Right hands, lefts, I was nailing him with everything."[21]

Johnson, with his undefeated record and the title shot against Galíndez gone, was despondent but respectful in the locker room. "I threw a lotta punches. But he took it. Some fighters can, some can't. That's what proves he's a good fighter—staying in there."[22] He lay on a rubbing table, still exhausted, his face lumpy and bruised. Briscoe surveyed him from a few feet away. "Sometimes you win, win, win. Then you lose, it learns you a lesson," he said to no one in particular. "Makes you smarter."[23] Someone asked Peltz how much Matt and Johnson got paid for the evening. "They didn't get enough," he said.[24]

The fans staggered out into the summer night and into the bars and row homes and tried to describe to their families and friends what they had just witnessed but they lacked the vocabulary. They had to get liquored up first. Peltz, along with Indiana Boxing Commission chairman Kelse McClure, in town to cheer on Indiana's only boxing star, headed over to the Penn Center Inn to check on Johnson. They found him laid out on the floor in the hallway outside his room, too exhausted and despondent to go inside. McClure took Johnson's room key and he and Peltz carried Johnson into his room and placed him on his bed.[25]

The local writers were unanimous in their praise. "The fight fans in this town crave a sequel to Hiroshima every time they plunk down six bucks and Matt Franklin never once quenched this thirst until awkward Marvin Johnson left him no alternative. For one night in his career Matt Franklin abandoned his crochet needles and reached for a Billy club. Philadelphia loved every gory minute of it," reported one.[26] "It had to be the most memorable, most savage, most dramatic fight since Sugar Hart and Charlie Scott waged their brutal war 15 year ago,"[27] raved another. One more: "That the Philadelphian did not falter throughout the siege, that never once was he knocked off his feet, was absolutely incredible."[28] Decades later, writer Nigel Collins recalled, "It was the only time in my

Chapter 4. Do You Want Me to Stop It?

career that I covered a fight from ringside where I thought both guys might die."[29]

Matt gained more attention from the Johnson fight than he did from all his other fights combined. "People are coming up to me now saying, 'Hey, Matt Franklin,' and I don't even know them. People are coming up to me and telling me my fight with Johnson was the greatest one they've seen in 20 years. It makes me know I'm finally beginning to be somebody." Someone asked him if it was worth it. "I looked like I went through a meat grinder," he said. "I felt pain all over my face. I felt like someone had thrown hot water on my face. That was the first time I ever looked like that." He smiled. "One time out of 21 fights, that ain't bad."[30]

Matt took a few days off to heal and celebrate his win. When the time came for him to get back to work, he didn't go back to Belfiore and the Juniper. He went to a different Philly gym. It turned out he was mad at Belfiore for suggesting between rounds of the Johnson fight that he quit, and going to a rival gym was his way of punishing him.

"It looked pretty bad but I left it up to him [whether to stop the fight]," Belfiore later told a reporter. "I asked him because I wanted him to make the decision. After the fight he got pissed off and went over to another gym because he thought I was going to throw in the towel. He was gone one day and then he came back to my gym. He's headstrong and stubborn. Sometimes he's very smart. Other times he acts like he's got the brains of a 15 year old."[31]

With Matt and Belfiore back on the same page, it was time to line up the next opponent. Belfiore and Gelb wanted to go a little easy. Matt had just been in a war for the ages. The title shot would come sooner or later. Why risk everything against a tough opponent, the way Johnson just had, and maybe have to start over? Matt and Peltz had other ideas. Matt had momentum. He'd been in the fight of the year. Take advantage of all that attention. Keep the momentum going. If he came back against some stiff, he might lose all that goodwill he'd earned with the win over Johnson. So they needed a tough guy. Not a top contender but a battle-hardened guy no one else wanted to fight. The answer was easy: Billy "Dynamite" Douglas.

Yank Durham, manager and trainer of Joe Frazier, among others, articulated the general consensus among fight managers when Peltz offered Douglas for Yank's middleweight, Willie "The Worm" Monroe, in 1973. Durham turned him down flat. "He [Peltz] wants to try and kill you with Douglas," Durham shouted at a reporter. "What does Douglas mean to us? He's the kind of fighter you don't gain nothing by beating, but he can get lucky and knock you dead."[32] Eddie Futch, one of

Durham's assistants, agreed. "I've watched Douglas once before, and I came away thinking, with this guy you don't get careless. He has an exceptionally quick right hand. He can take you out with one shot, so the strategy is to not give him that shot."[33]

Douglas had been fighting all his life, the kind of man who "is supposed to be chained up," he once said with a big smile. Those who knew him were never quite sure if he was kidding when he said things like that or when he said he was mainly about "violence and music, music and violence."[34] He said music came first, that he was in the concert band in high school and marching band too back in Columbus, Ohio, and was good at it until he got into sports and he was even better there. Football was his thing then, until one time they were scrimmaging and he ran over defenders like they weren't there and one of them, a linebacker, told him, "You better not come through this hole again." He did on the next play, but he came through punching. "The coach saw me and the next day I was back in the marching band," he said.[35]

He ended up in the Navy ("I don't know how I got in the Navy anyhow. I hate water") and was in the brig for fighting while stationed in Orange, Texas. He wanted to go out dancing and the guard, a friend, let him sneak out. "Trouble was, there I am dancing and an MP spots me. Next thing I know there were seven MPs. Next thing I know the eight of us are in the back of one of those guard trucks. Only one came out."[36]

After being discharged, Douglas landed back in Columbus and started fighting for real, turning pro in 1967 in Newark, New Jersey, then for the next year fighting almost exclusively in Ohio. He went through managers like water, averaging a new one almost every year. The second one, Chris Cline, was reluctant to part ways. "He wasn't getting me any fights so I handed him a release and told him to sign it. He refused," Douglas said. "So I drew back my right fist and told him to sign. He signed." (Cline was later involved in the Don King tournament scandal.) Douglas was 14–4 (9) when he won a split decision over Don Fullmer in July 1970. The next day, Fullmer's well-connected manager, Angelo Curley, strode into the local commission's office and convinced them to change the decision to a draw.[37]

Douglas went on the road to Europe and Puerto Rico in search of big fights before eventually landing in Philadelphia. He dropped a few but won more than he lost while the big fights mostly continued to elude him for the very reason Yank Durham had articulated. He wasn't worth the risk. Too dangerous. Bruce Trampler, one of Douglas's managers, watched one fight after another fall through for dubious reasons. One was against Curtis Cokes in Washington, D.C., in 1969, when Cokes was thinking of moving up from welterweight to middleweight.

Chapter 4. Do You Want Me to Stop It? 51

"Four days before the fight Douglas is working out at a gym in Alexandria, Virginia. Cokes is watching. Billy is sparring with an undefeated heavyweight from Washington, hits the guy on the chin and the guy goes out." A few minutes later, the phone rang. Cokes had sprained an ankle. The fight was off. They rescheduled it for March 1970 in Columbus. "Cokes backed out three days before that one," said Trampler. "This time it was a broken ankle."[38]

There were others. Luis Rodriguez, Trampler said, backed out of a fight with Douglas in Miami Beach because a couple of weeks before, he had been floored by Bobby Cassidy (Rodriguez won on points anyway), and Angelo Dundee, Rodriguez's manager, thought maybe his guy had lost his chin and wouldn't be able to handle Douglas. They claimed he had the flu. A little later, Trampler had Douglas signed to fight Willie Monroe—yes, Durham's guy—at Madison Square Garden, when a week before the fight, his phone rang.

TEDDY BRENNER, matchmaker at Madison Square Garden: "The fight's off. Monroe has the flu."
TRAMPLER: "Fine, we'll wait till he gets over the flu."
BRENNER: "Between you and me, I think it's gonna be a pretty long flu."[39]

"To make it worse," Trampler said, "Duke Stefano, also of The Garden, calls later. He doesn't know I've talked to Brenner. He tells me the fight is off because Monroe hurt an elbow." (Note: Douglas and Monroe ended up fighting on August 19, 1974, at the Spectrum. Monroe survived an eighth-round knockdown to win a unanimous decision.) The managers of contender Denny Moyer also had a tentative date lined up with Douglas but found as the fight approached that he had "prior commitments." Fight off.[40]

Between fights, Douglas taught ghetto kids how to box in an old gym in the worst part of Columbus. He made his Philadelphia debut in February 1972, stopping Bill Lloyd in the first round. Lloyd was a replacement for Bobby "Boogaloo" Watts, whose managers called Peltz on January 21 to tell him Watts would be unable to fight. "They were sure he was coming down with the flu," Peltz said. After Douglas knocked out Lloyd, Peltz spotted Watts and Monroe in the arena. "It's a shame they had to come to this fight," he said. "I predict a widespread epidemic of the flu in the Philadelphia gyms about the time I start trying to find another opponent for Billy Douglas."[41]

After beating Lloyd, Douglas knocked out eight straight second-tier opponents to earn a showdown with fellow badass Briscoe, who stopped him in eight rounds. Over the next several years, Douglas went 8–5 (7), including a fun upset win over hot prospect Pedro Soto at Madison

Square Garden in '76. By the time Peltz matched him with Matthew in September 1977, Douglas was, at 37 years old, well past his best days and, after having spent almost his entire career at middleweight, was now at light heavyweight. (He'd moved up in 1975.) It was not the best Billy Douglas that Matt was facing, but he was still a risk, especially so soon after the Johnson fight. Gelb was against it from the start and went along with it only after Matt convinced him he wouldn't make it a war.

"I personally wasn't in favor of this fight. It's only eight weeks after the Johnson bout and that was brutal. But Matthew sat here in my office for three hours persuading me I should let him fight Douglas. I was afraid he'd have to mix it up again with this guy but he assured me he intends to come out and just box as opposed to the war he fought with Johnson," Gelb said.[42]

"I would have preferred he fought a donkey. He's number nine now in the WBA and number 10 in the WBC. Two easy wins and we could have backed into the number seven position rather than a tough fight with a seasoned veteran."[43] Jimmy Hayes, the one-time pro heavyweight who had been Tyrone Everett's confidant, had recently been hired on as Matthew's conditioning man. He too was leery of taking on Douglas so soon after the Johnson fight but assured Gelb that so long as Matthew was in shape, he'd be ready, and Hayes would see to that.

Matthew played the part. "I don't like to slug. But Johnson was so awkward I had to. But it won't be like that [against Douglas]. That was once in a lifetime. I'm not even looking for a knockout. The fans who know me are only worried that I win."[44]

It almost became academic. Franklin-Douglas was the semifinal to WBA lightweight champion Roberto Duran's rematch against slick contender Edwin Viruet in the main event, which was to be broadcast on ABC. If that fight ended early, plans were to show Franklin-Douglas. The day before the show, the WBA told Peltz and Don King, Duran's promoter, that they wanted to bring in their own officials. Two of the Pennsylvania commissioners insisted on using local officials. That was resolved by a call from Spectrum officials to the governor's office and a subsequent call from Attorney General Bob Kane, who told the Pennsylvania commissioners to back off. But then ABC—already wary of King because of his corrupt and disastrous U.S. Boxing Championships tournament that ABC had launched—thought the maneuvering was King trying to protect Duran. They didn't want to televise the fight. Even Howard Cosell said he wouldn't commentate.[45]

At noon the day of the fight, ABC officials told Peltz there was a 90 percent chance they would not be televising the fight. If there was no TV, King wouldn't have the money to pay any of the fighters. The

Chapter 4. Do You Want Me to Stop It?

Billy Douglas slams Matt with a right cross in their memorable slugfest in September 1977 in Philadelphia. Douglas floored Matt in the fifth round. Matt stopped him in the sixth (photo courtesy of John DiSanto).

whole card would have to be scrapped. By chance, Peltz ran into Spectrum owner Eddie Snider coming out of the building and told him what was going on. Snider called the governor's office again; they got in touch with ABC again and explained the problem was with the Pennsylvania officials and not with King. ABC relented and the broadcast went ahead (Cosell commentated).[46] Duran retained the title with a unanimous decision over Viruet, and in the semifinal, Matt Franklin and Billy Douglas, to the surprise of almost no one, went to war.

Matthew tried to keep his word. He really did. For the first two rounds, he did what he'd promised Gelb he would do—he circled on the outside and jabbed, played it safe while Douglas stalked him, looking for a chance to land the right. He found it early in the third and landed several, right on Matt's jaw. Matthew took them and near the end of the round replied with several crackling hooks that let Douglas, 34–12–1 (25), know *he* could punch too. The fight was on, and in the fourth, they traded bombs for the duration of the round, bringing the crowd of 7,910 to its feet. Shades of the Johnson fight. In the fifth, a series of thundering rights and a hook put Matt down. Plenty of guys would have stayedthere,

Billy Douglas follows through with a left against Matt after flooring him. Referee Hank Cisco was criticized for stopping the fight when Matt hurt Douglas in the following round (photo courtesy of J Russell Peltz).

but Matt got up and took a long thrashing against the ropes, a dozen punches at least, as Douglas tried to end it.

But 37-year-old prizefighters have to end it quickly if they're going to at all, and when Douglas started to run out of steam, Matt fought off the ropes and drove the old man across the ring. The crowd exploded. It was the best action anyone had seen in … eight weeks. Douglas tried to press at the start of the seventh, but Matthew, younger, fresher, and stronger, fought him off and soon pinned him on the ropes. Douglas bled from the nose and mouth, and as Matthew assailed him, the referee, Hank Cisco, jumped between them and called it off. The crowd erupted in boos; they wanted the referee to afford Douglas the same opportunity to recover that he had afforded Matthew the round before, and they were right to. Peltz went ballistic. Citing an apparent relationship Cisco had with Gelb, he told the press Cisco should never be permitted to referee another fight in which Gelb had an interest. Gelb, in reply, threatened to sue Peltz unless he recanted. Peltz recanted.[47] Cisco told one of the Philadelphia writers that the ringside doctor, Alfred Ayella, had come to him after the fifth round and told him that both fighters were in such bad shape that he should stop the fight at the first opportunity. Ayella later confirmed that he told Cisco to watch both fighters carefully but didn't recall telling him to stop the fight. The referee defended the stoppage.

"I looked at Douglas—his expression, his eyes, his hands, which had dropped. I know the signs. I fought amateur and pro. I know what a TKO feels like."[48] It went into the books as stoppage at 2:44 of the sixth.

Later, Belfiore broke it down.

"Douglas began to pour it on and Matt began to pour it on and both of them went for the kill. Douglas came on like a wild man and Matt's not gonna run and it wound up like it did." For his part, Matthew wasn't thrilled to have been in another war. "I don't enjoy this new style. It takes a lot out of me. I feel a fighter should last a long time. I have the strategy of being able to combine two styles. I enjoy the recognition, but I don't want to be recognized as a bomber. I want to be recognized as a skillful boxer."[49]

It was too late for that.

Chapter 5

Neanderthals Throwing Rocks

"I got stopped and I enjoyed it."
—Dale Grant

The fight was five days away and Matthew had hardly been in the gym over the last two weeks. Belfiore was furious. Gelb wasn't happy either. Matthew's career was finally in high gear following his wins over Johnson and Douglas and looking past a lesser fighter next time out could lead to disaster. Lee "Junior" Royster was a tune-up for a big fight Gelb was working on for a couple of months down the road, but they had to be careful. Tune-ups could backfire on a fighter who was coming off a big win or two and Matt's wins over Johnson and Douglas were the biggest of his career. An emotional letdown was almost inevitable, and Royster was the kind of fighter who could surprise you.

It was true that in 23 fights, most of which had taken place in Miami, Royster had never put together three straight wins. He'd win two, then lose two, then draw. Win one, drop one, then win two more. He was all over the place as a fighter—one night, he looked like a world champ, the next like a palooka. You never knew which Royster was going to show up. Would it be the one who went down to New Guinea and starched Australian and Commonwealth light heavyweight champion Tony Mundine in the first round (and lost an unpopular decision in the rematch) or the one who lost to 10–12–3 (3) Bobby Lloyd? Would it be the one who drew with undefeated prospect James Scott in Miami (more on him later) or the one who lost to 16–5-2 (6) Walter White? Either way, Royster had to be taken seriously, if for no other reason than the night in July 1976 when he stopped Wayne McGee—the guy who'd handed Matthew his first pro loss—in five rounds.

The problem was Matthew's personal life was a shambles. He was engaged in a custody battle for his twin daughters, Rashidah and Sheena, now four years old, and every day was a roller coaster. He rushed through the final press conference for the fight, staying only long enough to tell

Chapter 5. Neanderthals Throwing Rocks

the press, "The mother keeps aggravating me. The court case is coming up after the fight. I'm tired and exhausted because I want to have my child. I can't train right."[1] He left halfway through, refusing a plate of roast beef and potatoes ("I have a bad appetite") and leaving Belfiore to answer for the writers, not just which Royster would show up but also which Matthew—the raw kid he'd melded into a smart boxer-puncher or the reckless puncher the crowds loved.

"I want him to box. I want him to be aggressive but also defensive. But Matthew never does anything he's told. When I started with him back in the amateurs I'd want to walk away from our corner, that's how disgusted I got with him. He's a 24-year-old who doesn't have the brains of a 15-year-old sometimes. But I always knew he had the makings. That's why I put up with it."[2]

"I don't want him to have a short career," Belfiore said. "Matt ain't had no soft touches and too many wars. He's gonna be the light heavyweight champion in less than a year. He's got the tools to do it." Royster quickly tired of all the talk about which style Matthew would employ. "He'd better decide in a hurry which style he's going to fight. Because I'm going to come out smoking on his head." Peltz had the line of the day: "There is nothing wrong with Franklin's new style if he'd just learn how to duck."[3]

Of near equal interest was the main prelim on the card in which Matt's two most recent victims, Johnson and Douglas, would meet in a 10-rounder, ostensibly for the right to a rematch. Johnson spoke at length about the loss to Matt.

"After that fight I was as depressed as I can get without someone dying in my family," he said. "I replayed that fight over and over in my mind every day. In fact, I still do it now. My manager had been negotiating a fight with Galindez for after the Franklin fight. It was close to being finalized. Losing was a big blow. I figure it set me back a year in my quest to be light heavyweight champion."[4]

Meanwhile, Douglas was still fuming over the ref's oddly-timed stoppage in his own loss to Matthew. "I still don't understand why the referee stopped the fight. I wasn't bleeding. I wasn't cut. [Note: Yes, he was.] I wasn't knocked down. Franklin never could have lasted another round. I always go into a shell the last few seconds of a round and the ref thought I was hurt."[5]

Half-assed training camp or not, Matthew had it all over Royster and on November 1, 1977, in front of a crowd of 6,317 at the Spectrum, Matt dropped Royster twice in the third, twice in the sixth, and twice in the tenth on the way to a unanimous decision win by scores of 49–40, 50–40, and 49–35. Royster managed little offense, though with 28 seconds left, he did walk Matt into a Hail Mary left hook that might have mattered had it landed earlier in the round. As it was, the only drama involved whether Matt would get the knockout.

"I was shocked he kept getting up. I was hitting him with some powerful punches. I wanted the ref to stop it. I was disgusted at the end that I hadn't knocked him out," he said.[6] He blamed it on his decision to box rather than slug. "I told you reporters I'd come out and box, and I did. In fact that might be why I didn't take him out early."[7]

Royster took solace in the only thing he could: lasting the distance. "My eyes can get knocked to the back of my head and I'll get up blind," said Royster. "My father was a fighter. He said if you get knocked down, forget it. Keep fighting." And as many expected, Johnson made a mess out of the 37-year-old Douglas in the main prelim, stopping him in the fifth round. A torrent of left uppercuts—the same punch Johnson landed hundreds of times on Matthew but to little effect—opened up Douglas's eyelid, his nose, and his mouth, creating a ghastly bloodbath that left both fighters' trunks covered in plasma. "I would have been ashamed of myself if that fight went 10 rounds," Johnson said afterward. "He's an old man."[8]

Later, Gelb revealed that Royster was a tune-up for a big fight he'd been working on for six weeks. It would be in February and the opponent was no joke.[9]

* * *

Richie Kates was 13 years old, 5'5", and about 129 pounds when he and his buddies headed out to the Millville Athletic Club. He'd been reading in the papers about all these allegedly great boxers they had over there. "I can whip anyone they got over there," he told his friends.[10] He'd never been in a gym or anything, but he'd grown up rough, with seven brothers and three sisters and all of them worked in the fields picking tomatoes and beans and loading them onto trucks.[11] He'd been born in Savannah, Georgia. His parents, John and Alice Kates, moved the family to rural Cedarville, New Jersey, then to Bridgeton in 1954, hoping to give their kids a better life than they could in the Deep South. They'd succeeded but just barely. Kates and his siblings worked long and hard in the fields.

"My parents were migrant farm workers, just like a lot of blacks in the South. You named it, we picked it. Tomatoes, beans, okra, asparagus. That's where I learned the value of hard work. Nothing was given to you. You had to earn it," he said years later.[12]

On Saturdays, he watched boxing matches on his family's tiny black-and-white TV. One Saturday afternoon, he was watching when

Chapter 5. Neanderthals Throwing Rocks

one of his friends came over. He said, "You know those guys get paid to do that." An epiphany. Kates thought, "I could do that!"[13] It wasn't much later that he and his friends cut school to check out the gym in Millville. It was only about 12 miles from Bridgeton, and they figured that once they got on 49 East and started hitching, someone would pick them up. Ten minutes into their trip, no one had, so they said to hell with it and decided to run the rest of the way.

The guys at the gym laughed at Kates and his friends when they showed up, but they let them fool around on the bags and jump rope. A trainer, Letty Petway, kept an eye on the group. One of them was harassing the fighters, calling them "sissies." It was Kates. Petway threw him out. He showed up again the next day insisting he could beat up Al Thomas, a local heavyweight. Petway threw him out again. The next day, there was Kates again, going through his act. Petway said to hell with it and put him in with Thomas to teach the kid a lesson. Thomas sent the kid back to Bridgeton with a broken nose, and everyone figured that was the last they'd see of him. They were wrong.[14] Kates showed up again, and that's when Petway started teaching him. Pretty soon, he was getting him fights in South Jersey and Philadelphia. Kates would walk into the ring wearing his mother's terry-cloth bathrobe. It was all he had. It wasn't until he was 13 fights into it that he got a proper robe. But he kept making the trip down Route 49. Sometimes, if he had a couple of extra coins in his pocket, he would catch the bus. More often, he had to decide what he wanted to spend those coins on—lunch at school or bus fare. When lunch won out, he hitched, ran, or caught a ride with a friend, but he kept on making the trip, and the spirit that kept him coming back to the gym took him over the next several years to a 57–7 amateur record that included a Mid-Atlantic Amateur Athletic Union (AAU) title in 1969.[15]

Kates lied about his age and turned pro in 1969 at age 16 and made his debut in December during his sophomore year at Bridgeton High School. It was out of necessity. He had gotten a girl pregnant and had a daughter whom he wanted to support. He went pro under longtime Philadelphia manager Joe Gramby and Bonnie Coccaro, the wife of local promoter Tony Coccaro. Ray Campbell assisted Petway in the gym and the corner. As Kates awaited the opening bell during his pro debut, he spied his opponent, Bobby Haynes, then turned to Petway and said, "That's a grown man over there." Petway replied, "You're a pro now. You're going to be fighting grown men all the time."[16]

Later, Kates told the press how important boxing was to him as a child. "Boxing is how I stayed out of prison. Some of my friends are there. And many of them got into trouble when they were 12, 13 years old. Right at the age when they shouldn't have been out on the streets with nothing to do. Society—adults, you, me, city government—forgets about these kids. Society has to create something for them to do. A kid with nothing to do is more likely to get into trouble than one who is kept interested in something—like I was with boxing."[17]

Kates went 18–0 before getting stopped by Eddie Owens in 1972 in Philadelphia. He won his next 14 straight, including a rematch with Owens, to get a shot at WBA light heavyweight champion Victor Galíndez in May 1976 in Johannesburg. In one of the more bizarre fights of the era, an apparent headbutt opened a gash over Galíndez's eye in the third round that would later take 20 stitches to close. Referee Stanley Christodolou immediately stopped the fight and sent Galíndez to his corner, prompting dozens of photographers and Galíndez camp members to storm the ring. It appeared the fight was over. Instead, Galíndez's corner was given five minutes to repair the cut and the fight continued.

A brute of a fighter, Galíndez ignored the rivers of blood flowing into his right eye and floored Kates in the seventh before stopping him with a pair of left hooks seconds before the bell ending the 15th round. Kates won a tune-up three months later in Atlantic City before taking on Galíndez again, this time in Rome. Thirteen months after their first fight, Galíndez won a unanimous 15-round decision. Kates beat Harold Carter in Vineland, then took a nice, long break. Behind the scenes, Granby and Coccaro were talking to Gelb.

"I think it would be a good fight for both of them. We've been working with Bonnie Coccaro and Joe Gramby for about six weeks now," Gelb said after Matthew beat Royster. "It looks like it will be set for January or February. The two guys know and like each other. They want to meet and it would be a great fight. They're both at the top of their careers and now is the time to get them together." Gelb had promoted Kates's fight against Carter, and Matt visited Kates's corner during the bout to share some advice.[18]

The fight was set for February 7, 1978, at the Spectrum and would be for the NABF light heavyweight title. With his custody dispute resolved for the time being, Matt started training in earnest in December. Kates was not just a slick, talented boxer but also the most experienced fighter he had faced in terms of competing on the big stage. Matt had nowhere near that level of experience. It's what Kates's team was counting on.

"I've been through big fights, championship fights, so this one is no big deal to me. It's important that I win, but I'm certainly in no panic. I respect Matt Franklin, which means I see nothing there that I can't handle," Kates said.[19]

Petway agreed. "This should be one hell of a fight," he said. "It's not an easy fight by no means. But I feel Richie has advantages. First of all, Richie has more experience. Those two shots at Galindez might come in handy. Second, Richie is in much better shape than I have seen him in a long time. Richie also punches harder than Franklin."[20]

Kates elaborated. "There is nothing I can do wrong in this fight. I'm not just basing that on my experience. I think I'm just a better fighter. He's putting himself next to God since he beat Johnson. I still respect him. There is no animosity in my heart for him. But we're fighters. I'm not going into the ring to shake his hand. I'm going in to fight him and beat him.[21] He thinks his win over Johnson made him a slugger, but Johnson made him fight the fight he wanted and I'm going to force him to do what I want him to do."[22] Two days before the fight, a blizzard dumped 16 inches of snow in Philadelphia, the most in a decade. Peltz rescheduled the card for the 10th. Matt, in high spirits, took advantage of the delay to get to know some of his neighbors.

"Tuesday morning I grabbed a shovel and went out into the neighborhood," he said. "I walked around looking for houses where there were old people, people who couldn't clear their own walks. Quite a few of them said, 'Hey, I know you, you're the fighter.' And I'd say, 'You want your pavement done?' I didn't charge. I did it for the exercise and because there are a lot of fine people in South Philly. I loved it. Maybe some of them will even come to the Spectrum Friday night."[23]

"I was out at 7:00 AM," Matt said. "Ran all the way up Broad, from Ellsworth to City Hall. Shadow boxing, waving to the people. I felt real good, just like Rocky. I'm ready for Richie Kates. A new era is about to begin."[24] Kates was equally unbothered by the delay. "What I'll do is use my left to keep Franklin away and see how he handles my right. I'm not sure he can, but regardless, I'm going after his body," he said. "When he began fighting, he was a counterpuncher. Now he's more of a free swinger, taking the initiative. He's a good fighter. I'll find out how good."[25]

Matt had to take off three pounds at the noon weigh-in to make 175. He told reporters his scale had him right on weight in the days leading up to the fight, so he was surprised to find himself over. (It was no surprise to those who had been covering him for a while, as he'd missed weight at least twice before.) He then revealed that along with heat, he employed bubble gum to drop pounds. "The bubble gum helps bring out the sweat," he said.[26]

The paid attendance was 6,586 at the Spectrum, but it should have been more. As in the Douglas fight, Matthew began by moving and boxing, as he promised he would. In those first two rounds, he was about as good a boxer-puncher as he ever would be. All the years Belfiore had spent on him making him a complete fighter in that hole of a gym in South Philly had fully paid off. This wasn't Matthew out-toughing a guy like in the Johnson fight. And it wasn't him outlasting an old guy like in the Douglas fight. He was outboxing one of the best and most experienced light heavyweights in the world. There was little Richie Kates couldn't do in a prize ring. And Matthew was taking him to school.

Late in the second round, Matt nailed Kates with four—four!—rapid-fire left hooks, each short, hard, and on the button. Moments later, he crashed a right hand off Kates's head and Kates fell into the ropes and to the canvas. The referee, Charlie Sgrillo, apparently missed the right hand and called it a slip, but everyone, Kates included, knew better. Matt battered him on the ropes and a more thoughtful ref might have stopped it there, with Kates almost out on his feet. Sgrillo wasn't that guy. He let Kates stagger back to his corner at the bell. The third round featured more straight, hard jabs and right hands from Matt and a left-hook, right-cross combination rocked Kates. He came back with a good right of his own near the end of the round, but Matt was in complete control. It didn't last.

With his head fully clear from the shellacking he took in the second, Kates attacked Matthew in the fourth. He landed one combination after another until a crackling right over Matthew's low left hand dropped Matt face-first. He fell like a man who had walked into a trip wire, and they say in boxing that when a man falls face-first like that, the fight's over. He doesn't get up. Everything has short-circuited. But Matt was up at the count of five, his nose bleeding, his legs unsteady. Like Kates had earlier, he looked out on his feet but ready to start swinging. The bell rang before another blow was thrown.

"I said to myself 'Matt, you been hurt,'" he said later.[27]

In an odd kind of replay of the first Galíndez fight, Kates and his corner started celebrating, thinking Sgrillo had stopped the fight. The crowd was so loud that they hadn't heard the bell. Between rounds, Belfiore did the best he could to clear the cobwebs from Matt's brain. When the bell sounded for the fifth, Matthew was still hurt and went to the ropes while Kates went to work on him.

"By the time we got back out there I knew exactly what I had to do," he said. "I played with him on the ropes, let him do most of the work. But I kept tap-tap-tapping, then I'd throw a couple smokers once in a while. You got to make sure the referee don't stop it."[28]

Matt spun Kates around on the ropes and hurt him again with an explosive volley, sending the crowd into yet another apoplectic frenzy. Kates battled back, landing hard shots of his own. With 10 seconds left in the round, a bazooka of a right sent Kates down again. The bell saved him, but he was done. Matt beat him all over the ring in the sixth until a right hand sent Kates staggering into Sgrillo's waiting arms. The time was 1:35. Matt jumped all over the ring, arms aloft, smiling widely.

"Richie Kates is a good fighter," he said, still out of breath, to the television interviewer. "He's the best fighter I ever fought. I can't take nothing from Kates. He hurt me. Then I got determination and guts. I had it all on my side and I want to thank Nick Belfiore and Frank Gelb and Jimmy Hayes and all my corner. I gotta have Galindez or Mate Parlov next."[29]

Matt blasts Richie Kates with a right hand during their war at the Spectrum in Philadelphia in February 1978. Matt climbed off the canvas to stop Kates in the sixth round (photo courtesy of John DiSanto).

While Matthew and the crowd were in a state of delirium, Kates was lapsing in and out of consciousness. He lost consciousness in the dressing room, regained it, then passed out again. He was taken by ambulance to Metropolitan Hospital and released after test results indicated nothing more serious than a concussion. Later, he blamed himself for the loss. "I'm going back to my old style," he said. "I got to the top by being a finesse counterpuncher. My undoing, so to speak, was in trying to be a slugger, a free swinger."[30] He continued, "I learned two things from this fight. You don't box with a boxer and you don't slug with a slugger. I tried to slug and I paid for it."[31]

Again, the Philly reporters raved about the hometown kid. "As you may have gathered by now, this was not just another ordinary prizefight. It was, in fact, another example of what is rapidly coming to be known as a Matt Franklin special," wrote one.[32] Another: "It was the most savage fight in Philadelphia in more than a decade. They fought like Neanderthals throwing rocks at each other. They staggered and slumped and

Top light heavyweight Richie Kates glares up at Matt from the canvas in the fourth round. The referee, Charlie Sgrillo, incorrectly ruled that Kates had slipped. One of the best overall fighters in the division, Kates had previously fought twice for the WBA championship, losing both times to Víctor Galíndez (photo courtesy of J Russell Peltz).

survived vicious punches and knockdowns. And when it was over Matt Franklin emerged as the NABF light heavyweight champion."[33]

Gelb talked afterward about Matt meeting Parlov again. Peltz had other ideas. He wanted to match Matt with Mike Rossman, a young, popular puncher based in Turnersville, New Jersey, 20 minutes from South Philly. Although Jimmy DiPiano, Rossman's father, was Italian, Rossman's mother Celia was Jewish and it was decided Rossman would fight under his mother's maiden name. Consequently, he fought with the Star of David on his trunks and was billed as the "Jewish Bomber."

DiPiano managed him and Rossman trained out of Seven Champs Gym in Pleasantville, New Jersey, which his father ran. Although Rossman had been raised around the corner from a locally famous roast beef joint at 20th and Jackson Streets in Philly and was, as one writer put it, "as Philadelphian as the Mummer's Parade, Freedom Week, scrapple, and hoagies,"[34] he didn't fight exclusively in Philadelphia or even regularly. He didn't have to. By the time Matthew stopped Kates, Rossman had 38 pro fights under his belt, 10 of which had taken place at Madison Square Garden.

"I can't get an agreement with the Spectrum," DiPiano told a reporter in November 1977, not long before Rossman was scheduled to fight perennial contender Yaqui López. "I have nothing against Russell Peltz. He knows how to put matches together, but if you can't come up with the money, what good is it? We can go somewhere else, fight the same guy he wants us to fight and make a lot more money."

"They never gave us a chance here," DiPiano said. "They think he can't draw. Can you imagine that—a white fighter like Joey Giardello and he can't draw? If TV can pay, if Madison Square Garden can pay, who are they to say he can't draw? In this business you go where the money is. We got $30,000 for fighting Mike Quarry, and 35 big ones for [Gary] Summerhays and we're gonna get better than $40,000 for Lopez."[35]

As far as Peltz was concerned, Matthew's win over Kates changed all that. He was certain he could build a Franklin-Rossman showdown that would do big numbers at the Spectrum. "I talked to Jimmy DiPiano and told him the Spectrum is now willing to pay him the kind of money he's getting from the Garden. He promised he wouldn't do anything after that next fight until he talked to us," Peltz said. "I hope he means it. I think he'll be pleasantly surprised."[36]

A month after Matthew stopped Kates, López stopped Rossman in the sixth round. In terms of a Franklin-Rossman fight, it didn't matter much. López was a highly regarded, well-respected contender. Rossman was still a young kid who would eventually have his day. He came right back three months later to stop Lonnie Bennet in the Spectrum and talk of a Franklin-Rossman match revved right up again. It reached a peak in the days leading up to and immediately following Matt's fight at the Spectrum in June 1978, along with many wondering when Matt, now ranked second in the world by the WBA, was going to get a title shot.

One Philly writer described a conversation between a producer at CBS named Chuck Milton and Tommy Kenville of Top Rank, the promoter. (CBS would be broadcasting an upcoming bout between WBC champion Mate Parlov and John Conteh.) Milton wanted to know the records of Parlov and Marvin Johnson, who was fighting Lotti Mwale on the undercard.

"Parlov's 23–1," said Kenville.

"Who beat him?" asked Milton.

"Matt Franklin," Kenville answered.

"How about Johnson?" Milton asked.

"He's 20–1," replied Kenville.

"Who beat him?"

"Matt Franklin."

"Franklin!" Milton cried. "How come *he's* not fighting for the title?"[37] That's what a lot of people wanted to know. What they didn't know was that Matt had been offered a shot at Galíndez's WBA light heavyweight title and he'd turned it down. Why? That was the real story.

Matt wanted out of his contract with Gelb (who was now Matt's comanager, along with Belfiore). He had over the last several months, at least since the Kates fight. That was the reason for the four-month layoff following the Kates win, and by June, the cat was out of the bag. Gelb and Matt hadn't been seen together anywhere in public since the Kates fight, and Matt had been grumbling that Gelb wasn't spending enough time with him. He complained that Gelb had too many other fighters and other interests.

This came as curious news to those who knew them both well. They knew that Gelb spent more time one-on-one with Matthew than he did with all of his other fighters combined. They knew that Gelb's wife, a schoolteacher and a counselor for troubled kids in Norristown, took him around to all the schools so he could counsel the kids against going down the road he had traveled and that she always accompanied the crew to Matt's out-of-town fights. Gelb's family didn't socialize with any of Gelb's other fighters, but Matt was invited to every family function. Gelb's sons played basketball with Matt and worked out with him at the Juniper.[38]

Matt was unmoved. "Frank, he's a hungry sort of man and he put me in with King Kong. Put me in with guys who could knock my head off. I got tired of that."[39] But there was more to it than that. In June, Matt told a writer named Ray Didinger that Gelb was taking 50 percent of his purses. Not so, according to Gelb. Gelb and comanager Belfiore each got 25 percent. Gelb said Matt got the other 50 percent. "My contract with Franklin is on file at the Pennsylvania Athletic Commission. Anyone who is interested can go to the commission office and see for themselves what I get from the Franklin fights," he said.[40]

Someone had gotten in Matt's ear, told him Gelb was ripping him off. It was a story as old as the sport itself: Tell a fighter his money man is screwing him so you can steal him away. Then *you* can steal from him. It worked so often because a lot of the time, it was true. Who's a fighter to believe? Whether or not it was true in Matt's case, he told his lawyer, Harry Rubin, to dissolve his relationship with Gelb.

Their contract was set to expire on October 20, 1978. But Gelb claimed Matt had signed a two-year extension that would take the contract to late 1980. Matt countered that Gelb had stuck a blank sheet of paper in front of him and told him to sign it. To get a shot at Galíndez, Matt would have to sign a three-fight deal with Bob Arum—and if Gelb's contract was still in effect, Gelb would get a big chunk of the purses. Either way, from this point on, it was Rubin who mostly worked with Peltz on Matt's fights, not Gelb.

So Matt turned down the Galíndez fight, which would have taken place on September 15 in New Orleans on the Muhammad Ali–Leon Spinks II undercard. The Ali-Spinks rematch ended up drawing 63,352 fans to the Superdome, was watched by 90 million viewers in the United States on television, and some 2 billion worldwide in 80 countries. It broke all the records. Matt would have become an instant worldwide sensation.

"I wasn't ready to be king under those [contractual] circumstances," he later said.[41]

So he took a couple of smaller fights to bide his time until, he hoped, he could get rid of Gelb. The first was against Seattle's Dale Grant, half brother of 1972 Olympic gold medal winner Sugar Ray Seales and owner of a purported 303–6 amateur record that included two national championships. He had won nine straight since moving up from middleweight to light heavy, but the only reason anyone could come up with as to why it might be competitive was Matt's four-month layoff. He was unconcerned.

"The layoff won't bother me. I've been doing a lot of boxing [in the gym] and running to build up my stamina. I don't know too much about the guy, but almost every guy you come up to you got to fight different. Sometimes it takes a little longer to solve a guy's style," he said. Then, by way of warning: "Anybody that takes it to me, they're in trouble if they make me fight."[42]

Belfiore said he had checked out Grant, and although he saw that he was a "pretty good boxer and a good puncher," he was confident Matt would prevail, even if it took him a couple of rounds to get going. "Matt was always a slow starter; it takes him a couple rounds to warm up. He's always had the tools and he can punch. But on defense, even now, he gets a little careless."[43]

In front of 4,707 fans at the Spectrum, Matt stalked Grant for the first few rounds before landing a right-hand bomb at 50 seconds of the fifth that sent Grant down. He beat referee Frank Cappuccino's count, but when another right sent him reeling, Cappuccino called it off. The time was 1:10.

"I felt kind of stale at the beginning. The layoff didn't affect me that much. I just wanted to take my time with him. I didn't want to do too much wildness," Matt said afterward. "He was always running. If he'd took it to me instead, it probably would have been a more exciting fight. He could punch. I felt him a couple times. But his style still was kind of funny. I finally figured it out about the third round. I would jab, feint the right, then jab. When I jabbed him, he blinked and started looking for the right. He knew the right was the bomb. He knew it was coming, he just didn't know when."[44]

"I got stopped and I enjoyed it," Grant said. "I know now what I have to do next time. It's a different style of boxing in Philadelphia than I'm accustomed to. It's way tougher to fight here than out in Washington. Also, I was fighting a guy who was a champion. I'd do my things for a few seconds and then I was watching him because it was the first time I ever fought a champion. It was good experience."[45]

Afterward, the local press hammered on a Franklin–Rossman fight harder than before. "In this city, it would be a fight to remember. The Gods on Mount Olympus couldn't draw a better pairing. It would set a new standard for boxing at the Spectrum. Matt Franklin versus Mike Rossman."[46] The people in the know—Matt, Peltz, DiPiano and Belfiore—knew it wouldn't happen. According to Belfiore, DiPiano had a grudge against him over an incident that had taken place at the Juniper.

"Yeah, big man—that's the way he used to come into my gym, like he owned the joint. He and Mike were welcome, but all of the sudden he was bringing along four or five guys to train, and 10 or 12 to watch. I told him, 'This is a small place. I don't have room for all these people.' I asked him why he didn't go around to the Passyunk Gym, where they could accommodate him."

"He sat there, never said a word the day I talked to him about it," Belfiore said. "Next thing I know I'm reading in the paper where he said I couldn't train a mouse to go up a cuckoo clock. We haven't talked since, and I ain't about to apologize to him for something I never did. But if he wants to bury the hatchet, I'm willing."[47]

But that wasn't DiPiano's only reason for avoiding Matt, according to Belfiore. "The real truth is, he knows Matthew could be champion tomorrow. He don't want his kid hurt, and I don't blame him for that. Matt and Michael used to spar, and at the start Matthew had trouble with Michael's jab. Later it was obvious Mike couldn't handle Matthew anymore. That's the real reason they left the gym."[48]

Tony Green, one of Rossman's early sparring partners who later joined Matt's camp, said he was with Rossman and DiPiano in a diner when someone brought up Matt's name as a possible opponent. DiPiano replied, "My son is never getting into a ring with that fucking animal."[49]

Shortly after the Grant fight, Matt agreed to face Newark's Bob Smith at the Branch Brook Ice Center in Newark, New Jersey, underneath

Chapter 5. Neanderthals Throwing Rocks

his old rival Eddie Gregory against Chuck Warfield in the main event. The promoter was Murad Muhammad's Triangle Promotions Inc., which had started out as Cornerstone Promotions, a group comprised of five men, each with some ties of undetermined significance to Muhammad Ali's camp and to Herbert Muhammad, Ali's manager. They were Akbar Muhammad, Sayyid Bilal Muhammad, Bahr Muhammad, Murad Muhammad, and Abdullah Muhammad. Murad had purportedly come close to making a deal with the government of Ghana to sponsor and host Ali–Ken Norton IV before Ali lost to Leon Spinks. When that fight fell apart, some members of Cornerstone left to form Triangle Promotions.

Ali and his wife, Veronica, attended the show in Newark as special guests of Murad. It was Ali's last scheduled public appearance in advance of his rematch with Spinks, which was to take place the following month. A sellout crowd of about 3,000 in Newark saw Gregory stop Warfield in a round and Matt take out Freddie Bright, a late replacement for Smith, at 1:30 of the eighth. At some point during Matt's time in Newark, someone introduced him to Bilal, who, through his work with Ali, had ties with Bob Arum.

Bilal asked him if it was true, as he had heard, that Matt was unhappy with his current management and looking to make a change. Matt answered that yes, it was true.

Bilal asked him, "What do you really want to do in boxing?"

Matt said, "I want to fight for the title."

"If I can put you in a position where you fight for the title can I manage you?"

"Yes."[50]

Over the next weeks, Bilal and Matt spoke frequently toward dissolving Matt's relationship with Gelb. But that wasn't all that Matt had going on. The year prior, he had begun seeing a woman named Shirley Mitchell in South Philadelphia. Their romance, which lasted years, produced a daughter, Zakiyyah, who was born in September 1978. Sometime earlier, another relationship had produced a son, Jamar, and there was another daughter too, Sophia. Later, another daughter, Tenille, from another relationship, brought the number of children Matt fathered to six. Although he married none of the children's mothers, he paid child support as a matter of routine and was a part of his children's lives to the extent that was possible and with the cooperation of the children's mothers.

In the meantime, Peltz and Rubin were working on putting together Matt against Yaqui López, but before that could happen, Rossman turned the light heavyweight division upside down when he stopped

Galíndez in the 13th round on the Ali–Spinks II undercard in New Orleans. Matt watched from his seat as Rossman captured the WBA light heavyweight title in a match that he, Matthew, had turned down. "I knew Galindez was ready to be taken but I was surprised that Mike Rossman was the one to beat him," Matt said later. "Flying home I found myself thinking, 'Matthew, you could have stopped him in five,' and that's what my friends have been telling me ever since. 'If Rossman could do it in 13,' they say, 'you could do it in half that time.'"[51]

While Rossman's team was trying to figure out how to make the most of his title win—that is, make the most amount of money while assuming the smallest amount of risk—Matt got lucky. The only contender ahead of him was Gregory, who, theoretically, was first in line to get a shot at Rossman's title since he had beaten Matt. Unfortunately for him, he took a fight against James Scott in Rahway State Prison in New Jersey (in a show promoted by Murad Muhammad) and was soundly beaten over 12 rounds. That was great news for Rossman and his team. They wanted no part of Gregory and couldn't have been happier.[52] The bad news was that instead of Gregory, his mandatory challenger would be the winner of the Franklin-López fight. Rossman had already lost to López and knew he'd be a big underdog to Matt, who wasn't sure the fight could be made, even for big money.

"There's a little problem there," said Matt. "If I beat Lopez, I think me and Mike got to fight. We can make a ton of money. Two Philadelphia area boys, a white boy against a black boy, they'd have to put that in the stadium. We could become the first million-dollar gate in this city. Even if Mike didn't have the slightest thought he could beat me, he'd have to take that fight. But we got a problem. Mike and I used to work out, afterwards we'd stand around and talk about a lot of things. That's changed."[53]

Matt said he tried to get into Rossman's dressing room before the Galíndez fight in New Orleans to wish him luck, and when he identified himself, the door was closed on him. And in early October, Matt went to the Passyunk Gym where Rossman was training in hopes of getting some advice about fighting López. "Mike kind of shrugged his shoulders like, 'Go find out for yourself.'"[54]

Matt remained hopeful. "I don't think those are real scenes. I'm sure there's gonna come a time when we're gonna fight each other. And some day, after it's all over I can see us sitting down, talking about the days when there was so much money hanging out there and we couldn't get to it because our managers were quarreling. We'll get together eventually. Mike's a smart guy and a better fighter than I thought. And I'd box King Kong if the money was right."[55]

Chapter 5. Neanderthals Throwing Rocks

Peltz, for one, remained doubtful. He told reporters he believed DiPiano would relinquish the title before he'd defend against Matt. "Jimmy is serious about not doing business with Nick," he said.[56]

Rossman wasn't so sure. "There are problems with that fight, but it still all comes down to money," he said. "If the money is there, we'll fight. What Franklin doesn't seem to understand is that he's not gonna end up with much, because most of it goes to the champion ... and that's me.[57]

"Fighting him is no bother. I boxed him in the gym when I was a middleweight and he was a light heavy. I've grown and improved since then, and he's the same. He's been on the deck a lot. In fact, I'd suggest he stop talking about me and start worrying about Yaqui Lopez, who can put him out of business real quick."[58]

Chapter 6

Tightrope

"I'm going Injun hunting!"
—Matthew Saad Muhammad

Matt strolled into the press conference for his upcoming fight with Yaqui López wearing a big smile, a cowboy hat, and a shoulder holster with a water pistol in it. After he sat down, someone whispered to him an unfortunate truth about López: he was not American Indian but Mexican. "What?" Matthew said. "I had no idea he was Mexican."[1] You couldn't blame him. The man's nickname was "Indian Yaqui" López, after all. He picked it up as an amateur in 1971 when he defeated a Native American fighter in Eureka, California, in front of a large, rowdy, Native American crowd.

Afterward, someone asked his handler if López too was Native American. The handler believed that all Mexicans probably had some Indian blood, and he knew too what they wanted to hear, so he replied to the effect, hell yes, he was Native American.

"What tribe?" they demanded.

The handler didn't know one tribe from another and the only one he could think of was the Yaqui tribe, so that's what he said. It was bullshit, of course, but bullshit in service of a higher cause, so naturally it stuck. The fighter was henceforth "Indian Yaqui" López.[2]

Someone turned off the lights at the press conference, and Matt, along with everyone else in attendance, watched highlights of López beating the living daylights out of Rossman during their match the previous March, won by López in six rounds. "I can see that when he starts putting punches together, he can be plenty of trouble," Matt said. "Mexicans are tough." But he also saw the man's weaknesses.

"Lopez is very good. One of the best. But every time he fights, he gets cut. He's got a reputation for cutting. Look at his face. It's all cuts and bruises. He's got a big gash right across the bridge of his nose. And I have developed the punch that will beat him. I call it the 'loop-a-doop.'

Chapter 6. Tightrope

It's a looping overhand right that, when it lands, it will press down on that gash on his nose. I've been practicing it for about two months now and I'm going to use it to try to re-open that cut. It could come at any time."[3]

Álvaro López was born under the bullring at the Plaza de Toros San Pedro in Zacatecas. It is no coincidence, then, that he grew up wanting to be a matador. He got his chance, sort of, at about 11 years old when he and a friend sneaked into an unguarded bullring where a pair of bulls were kept for aspiring matadors to "train" on. Young Álvaro used his shirt as a capote (the red cape the matadors wave at onrushing bulls) and mimicked the bullfighters he had seen. The first two passes went well enough, which is to say, they resulted in no broken boxes. On the third, the bull caught Álvaro's right ankle and broke it into pieces.

Unsurprisingly, this cured him of his bullfighting fantasies but did little to eradicate the instincts that led him to the bullring in the first place: his instincts as a fighter. Whether or not he knew it, he would be a fighter of some kind. Maybe not of bulls but a fighter of something, and this instinct surely was abetted by the fact that he spent much of his time selling magazines on street corners in hopes that he could make enough money to eat.

Not long after his ankle healed, López's parents, Raul and Raquel, got word to Zacatecas that he was to join them in Stockton, California, where they worked the fields. He lasted for six months at the local school before dropping out and joining his parents on the farms. Soon, he took up with a girl named Beatrice whose father was a local fight promoter. Álvaro asked the man to teach him how to box. The man, Jack Cruz, took him to the gym, and two weeks later, Álvaro had his first amateur fight. "He was the worst-looking amateur ever," according to Cruz. "They wanted to put me in jail after his first fight. He lost it, but all the little kids liked him and followed him to his dressing room for autographs. He won [most of] his amateur fights but he looked so bad we decided to turn him pro [in 1971]."[4] López married Beatrice, and probably not coincidentally, Cruz remained his manager for the rest of his career.

By the time López and Matt faced each other at the Spectrum on October 24, 1978, everything there was to know about López was known. On the way up, he'd lost the occasional fight here and there but only to the guys everyone else respected or feared: Jesse Burnett, Al Bolden, and Lonnie Bennet. And he'd already had three shots at the two available championships, losing on points to England's John Conteh in 1976 and twice to Víctor Galíndez in '77 and '78.

López occupied, indeed seemed to have been permanently sentenced to, a no-man's land just below the best in the weight class and demonstrably better than those rated below him. If you weren't at his level, López would take you apart—ask Rossman. But when he faced the best 175-pound men, the scar tissue around his eyes betrayed him, or his lack of world-class punching power encouraged bravery in his opponent that didn't exist against other men. His wooden legs and slowness of hand were found out and exploited. At those moments, he tried to compensate with balls and guts, but at the top level, everyone had those. They weren't enough.

To be sure, many of the men López whipped envied and revered him. What a fighter! And the slums in Zacatecas were full of pugs who would have given everything—and in some cases, did—to fill as many arenas as he did, to collect as many purses, and to see, feel, and know that they were better than so many who wanted to be what he was.

But to the man himself, it could only be torture to have gotten so close to the top, more than once even, and found himself lacking in just this area or that and to know too that at a different time, in a different era when 175-pound men hadn't all seemingly conspired to make his the best group ever, he could well have been, for a short time anyway, the best of all of them. He shared this terrible space with Richie Kates, Burnett, and others who sooner or later were forced to acknowledge that our fates frequently are owed to luck and timing and that no amount of push-ups or rounds on the heavy bag are sufficient to undo them.

A full 8,877 spectators crowded the Spectrum to see if López could overcome his lot, but not before Matt had to take off three pounds the morning of the fight—again—to make the contracted weight of 175 pounds. Nevertheless, Matt started quickly, double-jabbing the bejesus out of López at the opening bell. This was not the stand-and-slug Matthew of the Marvin Johnson fight, the Billy Douglas fight, or others that were the result of the epiphany he had after getting screwed over against Eddie Gregory. He moved quickly and sure-footed around the ring, walking poor López into right hands and left hooks after the jabs blinded him. Every once in a while, he stood still and blasted López simply because he could, but in the main, he outboxed him and absorbed López's occasional and earnest retorts with little trouble.

In the third, a right hand caused López to wobble, and in his hurry to recover, he twisted his ankle, aggravating an old injury that had popped up in the lead-up to the second Galíndez fight and hampered his effort that night. "I twisted my ankle in the third round trying to go to my right. And that changed everything around,"[5] he said later, because when things go to hell, fighters have to find a reason for it that is outside their control or they would never fight again, and then what would they do? In fact, López came out guns blazing in the fourth and had his best round of the fight. Go figure.

López's success was temporary, and Matt was soon blasting him again with double and triple jabs and winging right hands. In the seventh, one such right busted López open over his left eye and blood streamed down his face for the remainder of the contest. Knowing he was well in control and having fun, Matt took a couple of shots, smiled, and waved López in. When López took the bait—because what else could he do?—Matt smiled and pounded him again. Jimmy DiPiano, lending his voice and "expertise" to the TV broadcast between chomps on a wet cigar, noted that he could hear Matt's corner—Nick, Sonny, and the hulking Jimmy Hayes—exhorting Matt to attack López's body. "Why should he go to the body?" DiPiano demanded, incredulous. "He's got the guy cut!"[6] It shouldn't have gone unnoticed to viewers that DiPiano's contributions, while colorful, were not what one would characterize as objective.

López's whole life had been a case study on the myriad benefits of persistence and spirit, and they afforded him a moment of success, finally, in the eighth round when he caught Matt with a right cross straight and true. Matt shuddered and grabbed at his left eye where the punch had landed. This was López's big chance and he hadn't gotten this far by letting such chances slip away. He jumped on Matt and, for the next full minute, hacked away at him with every punch the rules of the sport permit a man to throw. But by this time in his life, Matt had been hurt so many times that he knew an inner voice appeared in his ear at such moments and got him through. It appeared in the Kates fight and it appeared now. "I was dazed. I exhort myself sometimes. I said, 'Matthew, get out of it. You're fighting for something.' It was one hell of a shot."[7]

López couldn't have heard this conversation, but one suspected he sensed it when Matt eventually sprung off the ropes with a shit-eating grin and proceeded to batter him all over the ring. This is what the crowd had been waiting for, the kind of moment that had defined Matt's recent fights against Johnson, Douglas, and Kates. Against any high-caliber fighter, the moment would arrive sooner or later when Matt stepped out onto the tightrope like a deranged Wallenda and the wind blew in from all directions and he would sway this way and that and there was no net underneath, and the crowd would gasp at the implausibility of it all.

Would he make it across this time, or would he finally topple over? And each time he made it to the other side and rejoiced in having made it (again), he also rejoiced in the crowd's delirium because there are few, if any, times in the life of an average man when he is able to incite the passions of thousands by the virtue of his will and one does not let such moments pass unacknowledged. And when the crowd quieted down and the round ended with Matt on his feet and smiling, you could almost feel the fight go out of poor López, who had done everything a man could do to write his own story and had just run out of ink.

The rest was academic. Matt returned to boxing and moving in the ninth and hammered López's right eye shut. He did the same in the ninth, and if you didn't know better, you'd have thought he was taking it easy on López, and why not? There was no reason to kill the man. He had a family. At 2:59 of the 11th, referee Frank Cappuccino called it off, and the party started.

"I am some fighter. Look at me—no cuts, no bruises. I am the uncrowned champion,"[8] Matt said. Press coverage was glowing as usual. "You come to Philadelphia to fight Matt Franklin, you are liable to leave town looking like the Liberty Bell,"[9] wrote one local reporter. Another: "The fight was Franklin's finest performance since his loss to Eddie Gregory on a hotly-disputed 10-round decision."[10] Another reported that Matt "staggered Lopez like he has never been staggered in three world championship fights."[11] The same writer observed that by the fight's end, "Lopez looked like a Picasso abstract. Right eye closed and purple. Left eye split open, with a bandage fighting to hold the blood from spilling onto the cheek. His mouth bled. His nose bled. His ankle was swollen."[12]

Belfiore said he was going to send a telegram to the WBA guaranteeing $150,000 for the right to have Matt face the winner of an upcoming bout between Mate Parlov and Marvin Johnson.[13] Rossman, who attended the fight at ringside with his father, was stingy with praise. "Lopez didn't throw no right hands. I knew Lopez would get busted up but I figured it would happen sooner. I know Franklin's gonna be hollering for me. If the money's right, fine. But my name is not Yaqui Lopez. I don't cut. I'm not gonna be bloody. And I punch harder than Yaqui Lopez."[14]

One could forgive Rossman for his arrogance. His win over Galíndez had exploded his celebrity. He and his wife, Maxine, were invited to the White House to meet President Jimmy Carter, and crowds and fight press attended their every move. There was even talk of Rossman challenging Muhammad Ali for the world heavyweight title in Jerusalem. In the meantime, Rossman defended the title against European light heavyweight champion Aldo Traversaro at the Spectrum in December, stopping him on cuts in the sixth round.

Four days before Rossman's win over Traversaro, Marvin Johnson stopped Mate Parlov in 10 rounds in Italy to claim the WBC world title.

Chapter 6. Tightrope

Typically, a new champion is afforded a soft opponent in his first title defense and no one would have blamed Johnson had he taken that route. But that wasn't his style. He wanted Matthew again and he got him. Johnson signed to defend the title against Matt in Indianapolis at the Market Square Arena on February 18 on national TV. He wasn't completely committed until Peltz told him he wasn't going to make that kind of money—$150,000, most of it from TV—against anyone else. Johnson agreed, and the fight was on.

"I can't erase the last fight from my record, but I am going to make certain the world knows there's a return bout that I won," Johnson said at the kickoff press conference. "I could have picked an easier opponent than Franklin. However, I chose him because I wanted my friends in Indianapolis to see me fight against the best competition available. This fight could have been in New York or Philadelphia but I insisted it be held here."[15] Johnson added that he already had plans for his next fight after beating Matt—a May 26 date in Monte Carlo against former champion John Conteh.

Matt, whose purse was $50,000, didn't mince words. "I want to be very blunt in talking about my upcoming fight with Johnson," he said. "I believe I will beat Marvin. I'm anxious to get back in the ring with him. He's going to suffer from a 'Big Matt Attack.'"[16]

"I beat Marvin Johnson once before and I'm a much improved fighter since then. I punch sharper and I punch harder but that doesn't mean I'm not expecting a tough fight," Matt said. "I beat the man once and if this was just a regular fight I wouldn't have taken it because it would be going backwards. But he's a champion now and I must prove myself against him."[17]

Before the fight could happen, the Indiana legislature had to write and pass a bill that would eradicate an old law that prohibited boxing matches on Sundays. "We do everything else on Sunday, including selling alcoholic beverages," said Kelse McClure, the same Indiana official who, along with Peltz, helped get Johnson to his hotel bed that terrible night back in Philadelphia. "About the only thing left in that old, antique law is boxing and selling cars on Sunday."[18]

It turned out the legislature could take their time. In late January, Johnson reported pain in his jaw following sparring sessions with Harold Jackson and J.B. Williamson. An examination revealed a hairline fracture and an impacted wisdom tooth that had to be removed. The fight was rescheduled for April 22. Matt was working out at the Montgomery Boys Club, a boxing gym in Eagleville, Pennsylvania, run by Steve Traitz, when he got the news that the fight had been postponed.

"I was disappointed but I'm already so used to the ups and downs in this business that I didn't let it bother me," he said. "I told myself, 'Pretend you just had a fight and you have another one coming up in a few weeks.' That's the way I approached it. Breaking down my training a little bit and building back up." Asked about a mental letdown, he said, "I don't really psyche myself up before a fight, so I don't have to psyche myself down."[19]

Eight days before Matt and Johnson met in their rematch, Rossman and Galíndez met in theirs, again in New Orleans. Rossman started well enough, but an apparently rejuvenated Galíndez mostly outfought him in the middle and later rounds. After an especially violent ninth round, Rossman told his handlers he'd broken his right hand and the fight was stopped in the corner. Many, including Galíndez, thought Rossman saw where the fight was headed and decided to get out before it went really bad. Only he knew for sure. Either way, the huge payday Matt envisioned was gone.

"I kept thinking that if I had an impressive win over Johnson and then beat Conteh, the money would be so big the Rossmans would have to forget any differences they think we have," he said. "It hurt me very bad to see what happened to Mike Rossman. The way I saw it, if he hadn't hurt his hand the fight with Galindez could have gone either way. If Mike wins, and I win, we have the perfect fight for Philadelphia. I was seeing Franklin-Rossman as a kind of Ali-Frazier type of showdown."[20]

"I know Mike Rossman," Matt continued. "I saw the fight and I think he broke his hand. I don't know how bad it was. I don't even know his doctors. I saw where Galindez was calling him 'chicken' afterwards. That doesn't make Rossman any less of a man to my way of thinking."[21]

In the meantime, while preparing for Johnson, Matt was running through sparring partners at St. Rita's Gym, sending at least a couple home early. Anthony Jones and Bernard McClain, the latter a former sparring partner of Johnson's, lasted one day. "I cut up Jones in a hurry. He wasn't much good," Matt said. McClain suffered a broken wrist. Kid Samson, from Philadelphia, took his share of beatings. After one gym session, Belfiore said to the press, "People around here haven't seen a puncher like Matthew."[22] He was right, but disaster looked imminent when Matt sprained his ankle doing roadwork at the Fairgrounds Racetrack. The night before the fight, he went to the local hospital and, using a phony name to prevent press coverage, had X-rays taken. They confirmed a sprain, and he and his camp kept it quiet and crossed their fingers. By fight time, he was ready to go.[23]

Johnson's confidence soared as the fight approached. "This fight will be entirely different from the first one," he said. "I did a lot of things wrong that night. I won't do anything wrong Sunday." He watched tape of Matt's win over López "because I wanted to see how much improvement Matthew has made since our first fight. I didn't see much. I want to win so bad I can taste it," he said.[24]

The Market Arena swelled with more than 9,000 fans on fight day, and if there were any Matthew Franklin supporters among them, you wouldn't know it from the sound of things. The crowd roared at Johnson's entrance and introduction and delighted in booing Matthew, as was their right and their obligation. It was not only that he was there to take the championship from their hero, and so soon after he won it (the nerve!), but that in their previous meeting he had proved himself, brutally, to be Johnson's superior. A no-hope challenger they could forgive, perhaps even greet him with polite applause. But Matt was a threat, they knew this, and by booing long and hard, they hoped, as all such crowds do, that their manifest hatred might swing things their way if it got too close. It couldn't hurt.

Johnson appeared in need of no such assistance at the fight's beginning, attacking immediately and expertly, and before any pacifists in the crowd could hope to slowly ease into the brutality, the two were already banging punches off each other's skulls. Immediately, Matt deployed a punch combination that would serve him well for the rest of the night, no doubt for its uniqueness: a right uppercut followed by a right cross. It thudded home several times in the first round, and if the crowd didn't see it, Johnson surely felt its effects. He returned to his corner at the end of the round looking like a man in the early moments of a terrible déjà vu whose ending he knows all too well.

It was cornerman Jimmy Hayes's job to position himself behind Matt, hands at Matt's armpits, and help him off the stool at the end of the rest period between rounds. A new observer might think this performative more than practical—how much energy does it take to stand up?—especially in a contest in which one's ability to lie is often the measure of victory. But they all had been there for Matt's first fight with Johnson and knew that Matt would need every bit of energy to hold Johnson off, to withstand his attacks, to discourage him and wear him out, and to hurt him back. What was there to lose? The energy it cost Hayes to lift Matt off the stool was cheap, but to Matt, it could make all the difference. Why take chances?

In the second, Matt stood still and the two traded bombs, producing action that was as good as anything they had done in the first fight. But in the third and fourth rounds, Matt mostly moved and boxed, which was precisely what Johnson had hoped for, and he took advantage of it, battering Matt with uppercuts, left crosses, and right hooks. By then, Matt's nose was bleeding and he was puffing up already around the eyes. After the fourth, Belfiore screamed at him in the corner. "Circle! Circle! Like we do in the gym! Circle! Move! Don't stand still, that's why you're getting hit!"[25]

But the fifth round was no better, and when Matt returned to his corner, he found Belfiore with tears streaming down his face. "I was crying because I seen him get hit with all those punches," Belfiore said later. "It was like watching my own son get hit. I don't want my fighters to get hurt."[26] The game plan had been to box Johnson until he tired in the late rounds and then go after him. But it wasn't working. Matt was taking too much punishment waiting for him to wear down. He told Belfiore, "I can't fight him backing up. You can't box him because he just keeps coming in. He don't ever stop." And then he saw the tears on Belfiore's face. He told him, "Don't cry. I'm gonna do it." He kissed him on the head and went out for the next round.[27]

Matt had a better sixth round, and with 10 seconds left in the seventh, he put everything he had into a straight right hand that caught Johnson on the forehead. It was the shot he'd been looking for all night. Johnson froze, wobbled, and did the dance of the doomed that all fight fans recognize as the beginning of the end. He nearly slid off his stool during the rest period. "I told my corner he had hurt me with that punch," Johnson said later. "It was a good punch, one he hadn't been able to get off all day, but it wasn't serious."[28]

The rest period rejuvenated Johnson and he looked fine again at the start of the eighth, pushing Matthew back and landing stinging blows. But prizefighters know when they have broken the other man, and they know too when they are close to breaking. Blood streamed down Matthew's face from a pair of cuts over his eyes. His nose bled too, and his cheekbones showed the effects of the blows that had brought Belfiore to tears. Matt gambled and pushed forward, throwing everything he had. The assault drove Johnson to the ropes and the two traded back and forth. Johnson needed just a break here or there to get his breath, to get himself together. Matt knew this and wouldn't give it to him. It was now or never.

"The blood was pouring down so fast I couldn't see out of either eye," Matt said afterward. "They could have stopped the fight at any moment. I think the reason the referee didn't was because I was the one who was still throwing punches."[29]

Matt poured himself into it, everything that was in him, and all of South Philly rained down on poor Marvin Johnson, the full length of the Ben Franklin Parkway, the Youth Study Center, the Daniel Boone School, Camp Hill, the rats, the foster homes, the hopelessness. Marvin Johnson got all of it and finally broke for good, slipping slowly and silently to the canvas, like a submarine slipping under water. He lay on his stomach for a moment, then grasped the ropes to pull himself to his feet. He made it in time, but the referee, George DeFabis, looked in his eyes. Referees know too sometimes when a man has been broken, the good ones do anyway, and he called it off. Johnson stared at him, incredulous. The crowd booed. And Matthew Franklin was the champion of the world.

Before the ring announcer told the crowd what they already knew, Nick and Sonny sat Matt down in his corner and pressed gauze and towels against the places on his face that Johnson's punches had split open. Matt looked into the TV camera, smiled, and yelled, "Allahu Akbar! I'm the champ! I'm the champ!" Across the ring, Johnson's handlers were tending to him as well. Matt looked over Nick's shoulder and said, "[Johnson] is a bad man. That boy is bad."[30]

When they'd cleaned him up, they pushed Matt in front of the TV cameras. "Every time I fight Johnson it's a hard fight," he said. "I think he's the best light heavyweight I've ever fought. Believe me all you light heavyweights out there, you all watch out for Marvin Johnson because he is *bad*. But I'm glad I'm the champion because I started off doing a lot of wrongness ..." and then he stopped and blinked a couple of times the way a man does when the regrets hit him all at once and he has to regroup before he sinks under their weight. He started again. "I'm just glad I'm champion of the world."[31]

When the interview ended, Matt told Sonny, Nick, and Jimmy to get him to his dressing room so he could see the damage Johnson had done to his face.[32] Afterward, there was plenty to talk about. Matt praised Johnson's toughness, saying, "He didn't want to go out in that last round even though I was hitting him with everything I had left. I sure was getting tired of throwing punches."[33] He thanked the referee for giving him a fair shake in the other fellow's hometown and discovered he needn't have worried. DeFabis said he never seriously considered stopping it over Matthew's blood being everywhere and was resolute with respect to the call he made to stop it in Matt's favor.

"He [Johnson] was completely dazed and out of it [after the knockdown]," DeFabis said. "Blood was just squirting from his eye. He was up at nine but his eyes were very glassy. He couldn't get his hands up to defend himself. I didn't think there was any reason for him to take another punch." Naturally, Johnson disagreed. "I think I was treated very unjustly. This is my hometown. I promised to bring my first defense here. I thought I'd be treated fair. But I got the bad break."[34]

Matt then announced that he would henceforth be known as Matthew Saad Muhammad, that he was Muslim, that his manager was Bilal

Muhammad. "Matthew is my given name. Saad means 'good future' and 'Muhammad' means 'worthy of praise,'" he said. "I think after today, those things apply to me." Someone asked him what he thought his birthparents might think of him now that he was the champ. "They didn't worry about me, so why should I worry about them?"[35] he replied. Another asked why he waited until now to announce his name change and conversion to Islam. "Muhammad Ali was always my idol. I saw what he went through after telling the world he was a Muslim. So I waited until after I had the title, and while still in the ring I let the world know that Matthew Franklin, who had never been born in the first place, no longer existed."[36]

CHAPTER 7

Thicker Than Water

"You're even crazier than I am."
—MUHAMMAD ALI

"We've always had problems with Gelb. He has no interest in Matthew," Belfiore said. "I didn't have much schooling but I ain't no dummy."[1] He sat to Matthew's left at the hearing that would determine how much of his $50,000 purse Matt would get to take home with him when he left Indianapolis after stopping Johnson. To Matthew's right was his lawyer, Harry Rubin. At odds was the "Memorandum of Agreement" that Gelb insisted extended his managerial contract with Matthew through September 20, 1980.

Matt's story was that he went to Gelb's office in March 1978 to "borrow a couple hundred dollars." He signed four or five pieces of blank paper that Gelb put in front of him that had Matt's picture stapled to them and was never told his contract with Gelb was being extended. Gelb claimed he talked with Matt for a full 90 minutes about the new contract and Matt understood what he was signing. Howard McCall, a member of the Pennsylvania State Athletic Commission, testified that after Gelb filed the contract extension with his office, he, McCall, spoke with both Matthew and Belfiore before approving the contract and that consequently, the Pennsylvania commission recognized Gelb as Matt's manager. (McCall further testified that he had arranged a meeting near the Philadelphia airport between Matt and Carl King, son of promoter Don King, and that Matt on two occasions flew to King's house in Ohio to discuss Carl becoming his manager. They failed to reach an agreement.)[2]

McCall's testimony, specifically that the Pennsylvania commission recognized Gelb as Matthew's manager, was the basis for their ruling in Gelb's favor. Richard Bossung, chairman of the commission, and Matt Walker, a commission member, determined that Gelb was due $11,250, his cut as Matt's "duly authorized" manager. "I feel justice has prevailed," Gelb said. "I just hope we can mend our fences and I wish the best for Matthew."[3]

That was only the first disappointment for Matt after winning the title. The second was his reception when he arrived back in Philadelphia. "I haven't gotten too much publicity since I won my title, not near as much as Rossman did," he said, and, he was right. There was no meeting with President Carter, no talk of a fight with the heavyweight champion. There wasn't a parade when Matthew got back to Philadelphia, no key to the city. "Most of the people who came down to the airport to meet me were the friends I grew up with," he said. "It makes me feel good that *they* care."[4]

On top of that, he needed surgery to repair the cuts he suffered in the Johnson fight. His title defense against John Conteh, which had been scheduled for July 22 in Monte Carlo, had to be pushed back to August 18. The venue was changed to Atlantic City, making Muhammad-Conteh the first title fight in that town since December 7, 1963, when Joey Giardello beat Dick Tiger.

The severity of Matt's cuts and the frequency with which he bled necessitated the addition of a cutman in his corner. Belfiore had worked hundreds of cuts over the years and was good at it, but Matt's was not a typical case. He was a bleeder. He was a young man still, just 25 years old, and he already had scar tissue over both eyes. Also, he was a world champion now. A lot was riding on him. There was big money at stake. What if he lost the title on cuts when a better cutman might have been able to get him more time? A good cutman could make the difference between winning and losing. It was an investment and an important one. Belfiore opposed it, as one would expect.[5] He felt he could do the job himself. He might even have been right.

Nevertheless, Bilal Muhammad got in touch with Angelo Dundee in early August, about two weeks before the fight, and asked for his advice. Dundee told Muhammad he remembered a cutman in Philadelphia who had kept Dundee's guy David Love in fights with Bennie Briscoe, Bobby Watts, Willie Monroe, and others. The guy's name was Adolph Ritacco.[6]

Ritacco was born in 1914 and raised at 10th and Emily in South Philadelphia. When he was a young kid, his father was sent to prison for three years after shooting two men, reportedly in self-defense. The neighborhood kids told Ritacco his old man was a "jailbird," an insult of the gravest severity and one that required in response the balling of fists. This sent Ritacco to the local fight gym so he could learn how to properly defend his old man's honor.

He became a prolific and highly skilled streetfighter, which was far more fun than sitting in a classroom, so he quit school at 14 and started fighting as an amateur. Topping out at 118 pounds, he went a purported 91–1 and turned pro in 1937, getting $6 for a six-rounder. He was undefeated, married, and had a two-month-old son when called on to fight the Nazis, which he did as a navy machine gunner. A shrapnel blast to the stomach took 190 stitches to close. "I had to hold 'em in or my guts would come out," he said.[7] They put a four-pound steel plate in his hip so he could walk again, but they couldn't do anything about the shrapnel still in his leg or the loss of hearing in his right ear. By the time he got out—with a Purple Heart and a Bronze Star—he was finished as a fighter.

It was too late for Ritacco to work in an office or on a construction crew. He was a boxing lifer. He started training guys and soon got a reputation as a cutman of the highest order, due in large part to a secret, dark-colored concoction that he applied in almost comic quantities around the eyes of his fighters. He used so much on Oscar Bonavena during Bonavena's loss to Joe Frazier in 1968 at the Spectrum that famed sports columnist Red Smith observed, "Little Adolph applied the black coagulant so liberally he might have been tarring his man preparatory to feathering."[8]

Ritacco worked with Rocky Marciano, Joey Giardello, Kitten Hayward, Bud Smith, top 1950s Philadelphia heavyweight Dan Bucceroni, and a slew of others out of the Passyunk Gym. He was a natural to join Matthew's camp, and his payday of $4,500 for the Conteh fight was the biggest score of his long career.

Ritacco's importance couldn't be overstated. Matt was almost certain to bleed and not just from punches. Conteh had a reputation as one of the game's dirtiest top fighters. His area of expertise? Headbutting. In a fight for the British and European light heavyweight titles in 1974, a sixth-round butt busted open Chris Finnegan's scalp, leading to a Conteh victory. A year later, a butt sliced open American Lonnie Bennett's eye, leading to a fifth-round stoppage. And a first-round butt against Len Hutchins in their fight in '77 led to a third-round win for Conteh. Everyone knew Conteh used his head like a third fist. "Conteh knows the only way he can beat me is to butt me and if he does that he'll be like a vampire looking for blood on the neck," Matthew said. "John is one of the best dirty fighters in the business. I can't take no chances."[9]

The thing was, Conteh didn't need to butt his way to wins. He was fast, athletic, with good legs and superb skills. There wasn't a light heavyweight in the world who could match him for pure boxing ability. Conteh's weaknesses were women, partying, and a fragile right hand, which was twice broken.

Born in Liverpool, Conteh started boxing at 10 years old and won numerous British and European amateur titles on the way to turning pro in 1971. He was 25–1 (20) when he outpointed Jorge Ahumada for the vacant WBC title in '74 and held the title until 1977, when, unhappy with the $233,000 purse, he pulled out of a mandated title defense against Miguel Cuello. The WBC stripped him of the championship. An attempt to regain the title failed when he lost a controversial split decision against Mate Parlov in front of 40,000 in Belgrade. In his three fights before meeting Matt, he beat second-raters Leonardo Rogers and Ivy Brown and survived a pair of knockdowns to draw against well-traveled American Jesse Burnett. He would get $50,000 for this shot at the title. Matt's end was $150,000. Of the predictions that he would try to butt his way to the title, Conteh replied, "They have a referee in the ring, don't they?"[10]

Matt and his team started serious training for the fight on July 16 but not at the Juniper and not at the Montgomery Boys Club. Matt's new management team used their connections to Muhammad Ali to get "invited" to Ali's famous facility in Deer Lake, Pennsylvania. Ali and Matt chatted it up for the press when camp opened. Matt even wrote a poem:

> We all know that one day Muhammad Ali will go.
> And that there's this new light heavyweight, I've been told,
> That will put boxing history back on its toes.
> And that new man and that great fighter is Matthew Saad Muhammad,
> Light heavyweight champion of the world.

It barely qualified as a poem even by the standards Ali set in his heyday, but when Matt read it to him, Ali laughed and told him, "You're even crazier than I am."[11] Everyone appeared happy with the arrangement, especially Matthew, who was now buddies with his boyhood idol, but that wasn't the impetus for the move to Deer Lake. It was part of Bilal's plan to improve Matt's commercial appeal. "Some more exposure and it will just be a matter of time," he told the press.[12]

Whether or not it was intended, the move also served the larger goal of separating Matt from the Juniper and the Belfiore brothers. As far as Bilal was concerned, Nick, Sonny, and Jimmy Hayes represented Matt's old regime, and even though Nick had gone on record supporting Matt in his legal battle against Gelb, Bilal wanted him out. It was nothing personal. It was business. And Matt was not the kind of man who needed grand explanations or some kind of "proof" that Belfiore was not who he needed anymore. He was a fighter, not a businessman. Yes, Nick had trained him since he was a young kid, drove him up and down the coast making him into a fighter, and had been there whenever Matt needed him, which was quite often in the early days.

They'd had their ups and downs, but Belfiore had cried real tears in the corner in the Johnson fight. How many trainers did that when their fighter was taking a beating? But business was business. Matt was a champion now and his new team—mainly Bilal and Akbar Muhammad—had his full trust. Of course, none of this was lost on Belfiore. He'd been around the game too long to think he was in a strong position. He said as much to Philadelphia writer Nigel Collins, who had come up to Deer Lake to watch Matthew train. Nick took Collins aside during a break. "People are trying to steal Matthew away from me," he said.[13] He was right.

Nevertheless, the atmosphere in camp was upbeat and positive and Matt was getting in his work. He woke every day at 6:00 a.m. and ran at least four miles up and down Sculps Hill Road, then chopped wood. He headed to the gym at 2:30 p.m. for calisthenics, sparring, and bag work, then it was dinnertime. After dinner, he'd spend the evening reading the Koran or chatting with visitors, his sparring partners, or with Sandra Alexander, a girlfriend he brought along from Philadelphia who, he said, he planned to someday marry. When the press crew raised their eyebrows at the presence of a champion's girlfriend in camp, he put their minds at ease. "Believe me, *it's* not allowed," he said. But going away to a real training camp was a change for Matt. It took some getting used to. "It gets a little boring sometimes," he said. "But that's okay. When I win I can relax."[14]

The visiting press wanted to talk in the main about Matt's conversion to Islam and he obliged them. "The old Matt Franklin is long dead. I've belonged to the community of Islam for some time now. I fight for the Muslims. If I lose it will be the will of Allah. But I'll tell you my way of thinking. I'm not going to let anyone take my crown. I've worked too hard for this."[15]

"Right now it's Conteh," he said. "After beating him I must take care of Victor Galindez, if he still has the title. I'll have to wait and see. But whoever is there at the time is in trouble. I'll lower the boom on him. My job is to put Allah's name up there to propagate the faith. Doing my job as a professional fighter I must go on and be victorious. Still, I am a Muslim. You must understand that and I must also be that."[16]

Without a religious conversion or a girlfriend or two in camp to talk about, Conteh contented himself with assessing Matt as a fighter. "I don't see him presenting any unusual problems," he said. "He doesn't bob or weave or anything like that. He's a straight, stand-up fighter. You can find him easily with your punches. He takes a good rap. He's got plenty of guts. And he's a really worthy champion. But I feel I can match him for all that and more as a boxer."[17]

The 1,593 that filled in the 1,700-seat Resorts International theater, producing a live gate of $90,000, saw Conteh start quickly, jabbing and double-jabbing Matt into knots in the early rounds while making him miss punch after punch. Matthew finally got going in the fifth and landed a few thudding blows, but a headbutt—surprise!—slowed his momentum and opened a deep cut over his left eye and another on the side of his nose. Conteh continued to outbox Matt through the middle rounds, darting in and out and stabbing him, almost exclusively, with jabs and hooks.

Matt did little in return but jab back at him, content, apparently, to bide his time. The great punchers can do that and the unusually tough too, and Matt was both. But his corner grew desperate, watching his championship, so brand new and so hard won, trickle away like the blood that ran in streams down his face and splashed onto his shorts. He'd taken them to the brink so many times already that they couldn't be blamed for worrying he might have run out of luck this time.

Jimmy Hayes screamed from the corner, "Let it go, champ! Let it go!"

Belfiore: "Bring the right hand! Bring that right hand!"[18]

In the eighth, Conteh began to blink repeatedly, as though something was irritating his eyes. At the end of the round, George Francis, Conteh's trainer, ran across the ring, yelled at referee Carlos Padilla about the gooey, black coagulant Ritacco had by this time smeared all over Matthew's left eye, and demanded that the local commission take a sample of it. He then hollered at Ritacco. "Hey remember the rules? You can only use certain things on the guy. Take that shit off him." Later Francis said, "Whatever it was, it got into John's eyes and got him blinking. I wanted [Padilla] to consult the doctor so he could rule on the fight. I don't like winning a fight on a cut, but that's my job. If you don't do that they go on their merry way, violating the rules."[19]

Francis complained after the 10th and 14th rounds too, which led to a New Jersey official grabbing a sample of Ritacco's solvent after the 10th round, a good one for Matt, who was finally fighting with some urgency, bombing away. He took the next three rounds, and in the 14th, a left hook hurt Conteh and a follow-up straight left dropped him. Conteh went down again before the end of the round and was hurt yet again in the 15th as the crowd, finally getting what they had paid for, chanted, "Matthew! Matthew!" The late-rounds comeback and the two knockdowns were enough to get Matthew the win by the announced scores of 144–143, 146–141, and 146–142. All three judges—Harry

Gibbs, Charlie Spina, and Padilla—had Conteh leading going into the 14th round. (The commission later found scoring errors on the cards submitted by Padilla and Spina. Their corrected scores were 147–142 and 146–139, respectively.)[20]

"I fought a man who outboxed me," Matt said afterward. "I slowed down a little bit during the fight but I paced myself. I knew I was behind, but I knew I would come back. John was a very unique, clever boxer, constantly keep me at bay with his jab." He said the key to beating European fighters is taking your time to figure out their weakness, even if it takes the whole fight. "I picked the lock and lowered the boom," he said.[21]

But really, the fight was just beginning. Francis renewed his protest over the composition of Ritacco's mystery salve, reminding everyone that it was agreed during a prefight rules meeting that only the British standard of a Vaseline and minuscule bit of Adrenalin would be allowed.

"We do have rules about that sort of thing. You're not supposed to use anything other than a small portion of adrenalin. I thought he might have been using glue. We've protested this to the commission."[22] Conteh jumped on the bandwagon. "Franklin would never have gone on if his corner had not covered his eye with some black stuff. I don't know what it was but it certainly saved him. It was agreed before the fight that only adrenalin could be used," he said. "I was pleased with the way I fought and I'm confident I could win a return."[23]

Ritacco remained defiant. "I can tell you exactly what they're going to discover. They're going to find the same thing I've been using for the last 25 years—a tannic acid, which is made out of tea leaves. And I don't give a damn whether they like it or not. What it comes down to, really, is whether or not we're gonna have boxing. With those two cuts today, I could have stuck Matthew's head in a pail of adrenalin and it wouldn't have done any good. If they ain't gonna stop a guy from butting cuts open like that, then they can't expect me to stop a two-inch cut with adrenalin," he said.[24]

"Matthew had a couple cuts you could stick your fingers in. I don't know why his eyes didn't heal better after the Johnson fight but I've been told the doctor who sewed him up left the sutures inside. And these weren't the kind that dissolve, either. They had to slit open his cuts and start over."[25]

Ritacco pleaded his case to New Jersey commissioner and former heavyweight champion Jersey Joe Walcott when Walcott visited Matt's dressing room after the fight, reminding him that Walcott had seen him use that same solution 25 or 30 times before with no questions asked.

And today, they had taken it right out of his hands while he was working in the ring. "What about my dignity?" he said. Walcott told him not to worry about it, that everything would be all right. It was not.[26]

A hearing was conducted on September 12, and on the 14th, Walcott issued a statement urging the WBC to order a rematch and suspending Ritacco and Belfiore for using "illegal substances" during the fight. "An analysis of the confiscated substances at the state police laboratory showed that something other than agreed-upon substances had been used on the eye cut," Walcott said.[27]

Moreover, Ritacco had admitted during the hearing his salve contained tannic acid, and WBC rules stipulated that only petroleum jelly or a mixture containing 1/1,000 of Adrenalin could be applied to an open cut. Ritacco was suspended in New Jersey for two months, Belfiore for three. They were both banned from working WBC title fights permanently, and Gelb and Bilal Muhammad, as Matt's managers, were each fined $7,500. The WBC mandated that the fighters rematch, or the title could be declared vacant and Conteh would fight the next highest-rated contender to fill the vacancy.[28]

Going for the rematch was a no-brainer, especially when Bob Arum put up a whopping $815,000. It was an amount unheard of for light heavyweights. Arum said he was willing to pay that much to keep the fight from going to England, where, he said, he was afraid it would get stopped the moment Matt's cuts opened up. So the fight was signed. But before it could happen, there would be a changing of the guard.

Tension between Matt and Belfiore was at an all-time high when Matt showed up at the Juniper in October. For the Conteh fight, he'd gotten $10,000 in training expenses from the promoter, from which he could have deducted $880, which is what was owed his sparring partners. Instead, he took the $880 out of Belfiore's cut of $7,000.[29] For Belfiore, it was the last straw. He threw Matt out and told him they were through. It had been coming for a while.

According to Belfiore, Matt had reduced his cut from 25 to 10 percent for his last two fights, and because they had never formalized their agreement on paper, Belfiore couldn't do anything about it. For the title fight against Johnson, Belfiore said he received just $2,300 out of a $50,000 payday. Matt told him, "We all took a cut." Belfiore asked what he would get for the next fight (against Conteh). Matt told him he would get 10 percent and that if he didn't take that, he would get nothing.

"Matthew lies like a rug," Belfiore told a reporter in January 1980. "He is the most ungrateful, lousy fucker I have ever run across in this business and I'm going to be 70 years old on Saturday. He came to my gym, I put clothes on him. Silk clothes, from my son-in-law. The last two fights, he cuts me down to 10 percent, he uses my gym to train, I'm paying for phone calls for his publicity. He uses tape like mad, he don't pay a nickel. I had an option to renew, I was too slow. Suddenly, Frank Gelb's got a two-year extension. Matthew signed a blank piece of paper. Now I've got nothin' to do with him. But I've still got headaches."[30]

Cornerman Jimmy Hayes was gone too. "I quit him. I'm the last carryover and I quit him today," he said. "I asked the man to put something on paper for me. He wouldn't do it. Let's see how he does with a whole new corner. The man is hard-headed."[31]

On another front, Matt's lawyer, Harry Rubin, was still working on dissolving Matt's relationship with Gelb. Instead of a flat fee for his services, Rubin asked for 15 percent of Matt's future earnings, with the stipulation that if he failed, Matt would just owe him for time spent. After both the Indianapolis and Pennsylvania commissions sided with Gelb after the Johnson fight, Matt started thinking the dispute might drag on for years. He consulted with Bilal, who hired a different lawyer. That attorney recommended settling the case with Gelb for 10 percent of Matt's earnings. "Matt called me from an attorney's office in Newark," Rubin said. "They turned round and made a deal with Gelb for 10 percent. What he did was break a deal for 50 percent, based on my brains and work, and now he wants to knock me out of my 15 percent. It doesn't work that way."[32]

Either way, Matt had the rematch with Conteh coming up and he needed a new lead trainer and new cornermen to replace Sonny Belfiore and Hayes. And he needed them fast. Bilal flew down to Miami and tried to talk Angelo Dundee into the job. Dundee turned him down. Bilal's second choice was Janks Morton, Ray Leonard's trainer. No dice there either. They were running out of time.

* * *

Sam Solomon had already wrapped a thousand gnarled hands and smeared Vaseline on a thousand broken faces when Matt asked him in early 1980 if he wanted to join the team. Solomon was working with Michael Spinks in 1977, and after Matt and Spinks beat the hell out of each other in a Philly gym, Matt told Solomon he liked the way he worked with his fighters.[33] Three years later, Matt hadn't forgotten.

Solomon was a South Philly guy, born there in 1915 and, like so many others, driven into the fight gyms by the thugs and bullies who ran the streets. He took to it quickly and over the next few years was a prolific amateur lightweight and semipro welterweight, reportedly logging around 300 fights in small social clubs, under tents, wherever the moneymen told him to go. He loved baseball as much as he did laying out opponents and spent several summers behind the plate for the Central Stars of the Negro Baseball League, pocketing $7.50 a game.[34] He quit fighting around 1937, at about the time he married.

When Solomon started training guys in 1950, someone asked him why he was doing it and he gave the best answer an honest man could give: "It's easier than getting punched."[35] He liked to tell people he was acquainted with the great old trainer Jack Blackburn, who turned Joe Louis into perhaps the most perfect prizefighter who ever lived. If it was true, "Chappie" didn't share any secrets with him, or if he did, Sam wasn't listening. Strategy and the game's finer points weren't Solomon's strong suit. He knew in general terms what a man should do to beat another man in a ring, but mostly he was a conditioning man and, toward that end, kept a notebook for every fighter he trained that detailed how many push-ups his man did every day in camp, how many sit-ups, how many rounds he sparred, and so forth. This was his stock in trade. He was not the emotional hollering type that Belfiore was but could be pushed to the edge when his fighter was wronged. When his heavyweight Ernie Terrell was robbed against Chuck Wepner in Atlantic City in 1973 in a blatantly corrupt decision, Solomon went after referee Harold Valan—the only scoring judge—with his cornerman's scissors. Wepner and ring officials held him back.[36] Terrell and Philadelphia middleweights Jessie Smith and Eugene "Cyclone" Hart were Solomon's primary meal tickets for a good while, though he worked with many others here and there, including a young Sonny Liston.

Solomon's relatively rudimentary understanding of the strategic end of things was the basis for his long feud with one-time middleweight contender-turned-trainer George Benton. Benton was Philly's resident ring genius until he caught a bullet to the gut in 1970, ending his fighting career. He turned to training, sharing with his students the critical subtleties and physical nuances that can render a fistfight a certain kind of art. His biggest triumph as a trainer was adding several years (and paydays) to the career of Benny Briscoe, who by all accounts was ready for the pasture when Benton took him on and showed him all the ways he could beat a man with a jab.

Benton was in Philadelphia in 1977 when he got a call from the promoter Butch Lewis, who was working on getting his fighter, Leon Spinks, a title shot at Muhammad Ali. Spinks was being trained by Solomon. Lewis knew Solomon didn't have the know-how to get Spinks ready for Ali, so he asked Benton to co-train him. "That was the second time I said no," Benton told a writer in 1978. "Lewis was after me from the start. But I had a funny feeling Sam Solomon wouldn't like it. I can work with the devil himself, but Sam wouldn't like it. Besides, I was working with Benny Briscoe, so I said no." Lewis kept after him until Benton finally phoned Solomon to feel him out. "I need all the help I can get," Solomon told him.[37]

In one sense, this was true. Spinks was a man-child of the highest order, an inveterate drinker and carouser who would disappear from training camp for days on end and eventually be tracked down at a disco or gin mill in the worst part of town. He wore poor Solomon down to a nub with his partying and excesses, to the point that Solomon had to hire a slew of tenders—one of them, Lawrence Turead, later found fame as "Mr. T."—to keep him in check. But that was only part of it.

"When he's training I have to start hours earlier just to wake him up," Solomon said in 1978. "To get him to the gym, I have to wake him at noon to get him there by three. For roadwork, I gotta get up at five to get him running by eight. He has no conception of time. And sleep? Man, does that boy sleep. One day I thought I would have to call the police to break down his door. I knew Leon was home but no one answered the phone. I let it ring and ring and ring. Nothing disturbs him. He'll fall asleep just sitting on the edge of the bed with his head in his hands. Or he'll walk in circles for a while and then sit down and fall asleep. When he goes to the bathroom and he don't come out after a while, you know he's fallen asleep."[38] One could forgive Solomon for believing he'd earned his trainer's fee and then some before ever taking a length of gauze to Spinks's wrist, but if he was going to beat Ali, the man needed more than a babysitter. He needed a teacher, and that wasn't Solomon.

Benton co-trained Spinks for his win over Alfio Righetti in November 1977, then went on the road with Briscoe. When he got home, Lewis was after him again. It was a few weeks before the Ali fight, and he relented, joining the Spinks camp. "I tried to tell him the things I'd do as a boxer if I were fighting Ali," Benton said. "We went over the whole thing about killing Ali's jab. But I was uncomfortable around Sam. I guess he thought I was trying to steal his job. Hell with his job. I got a conscience and it's clear. I did a good job with Leon. That's what is important." That he did. Spinks pulled off the upset, but Solomon refused to give Benton any credit, telling the press, "He just got in the way. He did nothing, nothing. Benton wasn't there in the beginning and didn't know the strategy, so how could he help?"[39]

Spinks's management was after Benton to join camp for the rematch, but he refused. He knew Solomon didn't want him there. Nine days before the fight, he again relented against his better judgment. "When I got there I saw Leon was doing all the wrong things," he said. "He'd forgotten all the things I had him doing for the last fight. The boy could be a hell of a fighter but he needs a teacher, and I can only do so much for him in a week or two. He'd lost his jab. He wasn't bobbing and weaving. I told him, 'Leon, it's about time you got to work.'"⁴⁰

Benton did what he could. In the dressing room, minutes before the fight, Solomon laid out for him how the night would go: Benton would be permitted to give advice only every third or fourth round. They would alternate. One round, Solomon would whisper in Spinks's ear; the next round, it would be Michael, Spinks's younger brother; then it would be Benton's turn. "Remember," Solomon told Benton, "if it's not your turn in the corner and you have something to say to Leon, just tell the guy whose turn it is and he'll relay the message." Benton said to hell with it and left after the fifth round. Spinks lost the decision and the heavyweight title.⁴¹

It may be that Solomon's generally low-key temperament appealed to Matt, especially after all those years enduring Belfiore's tantrums and insults. Where Belfiore had hollered, Solomon whispered. Where Belfiore threatened, Solomon coaxed. And soon it became clear that in the gym, Matt was in charge. He called the shots and this wasn't entirely bad, as he rarely needed to be cajoled into getting into shape. He was a fanatic about conditioning, even if he did miss weight on occasion. But it was a big change. When Nick Belfiore was in the gym, Nick Belfiore was in charge. It was his way or the highway. Solomon had no such hang-ups. He was happy so long as he got his trainer's fee. He could be counted on to keep the boat steady. He brought along his longtime assistant, Milt Bailey, a revered Philadelphia cutman. And when Matt's old reform school and jailhouse mentor Saleem El-Amin finished his obligation to the state, he joined the team too as an assistant trainer and cornerman.

It was around this time that Mustafa Ameen, who had made inroads with Matt at Deer Lake toward handling some of his financial planning, was frequently at Bilal's office in Newark, trying to get signatures and lock down deals. It was always a torrent of chaos: phones ringing, people coming in and out, piles of unopened mail. Quite innocently, he answered one of the ringing phones while Bilal was putting out a fire elsewhere, and then another, and then he was taking messages and promising return calls and helping Bilal, who clearly needed it. Before long, he was offered a job as Bilal's assistant. This evolved into a kind of camp coordinator/financial manager position reporting directly to Matthew, and for the rest of their journey, he was Matt's go-to man: traveling companion, roadwork partner, wingman, closest ally, confidant, and de facto manager. When they flew, if Matt was sitting in seat 1A, Mustafa was in seat 1B. When the whole team traveled in a caravan, it was Mustafa who rode with Matt.⁴²

Chapter 7. Thicker Than Water

Over the next weeks and months, Matt's team solidified. The primary sparring partners were Tony Green, Jody Ballard, Tim Witherspoon, and Cyclone Hart. Matt hired Ali's chef, Lana Shabazz, to cook for the team. Security was handled by Wayne Sharif, a Newark, New Jersey, police officer. Matt hired childhood friend Tim Sams—"Blue" to his friends—to be his driver, take care of his equipment, do odd jobs around his house and at camp, and other ad hoc duties. Bilal hired photographer Paul Trace to document Matt's career in pictures. Imam Shamsud din Ali, an influential religious and political leader in Philadelphia (and reportedly a member of Philadelphia's Black Mafia in the 1970s), was an honorary member of the camp and sat ringside at all of Matt's fights. So too was Matt's adoptive father, "Pop" Santos, along with Yusef Shah, at one time a high-ranking member of the Nation of Islam going back to Malcolm X and Elijah Muhammad. He helped on and off with security. Down the road, Matt's entourage would swell to 22 men, more or less, in camp as a fight approached. With the new team in place, Matt was ready to start the next phase of his career and his life.

Chapter 8

Guns and Switchblades

"Smile now. After Saturday they'll be very sad."
—SAM SOLOMON

"Cheerio, John!"

Matt and Solomon cracked up at Tony Green's impression of John Conteh's countrymen. So did everyone else at Montgomery Boys Club, where Matt was training for the rematch. (He was happy to be away from Deer Lake and the chaos and scrutiny that came with it.) A little while before, Green had gone three hard rounds with Matt and took some lumps (as did Charley Singleton before him), but his put-on British accent was perfect. A first-time visitor might have guessed him British born and raised, but the smile on his face and delight at everyone's reaction would have given him away.[1]

Green was from Miami. His older cousin, Willie Johnson, boxed out of the famed Fifth Street Gym alongside Muhammad Ali around 1963 and sometimes he'd take Green to the gym with him. The kid fell in love with it but, at 16, took part in an armed robbery and got sent away. He started boxing in prison and writing letters to Angelo Dundee, who remembered him from his visits with his cousin. Dundee wrote back to him, telling him that when he got out to come to his office. Green was released in 1972 and went right to see Dundee and his brother, Chris, who became his manager and promoter, respectively. He turned pro in March '73 with no amateur experience beyond what he'd gained in prison but fought 12 times that first year, winning nine.

Not long after fighting Mike Quarry to a draw in Florida in 1976, he sparred with Mike Rossman while Rossman was training in Miami. Sometime later, when Rossman was preparing to defend the title against Aldo Traversaro in Philadelphia, he remembered Green, looked him up, and asked him to help him get ready. Green obliged. It was while training in Philadelphia that he ran into Matt, who was training for his second fight with Marvin Johnson. They hit it off, and Matt asked him if,

Chapter 8. Guns and Switchblades   97

when he was done with Rossman, Green wanted to join his camp. "I told him to get his manager to talk with Angelo and get me six bills a week and that was it," Green said in 2020. "In Philly I worked with him and we became really good friends."

"When I first went up there with Matt, sparring every day you had to fight for your life," Green said. "But I was sparring with Roberto Duran, Jimmy Ellis, Quick Tillis, I sparred with all them guys so you know, that rough-house stuff, I was used to it. And we became good friends because he would dish it out and I would dish it back to him."[2]

Despite Green's comedy, tensions were higher than normal in Matt's camp in the days leading up to the Conteh rematch. For one, Matt was steamed at the purse split that the WBC had mandated in response to Ritacco's having used illegal substances in the first fight. Instead of the typical 70-30 split in the champion's favor, he would get 55 percent to Conteh's 45 percent. "Ain't that somethin'?" he said to a visiting writer, adding that he would make Conteh pay for the insult. "They [the WBC] made me fight this man again. I beat Conteh fair and square. You're going to see me fighting like a man possessed. You hit me once and that's it you can start making a grave for yourself. You can find a place to lie down."[3]

That wasn't all. Nine days before the fight, Matt was convinced he'd overtrained, peaked too soon. He said he felt sluggish and couldn't get off during sparring, that his timing wasn't there. In response, Solomon broke open the notebook. "[You sparred] 104 rounds since February 26," he said. "Just a little more." He then noted that Matt had run every day from 2½ up to 12 miles.[4] They agreed he had to back off training over the last week or he'd have nothing come fight time.

If that wasn't enough, Matt's adoptive mother, Bertha Santos, had died in October and he was mourning her. His adoptive father, her husband, John Santos, would be in the hospital having surgery right around the time of the fight. Also, Bilal's list-ditch legal effort to force the WBC to reinstate the customary 70-30 purse split failed. Matt sought comfort, or perhaps distraction, four days before the rematch by buying a $23,000 antique Louis XV medium grand piano and having it delivered to a house he'd recently bought in Jenkintown, a suburb about 10 miles north of Center City, Philadelphia. He had no idea how to play piano and had told fight publicist Chet Cummings he wanted to learn. Cummings introduced him to concert pianist Francisco Aybar, who took Matt to a store on West 57th Street in Midtown Manhattan, suggested the Louis XV, and told Matt he'd give him lessons.[5] "Boxing is boxing. But I want to learn other things besides being a fighter," Matt said by way of rationalization.[6]

Conteh's trainer, George Francis, tried to add to the distractions by saying at the final press conference that Solomon was "too fat to be a good trainer." This type of insult might have led to a brawl had Belfiore still been at the helm, but Solomon was a different type of man. He grinned and told the press, "Smile now. After Saturday they'll be very sad."[7] He then reminded everyone, as he had all week, that Conteh's first career loss was to a North Philly fighter named Eddie Duncan, who outpointed Conteh—in Wembley, no less—in 1972. Who was in Duncan's corner that night? None other than Sam Solomon.

Finally, in the last bit of prefight drama, Bilal and Matt tried to bring Ritacco in to work Matt's corner despite his lifetime ban from working WBC title fights. Following a closed-door meeting, WBC boss Jose Sulaiman agreed to reduce the length of the ban to one year, which would still preclude Ritacco working the rematch. Solomon and Bilal expected as much so had arranged to have local cutman Eddie "The Clot" Aliano as a backup and he stood at the ready in Matt's corner. Matt's hope was to make his presence unnecessary.

"There's a lot of politics going down, so that means I'm going to have to put him away," Matt said. "Destroy the man, not physically, but mentally. There will be no doubts and no stopping me this time. I have to go all out. You go out and give your blood and they're out there taking away half your money behind you. I'm the champ of the WBC but right now everyone's behind Conteh. It won't make any difference, though, because I'm gonna put Conteh down. With a knockout there can be no controversy."[8]

Indeed, Aliano's services weren't needed. After a slow first round, Matt, who had to lose a quarter of a pound the day of the fight, followed Solomon's instruction in the second to throw the overhand right over Conteh's jab and rattled the challenger. In the fourth, a right hand followed by a pair of cuffing left hooks sent Conteh down. Four more knockdowns followed before referee Octavio Meyran stopped it at 2:27 of the round, much to the delight of the crowd at Resorts International. Afterward, Matt went on the air with Howard Cosell and dedicated the fight to his late adoptive mother and her husband, who was recovering from surgery. "How ya doin', Dad?"[9]

He smiled into the camera, and when he did, all the warmth, love, kindness, gratitude, and innocence that was in him and that he stamped down when he had to, poured out, and one could see why the people who knew him loved him so much and wanted to be near him. And you had to wonder where he found the rage, strength, and the hardness of mind to be what he had to be when the bell rang. He was indeed a child, a loving one at that, in a prizefighter's body.

Chapter 8. Guns and Switchblades

He changed gears. "I will never let my title be taken by no man," he told Cosell. "I told you that I would be in tremendous shape and that Conteh would be destroyed."[10]

Later, Matt said although he had been prepared physically for his first fight with Conteh, all the distractions in his camp—the financial and contractual battles with Gelb and Belfiore, the circus-like atmosphere of Ali's camp in Deer Lake—affected his performance. "And every problem came to me because I'm the owner of my corporation," he said. "Now, I have a totally new staff."[11]

About the fight, Matt said, "Conteh was easy to hit with the left jab as well as the overhand right because he kept dropping his hands. I could see his legs getting wobbly and knew I'd get him. He didn't come as hard as last time. I was very upset about the purse. It was a political situation. They made me go through a lot of changes. But the next time I fight it will be for one million. Maybe two."[12]

Unbeknownst to most of the media, Bob Arum had been working for several weeks before the Conteh rematch on getting a softer defense for Matt, something that wouldn't be a war, leading up to potentially a third fight with Marvin Johnson. In November 1979, Johnson had regained the WBA light heavyweight title by stopping Víctor Galíndez in the 11th round, and a third match between Matt and Johnson, this to unify the title, seemed a natural. That was until March 31, 1980, two days after Matt stopped Conteh, when Matt's one-time rival Eddie Gregory knocked out Johnson in the 11th round to win the title in Knoxville, Tennessee. Like Matt, he later announced he had converted to Islam and taken a new name—Eddie Mustafa Muhammad. And the next potential big-fight opponent for Matt was he, not Marvin Johnson.

In the meantime, Arum landed on Louis Pergaud, an earnest but pedestrian light heavyweight from the Republic of Cameroon in Central Africa who had relocated to and was fighting out of Dusseldorf, West Germany. The selection of Pergaud was evidence of the malleability of the WBC and WBA ratings committees (they rated him fourth and ninth, respectively) in the face of the charms and connections of Pergaud's manager, the powerful Mickey Duff. Pergaud, 17–1 (7), had fought in the United States just once, outpointing Brooklyn, New York, trial horse Willie Taylor underneath Víctor Galíndez's rematch victory over Mike Rossman.

Arum was thinking about a June fight. In late April, ABC executives called him to say they had a spot open in their schedule on their May 11 Wide World of Sports telecast and would Matt be interested? Of course he would! Matt signed on for the $125,000 payday (Pergaud got $20,000). They put it in the 11,000-seat Metro Center in midtown

Halifax, Nova Scotia, and had 13 days to promote it. Matt had 13 days to get in shape. It had been only six weeks since his defense against Conteh. Everyone had the same question: Why was he fighting again so soon—and on such short notice?

"Why not? He is a legitimate-type contender," Matt said. "I told people I would destroy Conteh and I did that. I dominated Conteh. I put a lot of training into that, and being as I only went four rounds I'm still in shape. I'll be ready for 15 rounds." Solomon agreed. "That fight was rather easy. He didn't do a lot. Matthew didn't get out of shape. This is just fine tuning. A guy like him needs to stay busy. He can't stay idle. This is all right. It's not that quick." Matt predicted he would stop Pergaud in the fourth round, regardless of Pergaud's odd style. "His style will throw me off for a while. He's a boxer. He's a runner. He runs faster than a rabbit. But I'm going to catch him. I always do."[13]

He did catch him, though it took a round longer than he predicted. Fighting in front of roughly 3,000 fans, Matt, who again weighed in heavy and had to take off two pounds to get to the light heavyweight limit, started quickly, blasting away at Pergaud's body with uppercuts and left hooks. Pergaud was a lefty, and Matt, having gone almost 20 rounds with Marvin Johnson, knew the weapons to use—left hooks and straight rights. He attacked Pergaud's flanks relentlessly over the first two rounds, landing booming left hooks and right uppercuts.

At the end of the second, a straight right cross left Pergaud drooping in a corner. Pergaud had some moments of success in the fourth, but Matt had noticed by then Pergaud's unfortunate habit of ducking his head down, right into the path of Matt's uppercut. Matt just had to keep throwing it until one landed the way he wanted it to. "That was my master plan. He kept dumping his head and I knew I had to throw the uppercut," he said later. "Whatever goes down has to come up. And I made his head come up."[14]

About a minute into the fifth, a screeching left uppercut crashed into the right side of Pergaud's jaw, dropping him to the canvas. He beat referee Rudy Ortega's count, barely, and was teetering like an old silo in a windstorm when Ortega waved it over at 1:19 of the round. Matt admitted later that the knockout punch had been intended for Pergaud's body, but the challenger ducked right into it. The bad news? Matt injured his right hand in one of the earlier rounds. He didn't mention it while being interviewed by ABC's Chris Schenkel, instead issuing a challenge to Mustafa Muhammad. "I'm looking for Mr. Eddie Gregory. Listen to me boy, because I'm after you. I am the man. I am the champion."[15]

Later, reporters wanted to know against whom Matt might defend next if a title unification fight with Mustafa Muhammad could not be

Chapter 8. Guns and Switchblades

made. He said he welcomed all comers with the exception of James Scott, the top-rated light heavyweight who for the last two years had been terrorizing upper-tier contenders from behind the walls of Rahway State Prison in New Jersey. The question was newly relevant, as Scott owned a one-sided victory over Mustafa Muhammad, who by virtue of his knockout of Marvin Johnson, was now a champion.

From a pure boxing standpoint, Scott had a clear case for a title shot. Over a 14-month period in 1978 and '79, he beat Mustafa Muhammad, Richie Kates, Bunny Johnson, Ennio Cometti, Jerry Celestine, and Yaqui López. That a prison inmate could be that good surprised a lot of people, but not Matt's main sparring partner and close friend Tony Green. Scott was raised in New Jersey, where he was a frequent resident of reform schools and prison cells, but he came up in boxing in Miami just like Green had, and Green saw up close, when they sparred, what Scott could do in the ring. Scott was 10–0-1 (4) when he left Miami to go back to New Jersey, where he was soon arrested and convicted of armed robbery (the jury hung, 11–1, on a related murder charge) and Scott was sent to Rahway, where he spent the next several decades.

"If Scott hadn't come up to Jersey and got in that trouble he would have been a world champion," Green said in 2021. "Everybody was telling him to stay [in Florida] and stay out of trouble but he wouldn't listen. He was from the streets and some guys, you just couldn't take the streets out of them."

Matt answered like he always did about the prospect of fighting Scott, saying he thought it would give kids, especially those already in bad situations, the wrong idea about what it was like to be in prison and the freedoms one could expect while incarcerated. On other occasions, he had joked that if he and his entourage went into Rahway, some of them might be recognized and not make it out. During an interview with writer Steve Farhood in 1980, he expounded on his opinion of Scott, saying essentially that being in prison was an advantage.

"I don't think he was ever a good fighter. He was confined. He don't see pretty ladies walking on the street. He can't get to them. If you put him on the street, he wouldn't win none of his fights. Put me in a prison. I bet I can win all my fights by first-round knockouts."[16]

It's true that Matt faced more temptations every day than a hundred average men, and not just the women, who were plentiful. By this time, he was a celebrity, especially in Philadelphia but in New York and Los Angeles too. Doors were open for him everywhere—backstage with Peabo Bryson and Patti LaBelle, box seats at the U.S. Open, all the parties and events where only the elite were invited, there was Matt, typically with Mustafa Ameen at his side. There was Matt with Dionne

Warwick, and there he was with Teddy Pendergrass. There he was with Dr. J. and Darryl Dawkins, and there he was rubbing elbows with Ali and his wife, Veronica, and now he was smiling and talking with jazz musician Grover Washington.

One day he was hanging with Philadelphia bantamweight champ Jeff Chandler, the next with Sasson Inc., founders Paul and Gerard Guez at a bash thrown in his honor in Beverly Hills. (He had an endorsement deal with Sasson and also Pony and wore their gear in many of his televised fights.) And in every photo, Matt looked like a kid in a toy store, his smile and easy charm lifting up everyone and everything around him. It was good to be well known and well paid, and Matt was both. And he didn't shy away from public attention; he had a personalized license plate on his BMW that read, "BAM." If you saw it, you knew it was him. He and Ameen were living large.

Even "The Greatest" sought Matt's opinion. In early 1980, Matt and Ameen were at Matt's house and the phone rang. Matt answered and was stunned to hear Ali on the line. As they made small talk, Matt whispered to Ameen to pick up the extension. Ali said he had gotten an offer to come back and challenge Larry Holmes for $5 million, and everybody in his camp was telling him he could kick Holmes's ass. He wanted to know what Matt thought. Matt hesitated, shocked that Ali wanted his opinion but also at how to answer diplomatically; he knew Ali was no match for Holmes at that point, but how do you tell Muhammad Ali to not do something? "Well," Matt said, "what do *you* think, champ?"[17]

When he wasn't hobnobbing with the stars or training for a fight, Matt was talking to kids in reform schools, warning them against taking the road he had taken. He said that after he retired, he wanted to open a camp for underprivileged kids where they could "learn boxing skills and a trade, like carpentry. I want to be able to give kids breaks early in life."[18]

Still, there were times it seemed he didn't pay attention enough to taking care of himself. One summer afternoon, he and Ameen were lounging in the yard at Matt's house in Jenkintown, which featured a giant in-ground swimming pool in the backyard. It was rather for show, as Matt couldn't swim. (Ameen: "He couldn't swim a lick.") Ameen was reading when he heard a big splash and thrashing in the water. He looked up to see Matt sinking to the bottom of the deep end of the pool. He jumped in and pulled him out.[19]

Afterward, they agreed they wouldn't share the story with anyone. A world champion boxer needing rescuing from his backyard swimming pool? It could get embarrassing. (The only other witness was Matt's dog "Popper," an Irish setter mix, and he wasn't talking.)[20] Nevertheless, when a reporter from *Jet* magazine visited the house the next day to do a story on Matt's childhood, Matt shared the whole story, highlighting the fact it was Ameen who had saved him.

It was not long after that Ameen and Matt got a call from some casting people in Hollywood asking if Matt wanted to audition for the role of "Clubber Lang" in Sylvester Stallone's third installment of the *Rocky* series. (Matt was acquainted with Sylvester's brother Frank from their time in Philadelphia.) Stallone wanted to cast an authentic Philadelphia fighter in the role of Lang and interviewed Matt and Joe Frazier. They were then invited to Hollywood to audition. Matt and Ameen got there a week early and hired an acting coach who worked with Matt in their hotel suite. With just a few days left before the audition, Matt got to the end of the script and turned to Ameen.

"Mustafa—did you read this whole script?"

"Yeah, I read it," Ameen said.

"They got me losing! I can't lose! You better call those folks and tell them I'm the champ, I can't lose."

"Listen Saad, it's just a movie. And, it's a *Rocky* movie, and *Rocky* is going to win."

"Well, you still gotta ask them [to change it]," Matt said.

"Saad, I'm not calling anybody and asking them anything," Ameen said. "I'm not gonna do it."

Matt left the room for about 30 minutes and gave it some thought. He came back.

"Mustafa, how about if you call them and tell them to make it a draw?"[21]

Neither Matt nor Frazier got the role. It went to Laurence Tureaud, otherwise known as "Mr. T," who became known in boxing circles when Sam Solomon hired him to babysit Leon Spinks before Spinks fought Ali.

Matt's celebrity and fight purses put him in a position to do something he had wanted to do for a long time. In early 1980, he visited the office of Tim Crawford, a powerful Philadelphia attorney, a kind of attorney to the stars in Philadelphia circles. With Crawford's help, Matt put in place plans to provide a $10,000 reward to anyone who provided information that led to the successful identification of his birth family and thus to his true identity. "I have always thought about doing something like this but I wasn't in a position when I was coming up," he said. "I wasn't financially equipped to do it. Now I figured that since I was a champion, being in the public's eye, I could say anything I want to say, and then perhaps I would find them."[22]

This might have seemed strange to some; what did he need them for now? He was successful, rich, and famous beyond anything he could have imagined or dreamed of when, as a kid, he was fighting off street thugs, rats, and other inmates. They'd missed the boat. If anything, it was *they* who should be looking for *him*, begging his forgiveness for having abandoned him to the streets and the foster care system. Indeed, the cliché was just that: when a man becomes rich and famous, he discovers family he never knew he had, for they show up like insects crawling out of the woodwork, hands out, looking to partake of the spoils of a success they had no hand in creating—unless all but condemning one to a life of hardship in hopes that he is the one in a million it motivates to succeed can be viewed as a kind of contribution.

There were some in Matt's universe who counseled him against his plan for fear not only that his natural family, if discovered, would seek to cash in but also that making the reward public would be to invite all manner of fraudulent schemers looking to convince Matt that they were his long-lost loved ones. For this reason, he kept out of the paper certain details that only he knew. "I have a few details that will clue me in on the real ones when and if they show up, but I can't peep all my cards just yet. They have nothing to fear from me. I have almost everything else in the world I want already."[23]

In the meantime, there were bills to pay and noses to punch. Bilal lined up Yaqui López for a summer title defense, and Matt started training on May 29, just 18 days after the Pergaud fight. López was not, on merit, a particularly deserving title challenger; in the almost two years since their first fight, he'd beaten seven unranked fighters with a combined record of 125–112–8. In his only fight against a top contender, James Scott mauled him over 10 rounds in December 1979. (López's manager claimed he had the flu at the time.)

Nevertheless, López was a tough, respected contender and had made an exciting fight with Matt in Philadelphia. The details came together slowly and by piecemeal. The agreement was in place by June 1, but the site and date were still pending. By June 6, they'd arrived on a date, July 17, and a TV network, CBS, but hadn't finalized the dollars or the site. The formal announcement came June 21. The venue would be the Great Gorge Playboy Club in McAfee, New Jersey. Matt would get $150,000 to López's $40,000.

Importantly, Matt's defense of the WBC title would be paired more or less with Eddie Mustafa Muhammad's WBA title defense the following weekend at the same venue against Jerry Martin. The goal was to then match the two winners—presumably Matt and Mustafa Muhammad—in a title unification fight. It was the biggest fight that could be made at light heavyweight and one of the biggest fights in the sport. It would also make light heavyweight the second of just two weight classes headed by a single champion (middleweight was the other), an unfortunate peculiarity that would be remedied, according to a high-ranking executive, by none other than Playboy Enterprises.

"Playboy is pledging its resources to bring about the unification of the divided titles in the boxing world," Playboy suit Ron Amos said at a press conference in July. "We intend to put a lot into this. We have the resources and we intend to use them. Our aim will be to match the winners of [Saad Muhammad–López and Mustafa Muhammad–Martin] and get an undisputed champion. We think we will succeed."[24] Easier said than done. For starters, Mustafa Muhammad wasn't buying it. "What for? I'm not interested in unifying the crown. The more titles, the more chance guys have to make money. Besides, I beat him already. He knows I'm champ."[25]

More hurdles would follow, but first things first: Matt had to get by López again. He was as dedicated as ever, putting in miles on miles of roadwork and hitting all the milestones in Solomon's notebook. By the time they closed up camp, he'd sparred 90 hard rounds. The injury he sustained to his right hand in the Pergaud fight still bothered him and he aggravated it in training, so Solomon wrapped a sling around it to protect it and to make Matt use his left more.

Matt worked nearly as hard drumming up publicity for the fight as he did in the gym, showing up at one press conference wearing a white suit and a flaming-red hat and brandishing an elephant trainer's whip, which he frequently snapped for effect. "I am very good at my game right now," he said. "I don't know what kind of strategy his camp has but it won't work. Nobody is taking my title. You got to knock me out to take my title, but nobody is going to knock Matthew Muhammad out. He's telling everybody that this fight will be different. He's right in that respect—I'm going to be better. This is not going to be Matthew Franklin, it's Matthew Saad Muhammad. I have punching power now," he said.[26] "Yaqui's a good boxer," Matt continued. "He'll do what he did before, perhaps come at me more. Yaqui can make you look bad. He's a thinker. There is meaning in everything he does. He doesn't *just do* anything." Someone asked Solomon if López might be easier the second time around, and the old trainer smiled and asked if the interlocutor had seen the second Conteh fight. A reasonable response. Then, "I didn't try to change [Matt], but I modified him," Solomon said. "He was already a good fighter. This is a man who was a champion when I got him. But he had some rough spots that had to be ironed out. He didn't have too much of a defense."[27] Rejoining the team in the corner was Ritacco, whom the WBC graciously allowed to participate, though he had served just 11 out of the 12 months of his modified ban.

López, whose wife gave birth to an 11-pound baby boy ("Yaqui") two weeks before the fight, was never known as a talker and didn't bother trying to keep up with Matt in prefight banter. "Not too many fighters get even one shot at the title and I've already had four," he said. "I beat Galindez [in Rome]—but, the judges. I don't know what to say. I beat him. I'm very happy to be fighting for the championship in the United States. I stayed in front of [Matt)] last time. I have to move more. Every move will be different."[28]

There wasn't a man within a hundred miles who believed López when he said he'd move more. López had one speed and one style, and asking him to do anything more than what he'd always done was like asking a donkey to try to be a racehorse for a day and that's no insult to the donkey. López was superb offensively and could do just about anything when attacking his man, but relying on his feet to make him more elusive wasn't in his makeup. And even if he tried, the first time Matt landed, he would revert to the balls-out fighter he'd been all his career because that's what all men do when threatened—resort to who they are.

López might be able to use his feet for short stretches here and there if he remembered, and when he did, his corner might get their hopes up and think maybe he's finally using his head, but he was all fighter. There was no way he could box for 15 rounds, and even if he could, there wasn't a chance in hell he was going to outbox Matt because Matt was a better boxer. If he was to have any chance, López would have to beat Matt up.

Nevertheless, López came out more or less boxing in the opening round, and Matt was content to jab with him. López opened up more in the second, as though suddenly aware of how easy it was for him to land jabs, hooks, just about anything he wanted to throw. He opened a small cut over Matt's eye in the second, a favor Matt returned a round later on the bridge of López's battle-scarred nose.

Over the next several rounds, López boxed some, punched some, and for him at least, looked almost giddy at how easily he was landing. Matt did not box and move the way he had in their first fight. He stood right in López's range and tried to fend him off almost entirely with jabs and occasional left hooks. When he threw a right, it was almost exclusively to López's body, and if you didn't know going into it that his right hand was no good, it was clear a few rounds in. "Every time I used the right against Lopez there was a very sharp pain, right in the middle knuckle," Matt said later. "I used my left even when I had a lot of energy. I used my right just when I had to."[29]

Certainly, López noticed it and it gave him more courage than was good for him. He gave it to Matt again and again over the first seven rounds, and it might have helped if someone suggested to slow it down a little so as to save some for later, but neither was this in his nature. Besides, all that activity gave him a good lead on the cards going into the eighth, a danger Solomon acknowledged with desperate mid-rounds pleas from the corner.

"Slide with him, champ! Slide with him!" and "Get off! Get off!"

Finally in the eighth, Matt woke up and bombed López with both hands, trapping him on the ropes. López spun him around and let loose with combination after combination, as the crowd—a mere 1,300— roared. López threw a good 40 punches over almost a full minute, landing most of them, almost an absurd amount, before Matt got off a single good counter and then he smiled at the end to let López know things were about to go badly for him. López seemed to know it too, as Matt backed him to the ropes and unloaded again, and it was the same as it had been in their first fight.

López had given everything he could give, which was quite a lot for any prizefighter and on most days and against most other men, he'd have been getting his hands raised. But he didn't win a single round after the eighth. The fight was effectively over in that round, as soon as López realized that for all his fury, all his desire, and all the hurt he had meted out, Matt wasn't going anywhere and that it had looked worse for Matt than it really was. "I started to feel a little dizzy. My legs didn't buckle or anything like that, but I knew I was hit," Matt said later. "I was waiting for him to slow up a little bit, but I said, 'Wow. This guy's not slowing up!'"[30]

Decades later, a lot of those who saw it would call the eighth round against López Matt's finest hour. But a man's finest hour is frequently also his ruin. It takes too much out of him. A man's finest hour, by its very definition, cannot be replicated. If it does not ruin him, it accomplishes something close. Of course, he doesn't know this when he's in the middle of it—how could he? All Matt knew was that he still had a fight to finish, and over the next six rounds, he ground down what was left of poor Yaqui López, who still had some fight left in him but knew the cause was lost.

Protecting his injured right, Matt beat the remaining resolve out of López with jabs and booming left hooks, until finally in the 14th, a right-hand, left-hook, right-uppercut combination sent him spinning to the canvas. López went down again and then again and kept getting up because a real prizefighter can accept losing to a better man but not staying down if he is able to rise. There was a limit to what a man like Yaqui López would surrender. But by now, Matt was bringing both hands, busted knuckle or no, and after the fourth knockdown, Joe

Walcott, the Jersey commissioner, got out of his ringside seat to make sure referee Waldemar Schmidt called it off.

The first sign that this was not the same as all the other wars, or maybe that all the other wars—Johnson I and II, López I, Kates, Billy Douglas—were catching up to him was when it took Matt an hour and half to show up to the post-fight press conference. And when he did arrive, he spoke softly and gingerly, as though any abrupt movements or excited speech might break in him something that was already on the verge. "I don't have a headache or anything like that. It's just that I'm a little exhausted today. I'm not used to going 14 rounds. I usually knock guys out in five or six. This is the first time I remember being swollen. I usually look pretty good after a fight."[31]

"The early pace was very fast and I got a little careless," he said. "He was hitting me at will on the ropes. And he was hitting hard. I felt he had me in some trouble but I knew I'd come back. I came off the ropes in that same round and had *him* in trouble. I was the aggressor after that."[32]

The writers, by this time used to such drama one hoped, struggled to find new ways to describe how Matt had once again traversed the tightrope between winning and losing and came out on the right end. "The war between Matthew Saad Muhammad and Yaqui Lopez could not have been much fiercer if they had been armed with guns and switchblades," reported one.[33] "It was a brutal brawl, a slugfest of the proportions of a 23–22 baseball game, a fight that had the look of, 'How can they still be standing?'" wrote another.[34] The *Ring* magazine called it 1980's Fight of the Year. Arum said it was "one of the greatest fights I have ever promoted."[35]

A Philadelphia columnist who had covered Matt from the beginning wrapped it up thusly: "Matthew Muhammad strides to victory like a guy strolling down the middle of the street during an air raid. He is the Lloyd Free of boxing. Bombs away, but don't expect me to play both ends of the court. He hits like Reggie Jackson, also plays defense like Reggie. Very little gets past him because his chin is usually in the way."[36]

There is usually a kind of pain that accompanies heroics and often tragedy too. The former arrives first and it visited Matt in the days immediately following the fight. Tony Green, who fought on the undercard at Great Gorge, losing a decision to Johnny Davis, saw it firsthand. "Matt beat him, but Yaqui put a whuppin' on Matt," Green said in 2021. "I know because I stayed a week after the fight. I stayed with him because he was hurt. After that fight he was hurt, man. He stopped Yaqui in the 14th round, but I'm sayin'—he took a beatin'. I stayed with him an extra week just to make sure he was all right."

The following week, Mustafa Muhammad wrecked Jerry Martin,

invigorating talk of a unification match between him and Matt. On the surface at least, Mustafa Muhammad continued to object to the idea, saying that Muslim principles prohibited brothers from fighting each other and that if Matt truly wanted to fight, it was because he was "putting money before God."[37] This was a curious position to take, as Mustafa later bragged that Jerry Martin had paid for his Rolls Royce and Marvin Johnson for his Cadillac.[38] "Eddie Mustafa is too materialistic but that's his mentality," Matt countered. "Money is only a way to help get me the things I need in life, a good home, food, and shelter. Money's purpose isn't for praising."[39]

"I know it's not right for two Muslims to fight, but let me say this," Matt continued. "Italians fight Italians. Jews fight Jews. We try to keep these types of things away. But we realize we're in a game, and there can't be two shares [champions] at one time. We will have to eventually fight. I would not fight Mustafa Muhammad for less than $15 million [total purse]. I know I'm in a position to ask for that type of money because I'm a very exciting fighter. People would come to see me. I don't know about him, but they would come to see me."[40] The two went back and forth in the press trading mild insults, but it was mostly for the purposes of driving up interest in a meeting. They were on very friendly terms outside the ring, having spent time together with Muhammad Ali at Deer Lake and at other Muslim functions.

The real impediment to a match, at that time at least, was Arum, whose philosophy on unification fights and other potentially very big fights was to let them marinate. "There are so many good fights to be made in this division that it's my feeling we shouldn't rush into the unification," he said. "Let the champions continue to build the public appetite, then, when everyone's tongue is hanging out, when we have a climate that is boiling hot like it was for Leonard-Duran, then it's time."[41] Also, almost as an aside, after all their grandiose plans and supposed deep pockets, Playboy Enterprises was out of the fight business.

It was around this time that another promoter was making a name for himself and had both deep pockets and little interest in letting big fights "marinate." Harold Smith, whose real name was Ross Fields, had been hovering around the fringes of the boxing world since the early 1970s, when Ali helped him obtain the closed-circuit rights to his first fight with Joe Frazier. Born in Alabama, Smith reportedly got close to Ali while organizing efforts to overturn Ali's ban from boxing following his refusal to be drafted into the U.S. military. It was through his association with Ali that Smith got to do some business with Arum and other minor league entertainment promotions when he moved from New York to California around 1976. Around that time, Smith read a newspaper article about Florida sprinter Houston McTear's family and offered to sponsor McTear on the West Coast.

Not long after, Smith founded Muhammad Ali Amateur Sports and declared himself a promoter of track and field meets, paying Ali 10 percent of the gross from all his promotions for the use of Ali's name. By 1979, he'd changed the name of the company to Muhammad Ali Professional Sports (MAPS) and, on May 25, promoted his first boxing event at a small club in Santa Monica, California. He soon became a major player in boxing promotion by the odd habit of drastically overpaying his fighters.

If Don King or Arum offered a fighter $200,000, Smith offered him $800,000. If he was a $300,000 fighter, Smith gave him $1 million. His modus operandi was to show up at the residence of a fighter he wanted to sign and dump a suitcase or airline pilot bag full of cash, usually in the hundreds of thousands, on the floor. This frequently worked. Soon, he'd signed nine world champions to promotional contracts while paying them far above the market value and losing money on virtually every show. Some wondered where he got the money, but no one cared as long as they got paid. It wasn't their business.

Smith flew Matthew and Ameen to Las Vegas where they sat ringside for Ali's challenge of Holmes in October 1980.[42] Twice in the preceding months, Matt visited Ali's camp at Deer Lake and sparred with him: the first time just after camp opened in July, the second time in September as things were winding down. The improvement Matt claimed Ali showed between the first and second of these sessions convinced him to opine, at least publicly, that Ali would win. He told the press that he suspected Ali had something up his sleeve that he would unveil during the fight that would lead him to victory.[43] Of course Matt was wrong, and after Holmes battered Ali on the way to stopping him after the 10th round, Smith, Matt, and Ameen were part of a small group invited up to Ali's suite at Caesars Palace. Ali sat on his bed, his face puffed and bruised, and they talked. After a while, they let the press in, and Ali launched right into the battle cry he'd used in press conferences and appearances leading up to the fight: "I want Holmes! I want Holmes!"

Ameen never forgot how wretched the spectacle made him feel and promised himself that when it was Matt's time to retire, he would tell him so, and if Matt insisted on continuing on, he would do it without Mustafa in his corner. He refused to be that insidious enabler who pervades every corner of the fight game, the man who assures his broken fighter that he is as good as he's ever been and is just a fight or a break away from recapturing everything he's surrendered to time. He'd seen up close what those guys had done to Ali by telling him what he wanted to hear. He couldn't bear seeing Matt done the same way.[44]

Chapter 9

MAPS

"Everybody looks for the biggest pile of money he can make. But my main thing in boxing is not to come out of it on my heels."
—Matthew Saad Muhammad[1]

Matt was a free agent following the López fight, which represented the last of the fights he owed contractually to Arum. He could sign with whatever promoter offered him the most money for his services. That promoter, of course, was Smith, who was working on a two-fight deal: a title defense against Zambian challenger Lottie Mwale, for which Matt would be paid $650,000, by far his biggest payday, plus a $300,000 sign-on bonus.[2] Smith would promote a unification fight in which he and Mustafa Muhammad, whom Smith had also signed, would split $2.5 million the following February. Mustafa would fight Rudy Koopmans the day after Matt's defense against Mwale. He finally agreed to the unification fight, reportedly, because World Community of Islam in the West leader Wallace Muhammad approved it, so long as the fight was held "in the name of sport and not greed or anger."[3] At Smith's request, Matt and his team flew out to the West Coast to train at Ali's Professional Sports Boxing Gym in Santa Monica. Matt and Ameen roomed together at a condominium in Marina del Rey.

Before training could get under way in earnest, Matt and Solomon had to settle on how much of Matt's purse would go to Solomon. They had always adhered to a flat fee of $10,000 per fight.[4] That was the arrangement. But Solomon thought $10,000 when Matt was making $650,000 was an insult. Matt wanted to stick to the original agreement. Solomon insisted on 10 percent. They went back and forth, loudly and in front of other camp members, until finally Matt acquiesced. Solomon got his $65,000, but it would come back to hurt him when Bilal discovered he had gone back on their agreement without Bilal's knowledge.

One afternoon while Matt was in the gym, a young woman named

Jolita stopped in and asked him to come outside with her to meet someone. Matt knew Jolita; she worked for and traveled with Ali and his wife, Veronica, as an au pair for Ali's daughters, Laila and Hana. Waiting in the car was Jolita's friend Michelle LeViege, an Alaska native and model, who, two months earlier had placed first runner-up in the inaugural Miss Black World pageant. LeViege lived in Los Angeles and was attending Los Angeles City College as a marketing major. Matt had no idea that for the past several weeks, Jolita had been planning to get the two to meet. During the same period, Veronica had been hoping to set up Matt with her cousin, Lenora. Too late. Matt was smitten with Michelle and she with him, and they started dating immediately.[5]

In the meantime, Matt had a fight to prepare for. He knew little about Mwale but enough to know that he wouldn't fight him any place outside the United States. Mwale had decisioned Matt's old rival Marvin Johnson in Yugoslavia in 1978 via controversial decision and Matt was afraid he might suffer the same fate. (Manager and trainer Gil Clancy: "Marvin was beaten in the first two rounds but he had the fight won. He just got a bad decision."[6]) Otherwise, he knew only that Mwale was a tricky guy and figured he'd watch video to see what he was about. "I'll have to look at the films. All I have to do is take one good look for about a week and I can tell you his whole history," he said.[7] There was one problem: There were no films. Right up until the day of the fight, they were still looking and couldn't find anything. At one point during camp, someone sent a tape, but when Solomon went to watch it, it was blank. "Someone erased it," he said.[8]

Like Pergaud, Mwale was managed by Mickey Duff and arrived in the United States with an interesting story that was almost certainly manufactured by Duff, who could spin yarns with the best of them. Allegedly, Mwale was a young man living and fighting in Uganda, when after a bout, he was visited in his dressing room by the brutal dictator Idi Amin, during whose reign of terror there occurred reports of cannibalism in some remote villages. Amin supposedly complimented Mwale's physique and said his body looked "good enough to eat." Mwale packed his suitcase that night and fled to Zambia, according to the lore, and then to London. Fairy tales aside, Mwale was reportedly 21–0 (17) and had nearly 250 amateur bouts. His most important victories, at least as far as American television audiences were concerned, were over Johnson, Jesse Burnett, and David Lee Royster. Mwale's trainer, George Francis, told the press his fighter had sparred 600 rounds to prepare for Matt, an absurdly high amount.

Mwale held the odd distinction of having been on two Zambian Olympic boxing teams but never fought a round in Olympic competition. In Munich in 1972, he came in overweight before his first bout and was disqualified. Four years later in Montreal, Zambia was one of 29 countries to boycott the Olympics after the International Olympic Committee refused to ban New Zealand after the New Zealand national rugby union team toured South Africa despite the United Nations' pleas for a prohibition on sporting events.

Olympic heartbreaks aside, Matt was a solid favorite to defend the championship for the fifth time and spoke like one. "I don't want to take anything from Lotte [sic] Mwale. I feel he's a good fighter. He has to be good to be the number-one contender. But check my record. I'm the best fighter in the world. Lotte gets no 'Lotte-Pop' this time. I'm going to jog him so hard it'll shake his kinfolk back in Africa," he said. "I'm strong in my mind. I don't think anyone can beat me except Allah, my god and your god. That's the kind of mentality you have to have going in."[9]

Matt and Mwale met on November 28 at the Sports Arena in San Diego in front of a crowd of just 2,197, which included Muhammad Ali. Mwale took the first two rounds with an anxious, jumbled style that was more seasoned amateur than anything, but Matt was content to take his time with him, absorb Mwale's punches and see what he had. He'd gotten to the point where he rarely won early rounds anymore. He loaded up on power punches occasionally and looked fairly silly himself when missing, but by the third, he knew Mwale had nothing with which to hurt him and started applying more pressure. With just under 30 seconds left in the third, a bomb of a left hook sent Mwale reeling, and Matt assailed him in Mwale's corner for the remainder of the round. A less courageous referee than Tony Perez might have stopped it there, but Mwale, to his credit, appeared mostly recovered at the start of the fourth.

At about 2:00 of the round, an overhand right to the side of the head and a left uppercut to the point of the chin sent Mwale's mouthpiece sailing into the second row and the fighter on his back. Perez began one of the most unnecessary counts in modern boxing history and continued it even after the ringside doctor and Mwale's cornermen were busy at the fighter's side trying to revive him. Dr. William Lunde, the onsite physician, told the press it was at least 15 seconds before Mwale opened his eyes following the knockdown. The official time was 2:25 of the fourth round. "That's the best shot I've ever thrown in boxing," Matt said afterward, on time to the press conference and all smiles. "I couldn't miss."[10]

With Mwale out of the way, all that was left to ensure the big-money unification fight was for Mustafa Muhammad to win the following day against Rudy Koopmans in Los Angeles. He did that, stopping

Koopmans on cuts in three rounds at the Olympic Auditorium. The "This Is It" card, promoted by Harold Smith and MAPS, was thus set for February 23 at Madison Square Garden and would include matchups between some of the best fighters in the world: Matt against Mustafa Muhammad, Thomas Hearns against Wilfred Benítez, Wilfredo Gómez against Mike Ayala, Hilmer Kenty against Alexis Argüello, and Ken Norton against Gerry Cooney in the main event. As written up, the promotion would cost MAPS $8.1 million. Ringside tickets would go for $1,000, the cheap seats $50.

Still, no one could figure out where Smith was getting all this capital. There was no way he could continue to do business losing money on show after show. For example, MAPS paid Matt $650,000 and Mwale $50,000 for their fight, but gross gate receipts for the card were just $41,785. There were no television revenues. Similarly, MAPS paid Mustafa Muhammad $300,000 for the Koopmans fight and $65,000 to Koopmans, but attendance in Los Angeles was a paltry 2,749, generating a gate receipt of just $37,000. The following week, MAPS paid Benítez and Pete Ranzany $250,000 and $75,000, respectively, for a fight that made $89,992.50. Some who were keeping track said MAPs was $10 million in the hole.[11]

Even Ali was getting suspicious. In January, he acted on the advice of friends who told him to have his lawyers conduct an audit of Smith's books. Smith kept putting him off. A few days later, Ali decided to remove his name from the organization. "The money he was paying all those fighters. The office buildings. Everybody flying around in a private jet. The hotel rooms. Flying those card girls, the ones who carry cards between rounds, all over the place. All that money being spent and nobody saying where it was coming from. It was too much for me," Ali said.[12]

The bubble had to burst sooner or later. It did, finally, in early February, when a routine audit at the Beverly Hills branch of Wells Fargo Bank uncovered an apparent embezzlement scheme whereby $21.3 million had been illegally transferred to MAPS accounts and had then vanished. Moreover, Smith and a bank official named Benjamin Lewis, who sat on the MAPS board of directors, had also disappeared. And just like that, Matt's big unification fight and his $1.5 million payday were gone. (Bilal would later say that when all was said and done, Matt's take would have been closer to $2 million.)

Efforts were made to save the card; promoters and new investors scrambled to convince the fighters to take a pay cut. Ali himself offered to promote it provided the fighters agreed to take less money. A few did. Matt did not. Bilal told Matt the news. "Muhammad Ali calling to ask us to take a pay cut," Matt said to a reporter in a mocking tone. "Now ain't that something?"[13] To another he said, "I don't think [Ali] was serious. Of all people to be asking fighters to take a cut in purses, the last one should be him."[14]

"They [MAPS] hadn't given us proper respect to begin with," Matt said. "How could they make Gerry Cooney and Ken Norton the main event? Why do they always play up to the heavyweights? People can think [what] they want about me, but I am my own man. And I said, 'No cut.'"[15]

It all came crashing down. Within days, all MAPS assets were frozen. Some fighters had already received advances. Most hadn't. The FBI was involved. Don King called Mustafa Muhammad. "I'm still your man," he told him. "Don't worry about nothing." He implied he could still get the unification fight done. Mustafa Muhammad knew better. "I knew the fight with Matthew was off," he said. "No other promoters would give us a million and a half."[16] He was right.

Disgusted, Matt wanted to shut down camp and go home. Solomon and Bilal convinced him to keep training while they looked for another opponent. Why let all the work they'd put in go to waste? They moved quickly, signing a promotional agreement with Bilal's old Cornerstone colleague Murad Muhammad, who had been promoting James Scott's fights at Rahway. Murad had worked his way into boxing circles years before as a member of Muhammad Ali's security detail. Along the way, he became friendly with the well-connected duo of Bill Cayton and Jim Jacobs and made other important contacts. Murad was not particularly respected among boxing insiders: a persistent characterization—"He's Don King without the brains." Nevertheless, he had ties with Bally's in Atlantic City and his association with Ali went a long way.

By the second week in February, they'd found a replacement opponent. The way Bilal presented it to the press, Murad showed the team four names on a sheet of paper, each of whom had committed to him (Murad) if he could deliver a championship fight. The names were Murray Sutherland, Jerry Martin, Vonzell Johnson, and Dwight Braxton. Supposedly, Matt put his left hand over his eyes and with his right pointed to a name. His finger landed on Johnson. "It was the second name from the bottom. That's all there was to it," Murad said.[17] It was more likely simply that Johnson and Matt found themselves in the same predicament: training for a fight that got canceled. Johnson was preparing for Scott in Rahway when Scott's retrial on a 1975 murder charge started, effectively ending his boxing career.

It probably didn't hurt either that Matt's buddy and main sparring partner Tony Green knew Johnson well. They fought at the Randolph

Air Force Base in San Antonio in 1977. Angelo Dundee was Green's manager. While Johnson was having his hands wrapped before the fight, Dundee, watching in the locker room, demanded that the wraps be removed and done over. It was an attempt to rattle Johnson and his trainer, who started to complain. Johnson stopped him. "Do whatever he wants. Take them off," he said. Then he looked at Dundee. "You just got your guy knocked out." After stopping Green in the third round, Johnson shouted to Dundee from the neutral corner, "You did that. I told you."[18] Sometime later when Johnson was trying to get out of a managerial contract, he and Dundee connected and signed a deal.

Dundee remembered it the same way sans the hand-wrapping incident. "I saw him a couple years ago in a tournament. He took on one of my fighters [Green]. I said to myself, 'Look what this sucker did to my fighter!'"[19]

Johnson started boxing at 16 years old. He was a high school basketball player in Columbus, Ohio, with no interest in boxing. One day, he got into a fistfight on the court. It was at a recreation center and the boxing coach broke it up and told him he should start boxing. "At the time I said, 'Oooh no,'" Johnson told the press. "But I eventually went over to the gym. I picked up boxing really quick and got to like the one-on-one competition."[20] He went on to a reported 80–10 amateur record and national AAU and Golden Gloves titles before turning pro in November 1974. Wins over top-10 fighters Johnny Davis and Ernie Barr got him ranked eighth by the WBC. By the time he challenged Matt at Bally's on February 28, 1981, he was 22–1 (11) with the only loss to tough Jerry Celestine, on points, in Celestine's hometown of New Orleans.

"I want to thank Murad Muhammad and Saad Muhammad, and all the Muhammads," Johnson joked at a press conference. "I've fought a lot of guys and I'm not concerned about Saad Muhammad. He's a banger, but I have more desire to win. He's had a taste of the championship, but I've never had a taste." About strategy, he said he wasn't planning to exchange punches very much. He conceded, however, that "at one point we'll be toe to toe but it will be when I decide, not when he decides."[21]

"He'll get frustrated," Johnson predicted. "He'll have to come in. Most definitely he can be hit. He's got one thing on his mind, and that's banging. When you hit him he goes, 'Oh yes, I love it.' The more you hit him the more he likes to fight. That's not the kind of guy you want to fight. I can keep him at bay, keep him away. I'm going to stick to my fight plan."[22]

The fight plan devised by Dundee and Johnson's trainer, Dell Williams, was to keep moving and countering for 15 rounds and hope that Matt wouldn't be as motivated as he normally was. It was a fair bet.

After all, Matt was going from a potential $1.5 million payday to about $300,000; the biggest fight of his career in Madison Square Garden to a ho-hum title defense against a 6–1 underdog at Bally's. "Maybe the other guy is gonna be down a little emotionally after the big fight went bye-bye," Dundee said. "I figure we got a shot. To be successful in anything you need proper timing and a little luck."[23]

From all appearances, Dundee's hunch was on the money. Matt talked like a fighter not just having a hard time getting up for his opponent but one approaching the end of his career. "I don't really want to fight anymore," he said. "But I must. I have to get my mind back together before next Saturday, get this boy outta there, and then I don't care what anybody says, I'm gonna relax." Then he reflected again on losing the opportunity to unify the title against Mustafa Muhammad.

"The only real goal I have left is to bring the two titles together. So after I beat Eddie, there would be no reason for me to keep fighting," he said. "Maybe one more fight then retire. Sit back and let my money go to work. The [unification fight] excited me. I'm getting bored with boxing, and this was a quick way out. I can assure you that Eddie was in a world of trouble. I've never been as prepared as I was for him. I was in an evil frame of mind."[24] It got worse when the fight started to go to pieces.

"The week the show was coming apart I was stomping around, raging inside. I felt like I'd been betrayed. I was hard to get along with. I started to get angrier and angrier. I took it out on my sparring partners. They were in the wrong place at the wrong time."

Indeed, Ken Ringo, a puncher out of Alexandria, Virginia, got a couple of busted ribs for his trouble and a temporary demotion to camp valet. Ballard, who routinely sparred with heavyweights, including Larry Holmes, had to take a couple of days off from the bruising Matt gave him. The other sparring partners in camp—Tony Green, Amir Ali, and Pete McIntyre—all caught beatings. Matt was never one to go easy in sparring and he didn't expect anyone else to. But this was different. "Matthew was vicious in the ring," Solomon said. "Several times we literally had to pull him off his sparring partners."[25]

It wasn't just boxing that was wearing Matt down. It was also the pressure that came with fame and wealth. "Money? I just want enough to know that I don't have to worry. Then I'll get into something else, out of the public eye. It's not easy living when someone hears you're making millions. Someone's always ringing the doorbell saying, 'Matthew, please help me, my baby needs milk.' I know there are a lot of people who make a lot of money without getting their picture in the papers and I want to become one of them. I had thought that I was about to write the end to Matthew Saad Muhammad the boxer," he said. "Instead, the way things have gone, I guess it will just have to be another one of those stories that says at the bottom, 'To be continued.'"[26]

Solomon tried to present an upbeat picture, telling the press, "Whatever it takes, we're prepared. We've been training for seven weeks now, so we're ready. Matthew knows what he has to do here. He knows Eddie isn't the threat anymore. Sure he's disappointed, but that doesn't have anything to do with this fight. That was then and this is now. Vonzell Johnson is the threat now." He broke out his trusty notebook. "Matthew's sparred 139 rounds. That's not playing around. He's run 136 miles. That tells us he's not playing. It's really no problem getting up for the fight. The championship is always an honor."[27]

There were more stressors. Matt's childhood friend from the streets Tim Sams, whom he hired out of a sense of loyalty to be his equipment man and assistant, kept showing up in camp drunk or high. When sober, he was fairly good at controlling his resentment of the "Jersey guys"—Ameen, Bilal, Sharif, et al.—who were running Matt's team. When under the influence, it was another story. When he got caught stealing and selling Matt's equipment, Matt fired him. Sams apologized. Matt rehired him. Another incident. Matt fired him again. Sams apologized. It became a small soap opera.

Adding to the apprehension among some in camp was Matthew's relationship with LeViege. He had always been a playboy, and he and Ameen, when not in camp, were always ready to avail themselves of female company, which was plentiful. When he met LeViege, Matt was dumbstruck. He stopped cruising. He talked about settling down. This wasn't necessarily a bad thing. Fighters who settled down at least stopped chasing girls at all hours of the night and got their rest. But some on the team—Bilal and Shamsud-din Ali in particular—thought Matt and Michelle were moving too quickly. And history had shown that wives often had a way of inserting themselves between a fighter and his team and causing trouble.

In front of a national TV audience and about 3,000 fans at Bally's, the fight couldn't have started much worse for Matt. In the first round, he walked into a short left hook that rocked him back on his heels. A round later, Johnson's jabs and right hands had bloodied his nose. Simply by moving and jabbing, Johnson made the most of his five-inch height advantage, keeping Matt outside and on the end of his punches. Matt didn't help his case any, ignoring Solomon's instruction to work in behind the jab and attack Johnson's body. Instead, he loaded up on overhand rights, which Johnson was slick enough and mobile enough to evade without much trouble. Johnson took the first four rounds easily, as Matt plodded forward heaving bombs, no doubt confident that sooner or later one would land to end the evening. This is what happens when one scores one-punch knockouts of the type Matt scored over Mwale and Pergaud. The trouble arises when such a puncher runs into a fighter of higher quality, and this was the case against Johnson. "He boxed me beautifully. He definitely surprised me," Matt said later.[28]

After the fourth, Solomon told Matt to stop winging right hands: rather, to feint the right and throw the left hook instead. Matt followed his advice but found Johnson equally adept at blocking his left hook or circling to the left to avoid it. Matt missed hook after hook, and if not for his long history of staging comebacks, one might have gotten the sense in the middle rounds that he was about to be dethroned. He loped after Johnson round after round, and one could not be blamed for thinking he was simply biding his time waiting for Johnson to run out of gas and come down off his toes, where Matt's natural strength and punching power would take over. This wasn't a terrible strategy, given Matt's ability to withstand another man's punches for however long it took and Johnson's lack of championship experience. But it was a dangerous strategy. The ranks were full of former champions who ran out of time waiting for a challenger to tire out. Gil Clancy, calling the fight with Tim Ryan on CBS, said late in the fight, "Unless Johnson runs completely out of gas, the champ is in a lot of trouble this afternoon."[29]

Matt got a break from an unexpected source: Dundee. During the break after the eighth round, he told Johnson to stop circling the ring and to fight Matt, back him up. "I thought he was getting nailed backing out. I told him to stay close, pop him, pop him, push him," Dundee said later.[30] Johnson did as he was told, and although he did well enough even in that posture, he was now fighting Matt's fight as well as burning up energy that might have better been deployed using the ring. Matt was now able to land his power punches. And when Johnson did move, Matt froze him with the jab and combinations, the way Solomon had wanted him to all along, and the right hands and hooks followed. By the 10th, Johnson was cut over the left eye and haggard. He appeared as certain as anyone that his gas tank would be empty well before the 15th round. He wasn't going to make it. Still, Dundee barked at him to back Matthew up.

The fighters were grinding away on the inside in the 11th when a series of overhand-right, left-hook combinations punctuated by a final straight left found Johnson's jaw and dropped him on his side in a neutral corner, exhausted as much as concussed. He beat referee Tony Perez's count but didn't have enough left to do anything but back into the same corner and hope for the best. All Matt had to do was let loose with overhand rights, and after several of them thudded off Johnson's skull, Perez called it off at 2:23 of the 11th.

During the post-fight TV interview, Matt dedicated the fight to the missing or murdered children of Atlanta. About Johnson, he said, "I knew he would get tired. He couldn't keep it up all night, he's not Muhammad Ali," and then announced his intention to retire if a unification fight wasn't made, presumably with Mustafa Muhammad, in the next year. "Put the two titles together. I'm talking about retiring because I fight a lot of fights and I don't want to end up talking like duh-duh-duh and walking on my heels," he said.[31]

Later, Johnson lamented the lost opportunity. "I know I hurt him with a couple shots. When I was moving around he was really frustrated. I was nailing him with good shots. I could tell he was frustrated." Solomon, ever the company man, argued semantics. "[Matt] was never frustrated. Anxious, yes, but never frustrated. I had to keep his spirits up, let him know we were behind him, to keep him from getting frustrated. At the end he was going to the body, throwing combinations like I asked him to. He was throwing the right too much, loading up on the right too much. He was just trying to knock the man out with one punch."[32]

Matt poses with his WBC light heavyweight championship belt, ca. 1981 (photo by Paul Trace).

Matt agreed. "Sam was telling me to jab first, then throw the right hand, the one I was missing so much. I think I was a little anxious, trying to get it over with. As the rounds went on I felt more pressure, more pressure, more pressure. The fight was either way at one point—Johnson was very good," he said.[33]

Most didn't know it yet, but the fighter who had made his name going to war with Richie

Chapter 9. MAPS

Kates, Billy Douglas, Marvin Johnson, and Yaqui López was forever gone and the Vonzell Johnson fight was evidence of it. There was no hunger in this version for heroics, risk, or brutality. Now fans would see only a version of Matt that was flat and bloodless compared to the one that had brought them out of their seats, out of their lives, out of their minds. He would no longer outfight opponents; he would hope merely to outlast them, offering up his chin, body, and brain as things on which they would exhaust themselves while he conserved energy. It was the same in the gym: take a beating for two minutes and a half, then blast away for the last 30 seconds.

You couldn't blame him. All those wars—they change a man. Plus, he had money now. He had fame, nice cars, house in the suburbs. He had a woman he loved. He was as far removed from the reform schools, the rats, the gangs, and the jails as he could ever hope to be. He had everything he had ever wanted, and a man who has everything has little lust for violence. There was just one thing left: finding out who he was.

Chapter 10

Roots

"Not knowing your real name is like being nobody."
—Matthew Saad Muhammad

Since hiring a lawyer and private investigator the previous May, Matt had spoken with several parties who claimed to be his relatives but were not. He knew this because he remembered details from his childhood that only his true biological family would know. If the stories didn't match up, he knew they were lying. By the following year, he was beginning to think he'd never find them, and the success he'd achieved somehow made the not knowing even worse.[1]

"I think people who do well in life have a tendency to reminisce but when I tried I really couldn't," he told a reporter. "There were blanks in my life. When you get in my position, being a champion, you start thinking, 'Where did this greatness come from? Could my father be Sugar Ray Robinson?'"[2]

Then, in early April 1981, about five weeks after the Vonzell Johnson fight, Matt's lawyer received a letter from a Philadelphia woman named Ann Young. Ms. Young wrote that she had read in *Jet* magazine about Matt's search for his roots and that it was like "seeing someone from the past when I saw his photo." She had, she wrote, known the family of a little boy she remembered as "Maxie Loach."

Subsequently, the investigator found a birth certificate with that name and several siblings with a mother in common. Philadelphia General Hospital, where the birth certificate said Maxwell Antonio Loach had been born on August 5, 1954, closed in 1977, but a heel print was found on microfilm in the Philadelphia archives. Matt had a new heel print taken to see if it matched. The results were inconclusive, but he met with the Loach family anyway and concluded they were, in fact, his siblings.

"It looks very good," he said in mid–April. "There are a lot of things I never told anyone. I told my lawyer, 'Let me talk to them myself.' I

Chapter 10. Roots

talked to each one individually. Pictures were brought to me that were definitely me as a child. It matched. It's unbelievable. So strange, you know?" Matt said. "I have to sit back and recoup, get myself together. After so long, when it seemed it never would come, I have to deal with it.[3]

"Here I was, the light heavyweight champion of the world and I didn't know how I got here, who my mother and father were, nothing. You gotta be in that position to understand what it feels like."[4]

Particularly painful for Matt was hearing the story from his new-found brother, Rodney, about the day he was abandoned. "It's deep, man," he told a writer. "The story made me cry. It shocked me. I'm still stunned."[5]

"If he's an actor he's a great one," Matt continued. "He looked really scared. But he had the heart to admit doing this thing to me."[6] Matt searched for a bright side to having been abandoned by his biological parents, and as is often the case in these matters, there was one. "If what had happened to me didn't happen, I don't know where I'd be today. But I know one thing: I came from a pretty bad family. I'd probably be in my brother's shoes. He's got a little piece of a job and is not doing too good."[7]

* * *

Matt then did something that to most would seem extraordinary, given the circumstances: he gave Rodney a job in training camp, assisting camp cook Lana Shabazz in the kitchen. It was a wonderful display of grace on Matt's part; after all, it wasn't Rodney's fault that Matt ended up alone, wandering along the Ben Franklin Parkway. He'd merely followed orders. Moreover, the directive that day included a warning to Rodney that if he returned home with his little brother in tow, *he* would be left to the streets.

So he was blameless. He owed Matt nothing and Matt owed nothing to him. But Matt gave him a job in the kitchen while training in Deer Lake for title challenger Murray Sutherland. It was not a comfortable relationship or a long-lasting one as it turned out. Rodney had a hard time looking Matt in the eye.[8]

Guilt, one presumes. Undeserved.

"He was very quiet and shy," Mustafa Ameen said in 2021.

After a couple of weeks at Deer Lake, Rodney approached Ameen and asked him if he could leave camp for a doctor appointment he had in Philadelphia and return the following morning. As the camp coordinator and Matt's right-hand man, Ameen knew Matt was strict about anyone leaving camp. His rule was when you're in camp, you're in camp and you stay there until camp is over.

"It means you don't leave to go visit your girlfriend late at night, or go back down to Miami over the weekend, you know? You're in camp," Ameen said. The situation with Rodney was unique, however, and Ameen, without mentioning it to Matt, told him to go ahead but come right back. Rodney left. The next morning, Matt wanted to know where Rodney was. Ameen told him he had to handle something in Philadelphia.

Matt blew up.

"What are you doing? What kind of camp are we running? You know the rules! You need to do your job!"

"He got on my case—I was thinking Rodney might catch a break because he was Matthew's biological brother, but Matthew wanted me to read him the riot act about leaving camp," Ameen recalled. "So I chuckled about that, that Rodney wasn't getting a break either."[9]

Ameen would have been happy to talk with Rodney if only he'd shown up back at camp the next day. Or the day after. Or the day after that. He didn't. Rodney never showed up at camp again. None of them saw Rodney again until Bilal used his friendship with ABC TV executive Alex Wallau to have Matt and the Loaches do a reunion segment on *Good Morning America*, one of the most popular morning television shows in the country.

But first things first: Matt had to get by Sutherland at Resorts in Atlantic City on April 25, 1981. A native of Edinburgh, Scotland, who emigrated to Canada in 1974 and then to Michigan, Sutherland was ranked second by the WBA and seventh by the WBC. He immediately gained the affection of the local fight press when he announced at the kickoff press conference, "There is a rumor that I'm changing my name to Mick Muhammad. It is not true."[10]

Sense of humor aside, Sutherland was not seen as a serious threat—not by Matt, not by the fight press. He'd lost three of his first five pro bouts, then went on a tear against seven nonentities before losing a decision to Richie Kates. Seven more wins followed against a group of mostly sub–500 opponents before he fought reasonably well—on six days' notice—in a losing effort to 1976 Olympian and rising contender Michael Spinks in May 1980. He scraped together 11 more wins over journeymen, 10 by knockout, to get the title shot. More interesting than his record was his journey from blue-collar worker to world championship title challenger.

Sutherland was a nondescript kickboxer when his manager, who also managed light heavyweight Gary Summerhays, offered to take him along to watch Summerhays fight Mike Rossman on the undercard of Muhammad Ali's title defense against Earnie Shavers at Madison Square Garden in 1977. Sutherland jumped at the chance. "This was a dream come true for me—I mean, the fight was nationally televised," he said. "So I went to New York, saw the fight, then went to the post-fight press conference. Ali's there, and Shavers and Norton, all these big names, and it's like a magnet, drawing me away. I figured I just had to get some of this."[11] It didn't hurt that he hated the alternative.

"I worked in a factory, eight-hour shifts, days, then afternoons, then nights, over and over, as a machinist. The whole time I kept saying I wasn't going to do this the rest of my life. Earlier, when karate was just a hobby, people would ask me what else I could do. I used to say I didn't know, but I sure as hell wasn't going to work in a factory the rest of my life."[12] He turned pro in 1977, and four years later, there he was fighting for the light heavyweight title.

Matt did most of his training for the fight at Deer Lake. Sutherland put in seven weeks in Canton, Ohio. The week of the fight, both camps shut down and wrapped up training with open workouts at Resorts, though the workouts weren't quite as "open" as advertised. When members of Sutherland's camp went to one of Matt's workouts, Matt's guys kicked them out. Later the same day, Matt sent a couple of guys over to spy on Sutherland. "Hell, we have so many tapes of Saad's fights, must be a half dozen, that he can go to the bathroom and we know what's going to happen," Sutherland joked. "But he throws us out of his workout anyway. That's just bush."[13]

Meanwhile, Matt was in a sour mood over the three-room suite Resorts had given him. He felt disrespected. "When Conteh came here to fight me, Resorts sent him to the Bahamas to train, but I'm still not accommodated like a champion. They don't have a proper publicity spread for me. You'd think Diana Ross was the only entertainer in the building. I'm very upset," he told a reporter.[14] He went through the motions necessary to build the fight, such as agreeing to be photographed riding on the back of Bombay, the 600-pound Resorts International tiger, but didn't do anything more than he had to. A contributing factor may have been that his purse—a reported $275,000[15]—was smaller than his other recent purses.

In Matt's previous fight, Vonzell Johnson's backers pinned their hopes on Matt's many distractions. Sutherland's did the same. You couldn't blame them. Matt had a lot going on: getting acquainted with his biological family, reportedly working with an author on his autobiography, taking singing lessons, working with a tutor to improve his vocabulary, bitching about the accommodations, and of course, retirement, which he brought up at every opportunity.

"All those things going on, especially the things he's said about retiring, they have to hurt his preparation for this fight," said Frank

Luca, Sutherland's trainer. "You have to be 100 percent enthusiastic about fighting to be good, and as soon as you start talking retirement, you can't be 100 percent enthusiastic." By now Matt was used to this kind of talk and replied with due menace. "Come early. You'll see how distracted I am."[16]

Those who took Matt's advice saw two unexpected things: Sutherland escorted to the ring by a bagpipe player and Matt's lower lip ripped almost in half by a Sutherland right in the first round. Matt said he was going to break tradition by starting fast, but the opposite was true. He plodded forward as if in a trance, just as in the Johnson fight. Sutherland, mobile and quick-handed but fortunately without a lot of hitting power, punched him around the ring. Matt never looked so slow and easy to hit. He slogged after Sutherland, guided by neither urgency nor skill, and took punch after punch. In the corner after the third round, Solomon begged him to get moving. "Don't worry, I'll get him," Matt said. Ritacco did his best to keep Matt's lower lip from falling onto the ring floor.

In the next round, Sutherland opened a cut over Matt's right eye. "He doesn't move and is very easy to hit," Sutherland said later, showing a keen grasp of the obvious. "He comes straight at you but he can take a lot of punishment."[17]

It wasn't until the sixth that Matt finally appeared warmed up. He bulled Sutherland across the ring with booming body shots, and for the first time, the challenger wasn't in complete control. Just when Matt had finally found his footing, the round was delayed so Sutherland's glove could be replaced. Matt opened the seventh charging forward again, bombing Sutherland with overhand rights and hard left hooks to the body. Midway through the round, a pair of right-cross, left-hook combinations put Sutherland down. When he rose at eight, blood leaked from a cut over his left eye.

Sutherland recovered enough between rounds to get through the eighth with Matt stalking him. "He's a champion. He doesn't want to lose that championship," Gil Clancy said from ringside, calling the fight for CBS. "They're going to have to practically kill him to take his title away from him."[18]

Matt looked like hell, but there was plenty of fight left in him. Almost midway through the eighth, he launched an overhand right followed by a straight left, sending Sutherland down in a heap in his corner. Referee Paul Venti issued the count and when he reached nine, Sutherland sprang to his feet. Instead of stopping the count there, Venti continued to 10 and waved his arms, signaling the fight over. Sutherland immediately protested. Luca charged Venti, then commissioner Jersey

Joe Walcott. The small crowd took great joy in booing and continued it long after the point of usefulness, but this was their right. Two of the three judges had Sutherland leading on points at the end. Charles Spina and William Kostraub had Sutherland ahead 76–75. Frank Brunette had Matt up 76–75.

Sutherland's team was still outraged at the post-fight press conference. "I was on my feet at nine," Sutherland said. "I knew exactly what the count was. The referee said, 'Nine, out.' He didn't even ask me if I was all right. I said, 'What are you talking about? I'm up.'" Sutherland's manager, Art Dore, threatened legal action, surely knowing that nothing would come of it but perhaps with the idea that if they could make enough noise, they could get the WBC to mandate a rematch, as they had with the Conteh fight. "We're going to the New Jersey Commission that appointed that referee. Murray's been hit by everyone and he always gets up," Dore said.[19] Luca, the trainer, got in on it too. "There are going to be all kinds of lawsuits," he said. "We're going to stir things up around here."[20]

Venti defended his decision. "In my opinion he never made the count and was in no condition to continue. If he had been up in time I would have talked with him and looked him over. I was closer than anyone else and I needed just one look at him to know if we let Saad Muhammad go after him we would have been in trouble. He looked like a drunk to me."[21] Back and forth they went, with Sutherland claiming, with some merit, that recent deaths and injuries had made referees gun shy, a reference to Fred Bowman. Two months earlier, underneath Matt's win over Vonzell Johnson, Bowman, a junior welterweight in his fourth pro fight, was stopped by Isidro Pérez in the sixth round and dropped into a coma. He never regained consciousness.

Conspicuously absent from all the drama was Matthew. He was at Atlantic City Medical Center, where doctors would sew four stitches into his lower lip. In the same emergency room was his man Tony Green, who drew with Rodell Dupree on the undercard. Green needed stitches too but over his eye. Plus, he had a cracked rib.

> **MATT TO GREEN:** "Damn, brother. You got fucked up!"
> **GREEN:** "Shit, you got fucked up more than I did!"

It was a light moment, gallows humor if you like, given the location, but Green saw the same thing everyone else did: Matt wasn't the same fighter anymore. "I had been with Matt so long I could just tell," he said in 2021.

The Sutherland affair was the first fight of Matt's that Michelle attended. She had watched others on videotape and was surprised at the difference.

"'It's different watching him live,'" she said. "'On film, I already know he won. When I saw the blood, I didn't know how bad it was, how deep the cut was. I know you get cut in boxing and I know he has to take a punch to deliver a punch. It's hard watching someone you love, but I know he's good at it."[22]

Matt was still healing from the Sutherland fight when he and his team went to the ABC studios in New York to tape the segment about the reunion with his biological family on *Good Morning America*. Meeting him there were Tondylea Loach Vaughn, 33, Desiree Loach, 31, Frances, 29, Andrea, 32, and Rodney, 30. Vaughn told host David Hartman, "It feels unreal. We're overjoyed with the idea of finding him. He definitely looks like us—his smile, his eyes." Andrea added that she "knew" Matt was their long-lost brother while watching one of his fights on TV and hurriedly called her sister Desiree to get her opinion, who agreed it was Maxwell. Added Frances, "It feels wonderful."[23]

There is evidence that over the years that followed, Matt and the Loaches did not develop the kind of close, loving relationship that Matt longed for and that is typically depicted as a given in movies and on television. Rather, it was a distant, uncomfortable type that is frequently the product of splintered families thrust back together by circumstance and/or the innate desire all men have to connect with their tribe. Helen Loach's children, now adults and several of them strangers to one another, didn't have anything in common beyond their shared blood, and that wasn't enough to bring them together.[24]

Adding to the difficulty was Matt's status as a sports celebrity, and being an orphan was almost beside the point. Wealthier, more famous men than Matt had hit it big and suddenly found themselves besieged by family they didn't know they had, getting asked for help they weren't morally obligated to give. Those relationships are rarely sustained, and eventually Matt confided to those closest to him that there were days he wished he'd never found his biological family, that each day brought a new request for a favor, usually financial in nature.[25]

There was some good news. In April 1981, Matt and Michelle got engaged, right before she left on a Department of Defense USO tour representing the Miss Black America pageant. When she returned, she left her apartment and car in Los Angeles and moved in with Matt in Jenkintown. In July, Michelle's father, Sam, called the house and asked to speak to Matt. Michelle handed him the phone.

LeViege: "Listen, my daughter's there with you; when are you going to get married?"

Matt poses with his biological siblings before an appearance on *Good Morning America* in 1981. Shown with him are Tondylea Loach Vaughn, Desiree Loach, Frances, Andrea, and Rodney (photo by Paul Trace).

MATT: "What's the date today?"
LeVIEGE: "It's July 2."
MATT: "We'll get married in 30 days. We'll get married on August 2."[26]

It was as simple as that.

Before that day could come, Matt decided to take his team to Anchorage, Alaska, so they could all meet Michelle's parents, Sam and Catherine, and so Matt could formally propose to Michelle with Sam's approval. He boxed an exhibition for a small group of fans and did some sightseeing. One afternoon, Sam offered to let Paul Trace, Matt's photographer, take his SUV over to Seward to take some portraits of Matt and Michelle by the river's edge. When they finished, they turned to walk back to the truck and Paul saw a grizzly bear nearby watching them. He said to Matt and Michelle, "Whatever you do, do not run. Just walk slowly like he's not even there." He hadn't even finished the sentence when Matt took off like an Olympic sprinter.²⁷

There were still members of Matt's camp who were against the marriage and, if not suspicious of Michelle's motives, then uneasy at how quickly the relationship had evolved. Still, they had to be comforted by the idea that they no longer had to keep an eye on Matt lest his wandering eye get the best of him in the middle of the night. Although completely devoted to his training, it was not unusual for him, in earlier days, to escape from camp under cover of darkness to meet with one of his many female acquaintances. Early on, Bilal had taken to sleeping on Matt's floor in his apartment in Philadelphia to keep him home. Bilal saw the marriage as chance to get himself a rest.²⁸ Trace often roomed with Matt when they traveled together, and on at least a couple of occasions when they were not in camp but in New York on business, he would wake in the morning to find that Matt had spent the night at a girlfriend's house in New Jersey.²⁹

Still, there were signs fairly early on that Matt's relationship with Michelle might turn out to be at best, a distraction and at worst, destructive. Like the wives of many well-paid athletes, Michelle took some interest in the business side of her husband's career. This frequently put her at odds with Bilal, and even if they never argued, it was an

Matt with Michelle LeViege in Alaska in 1981. They met while Matt was in California training for Lottie Mwale in 1980 and were engaged by April the following year. They married in August 1981 and divorced in March 1985.

open secret in camp that they were unhappy with the power the other wielded over Matt's finances and how they were spent. A prime example was Michelle's insistence that her mother help out with cooking in the camp, thereby displacing Lana Shabazz and saving the salary Matt paid her. Some in camp felt that Shabazz's long experience with Ali in fight camps not only taught her how to cook for fighters but also gave her valuable experience and wisdom that could only benefit Matt.

There were signs too that Matt's spending was far above what it had been before he and Michelle got serious. Depending on his mood, he could be at once thrifty and free-handed when it came to spending the money he earned, quite literally, with his blood. It was true that he'd blown $23,000 on that antique Louis XV grand piano back before the Conteh rematch, which he never did learn how to play. He'd also hired interior designer Marilyn Cutler to renovate his house in Jenkintown to the tune of $65,000. It included a formal living room using "jewel tones" inspired by the piano, a library/TV room with "purple lacquered walls and a mirrored niche" for Matt's trophies, and throughout were "rugs custom-designed by Nigerian artist Emanuel Okon." Matt designed the basement disco himself.[30] On the front lawn, a small sign read, "Muhammad Summit."

When Michelle moved in, she added a woman's touch. "When I moved in Matthew was already set into it ... with a planned place for everything," she told a writer. "But I have lots of clothes and pretty French perfumes I'd like to put on display." She planned to turn one of the unfinished rooms into a dressing room "in peach/pink, with frilly, *frilly* curtains so you can walk in and say, 'Yes, a woman lives here.'"[31]

It was not uncommon, according to one camp member, for Matt and Michelle to spend $10,000 on a weekend shopping trip in New York. And there were other expenses. Michelle was an aspiring pop singer and Matt felt that with the right instruction, she could succeed. He hired renowned music producer James Mtume to give her lessons, and his tutelage was not inexpensive.

Nevertheless, Matt and Michelle were married on August 2, 1981, at the Jenkintown Country Club. (The announcement came as a surprise to Shirley Mitchell, Matt's longtime girlfriend in Philadelphia and his daughter Zakiyyah's mother.[32]) Mustafa Ameen was Matt's best man. The day before the wedding, Murad and Bilal announced that Matt's next title defense, his eighth, would be against Jerry "The Bull" Martin on September 25 on ABC. Matt and Michelle went on a Caribbean cruise for their honeymoon. Matt did roadwork running laps around the ship's deck.

The first order of business when Matt returned to work was

explaining to the fight press that he was done with Sam Solomon. He framed it as a desire to improve his style, particularly his defense. "Sam's a good man, I take nothing from him. I am established as the best fighter in my division. It's time to look for new and different ways to develop," he said. "Sam wanted me out there aggressive all the time. Now I think in terms of slide, slip a punch."[33]

This was largely subterfuge. Solomon was fired in large part because Bilal found out that Solomon had gone behind his back and badgered Matt into paying him $60,000 for the Mwale fight the previous November instead of his usual $10,000 fee. They met about it at the end of July, during which Solomon reiterated his demand for 10 percent going forward. Bilal offered him 5 percent. "We had a disagreement over money," Solomon told a reporter. "They seemed to think I'm not worth the money I was getting. Bilal seemed to think I was not worth 10 percent off-the-top money. I thought I was."[34]

Solomon attended Matt and Michelle's wedding two days after the meeting, but the relationship was effectively over. Solomon blamed Bilal. "We haven't gotten along since I've been there," but as far as he and Matt went, they "never had any bad feelings between us. There still isn't. I'm disappointed with Matt in a way because he knows what I put in. We have a friendship as well as being a trainer and fighter."[35]

Bilal again reached out to Angelo Dundee, who again passed. As the Martin fight approached, they settled on promoting Ritacco to head trainer, but everyone knew Matt was all but training himself, with an eye toward returning to his roots as a boxer-puncher. "Watch me. You're gonna see the new Matthew Saad Muhammad. Slide and glide. Toes and nose. Hit and not be hit," he told a writer before going five hard rounds in the gym with Jody Ballard. "The matador comes back. Martin calls himself 'The Bull.' Well, I will box him. I am now a boxer-puncher and it won't go past nine rounds," Matt said.

Ballard chimed in after the sparring session. "He is the type of fighter who says, 'So what? You hit me.' But that's why he's a champion. You just got to hit him. But once he feels you trying to hurt him, he comes back. Punches glance off him. So, sometimes he looks a little shaky but he always gets the job done. He'll knock out Martin any time he wants to."[36]

While Matt worked himself back into shape after five months off—one of the longest breaks he'd taken since winning the title—Murad Muhammad worked to find a location and venue. For a while, the unlikely front-runner was Pontiac, Michigan. Backers of the Silverdome were eager to host a big, televised sporting event, and as illogical as it was to hold a fight between two Philadelphia guys in Michigan, Muhammad would have done it if the parties involved had been able to demonstrate that they had some of the money necessary to guarantee Matt's $425,000 purse and Martin's $60,000. Alas, they were not, and Murad went scrambling back to Philadelphia and Atlantic City. The Spectrum and Convention Hall in Philly were booked. He thought he'd gotten a deal with Resorts, but that fell through when it was discovered he'd forgotten to apply for a vendor's license.[37]

The fight finally landed in the Opera House at the Golden Nugget Hotel & Casino in Atlantic City, with the furniture configured to seat 812 spectators and not until September 20—six days before the fight. This prompted a prominent Philadelphia sportswriter to observe, "Matthew Saad Muhammad has accomplished boxing's hat trick. He is the most mismanaged, mis-promoted, and now mis-trained championship fighter in America. The most exciting boxer, pound for pound, in action and they move his fights around like floating crap games."[38]

Years later, Bilal recalled that there were frequently problems like this with Murad that didn't exist with other promoters. "Murad paid more but you had to be on your toes with Murad. There was always something that wasn't completely confirmed with him. He always paid and he paid more. But there was always some issue. You had to stay on him."[39]

Matt was equally frustrated. "I'm an American fighter. I'm an international champion. Yet I'm not getting the recognition I deserve," he said. "I'm not getting the recognition money-wise. You shouldn't have to be an Olympic fighter to get a million dollars. Even if I never fought in the Olympics, I am an American, this is my country. I fight for all the people."[40]

Few knew it, but Matt and Ameen had already decided to leave Murad and sign a contract with Don King. They both felt like Matt had largely made Atlantic City and now had outgrown it. King was putting on big fights in Las Vegas and paying fighters the kind of money Matt believed he deserved. King was big time. Murad was not. Bilal, for his part, was opposed to the move, as he had given Murad his word that Team Saad would honor its contract, which gave Murad one more title defense after the Martin fight.

Martin, in the meantime, was no slouch. Born in Antigua in the West Indies, he immigrated to North Philadelphia as a teenager, bringing along the nickname "The Bull," given to him by friends based not on any fighting style necessarily but on some physical characteristics they said he shared with the animal. When he started fighting—at age 22 and without the benefit of a single amateur bout—it fit his style, so it stuck. He was broad-chested, powerful, and raw, and when he barreled forward, top-heavy on spindly legs with the intention of mauling his man, there wasn't a whole lot the average opponent could do to dissuade him.

Martin wasn't pretty in the ring or electrifying the way Matt had been at his best, but his bulk and strength smothered guys and he brought the right hand all the way from Antigua. If he caught his man square with it, it changed things. In his 12th pro fight, he beat world-ranked Jerry Celestine on points at the Spectrum in a brawl, and that's when fight guys knew he had something. When he wasn't in the gym sparring with more experienced Philly light heavyweights—Mike Rossman and Matt, among them—he worked on an assembly line putting together boxes. He and his wife lived in a row home in North Philly.

Things went sideways for Martin a short while after the Celestine win when he decided to tinker with his style such that he would box more and slug less because "I like the idea of not being ruthless and evil," he said.[41] He promptly struggled in wins over faded veterans Jesse Burnett and Billy Douglas and switched back to fighting like a thunderstorm just in time for a showdown in Rahway with James Scott. His unanimous-decision win in a big upset earned him a title shot at Eddie Mustafa Muhammad, who exploited his relative clumsiness and inexperience to stop him in 10 rounds. Three subsequent knockout wins landed him the shot at Matt. Martin's manager and trainer, Leon Tabbs, focused on putting the loss to Mustafa Muhammad behind them.

"It's a year later. He's got three more fights under his belt. And they were meaningful wins. He's been there before. There's not the newness of fighting for the title. He's greatly motivated and had excellent preparation," Tabbs said.[42]

Martin, recalling his days in the gym with Matt, said he would concentrate on body punches, as "he has no body and can be hurt there. If you hit him in the body he will fold." He also assured the press his days of trying to be more of a boxer were over. "That's all I am, a puncher. I'm not a boxer. That's all I know. I know that's all I'm going to be. I'd be lying to you if I told you anything else."

"I guarantee you, if I hit Saad like these [other] guys hit him he's going out," Martin said. "If he doesn't go down he's a miracle man. I've got power those other guys didn't have. Power and smarts are the keys to this fight.[43] I respect Matt a whole lot. I hope he can change his style so he doesn't get hurt. The first few rounds he'll come out and try to run then go back to the old Saad Muhammad after he's been banged around." Tabbs agreed. "Hit Matt and he's back to the same style. Saad is Saad in any town or country you fight in."[44]

Matt was resolute about how he would fight Martin. "In the first

Martin takes a straight right from Matt on the way to getting stopped in the 11th round. It was Matt's eighth and final title defense. In his next fight, he was stopped by Dwight Braxton (photo by Paul Trace).

round I see Jerry coming to me, pressing me. This is why I have adopted a style that will keep Jerry Martin at bay. He always comes in. It's the only fight he knows. There's no other way he can fight. If he backs off it'll be like picking flowers," he said. "He hasn't changed. He still does the same things."[45]

Matt was good to his word, opening the fight by moving and jabbing while Martin plodded after him. It wasn't long before Martin bull-rushed him to the ropes and, as promised, started digging in with short thumping uppercuts to the body. The second round was similar in all respects, and soon a pattern emerged: Martin rushing in with the hope of trapping and smothering Matt on the ropes, Matt jabbing, moving, and trying to catch him on the way in with a left hook or overhand right.

When Matt had room to punch, he found Martin to be easy pickings. But too frequently, Martin bulled him to the ropes before Matt could pull the trigger. Matt got there first in the third, when a crackling left hook froze Martin in his tracks. Near the end of the round, a right hand staggered him, but in the fourth, he pinned Matt on the ropes again and mauled him, opening a cut over Matt's right eye.

Over the next several rounds, their dueling strategies exhausted Martin, whose chest heaved from the exertion while Matt appeared

Matt waits for the bell during his title defense against Jerry Martin in September 1981 in Atlantic City. From left to right: Cutman Adolph Ritacco and assistant trainers Milt Bailey and Saleem El-Amin (photo by Paul Trace).

fresh and if not in control, then comfortable in the knowledge that Martin was gassing out and would become ever more susceptible to power punches. Back and forth they went: Matt gets worked over on the ropes, then comes to life and rattles Martin with ringing head shots. Just when it looks like he can't last another minute, Martin finds the energy to push Matt to the ropes and club away. Around and around they went.

Finally, with 20 seconds left in the ninth, a left hook shook Martin down to his bones. He teetered around the ring in the 10th in slow motion, surely on the verge of collapse as Matt lined him up for the finishing blows. Before he could get there, Martin sprang alive yet again and spent every last bit of what he had beating Matt around the ring for a full minute. With 30 seconds left, Matt took over again. After the round, referee Larry Hazzard checked on Martin in the corner. Later, he said Martin appeared to have been "getting weaker all the time."[46]

Twenty eight seconds into the 11th, Matt walked Martin into an overhand right. Martin's hands dropped to his sides and he lurched forward and stumbled. Calling the fight for ABC, Howard Cosell screamed from ringside, "He got him! Muhammad got him!" Matt missed two follow-up punches, and before he could wind up another, Hazzard jumped between the fighters and waved the fight over.

The crowd exploded in boos, convinced Hazzard had stopped it prematurely. Martin and his corner agreed and together, they rushed Hazzard, screaming all the while. Just as in the Sutherland fight, the small crowd booed long and hard, not only in objection to an official seemingly working in Matt's favor but also to his robbing them of the kind of conclusive end which seemed the whole point of prizefighting to begin with. You couldn't blame them. At the time of the stoppage, judges William Kostraub and Richard Murry had Matt up by scores of 96–94 and 97–93, respectively. Harold Lederman had it even at 95–95.

Martin sobbed in the ring and later in the locker room. "It was highway robbery. I am not a sore loser and I always congratulate my opponent but this was highway robbery," he said. "He [Hazzard] walked to me, I tell him 'one-two-three-four-five-six—I can count. I'm all right.' I saw him coming to me. I just knew something stunk."[47]

"He got hit, no question about that. But let him go down," Tabbs said afterward. "They waived the three-knockdown rule. At least give him a chance for an eight-count." Tabbs had complained before the fight about Hazzard getting the assignment, as he felt Hazzard had a history of stopping fights quickly. (Tabbs was later suspended for "bumping" Hazzard when he charged into the ring at the time of the stoppage.[48]) In a move that would prove to be career-defining, Hazzard accepted Cosell's invitation to share on-camera his rationale for stopping it when he did.

"As you know there have been a lot of deaths, ring killings of fighters who were unable to protect themselves at any particular time, getting concussions," Hazzard began. "This man suffered what is known as a 'concussive episode.' ... Now, it doesn't matter if he goes down or not. The referee has to be courageous enough to step in and do what he thinks is necessary. A man in this condition can get killed or seriously injured by a man like Saad Muhammad. I felt this man could have been seriously injured if I let this bout continue."[49] Hazzard included a long, impassioned homily about the responsibility boxing officials have to protect vulnerable fighters. And even if the crowd and Martin's camp disagreed with the stoppage, Hazzard had supporters.

"Those in the crowd at the Golden Nugget Casino Hotel yesterday were not close enough to see Martin's face," observed one Philadelphia writer. "And the ABC TV camera had a view only of the back of his head. If the camera had shown Martin's glassy stare, his obvious oblivion, then only sadists would have questioned Larry Hazzard's wisdom."[50]

Matt, too, wondered what all the fuss was about. "I saw very clearly that he was easy to hit with the left hook. I must have had him about five times. But you don't try to rush him and kill him. You try to set him up," he said.[51] "When I hit Jerry [in the 11th], he dropped his hands down. I was ready to hit him with another combination. It was plain to see he was going to get hit again."[52]

Chapter 11

The End of Miracles

*"I don't have fond memories of it,
but I don't have fond memories of the ghetto, either,
and I go back there after every fight."*
—Dwight Braxton

In July 1981, Michael Spinks, middleweight gold medal winner on the 1976 Olympic boxing team and younger brother to Leon Spinks, dominated Eddie Mustafa Muhammad over 15 rounds in Las Vegas to win the WBA light heavyweight title. This quashed Matt's hope, again, of a big-money unification fight with Mustafa Muhammad and forced him to change his target to Spinks. Where he used to talk about retiring after a fight with Mustafa Muhammad, he now chided Spinks. "There is one big-money fight left on the horizon. That's me and Michael *Stinks*. Uh, Spinks,"[1] he said a few days before the Martin fight. "That's an attraction. After that I'm going to retire. I'll be happy, and everyone else will be happy because the title is unified."[2]

Matt and Spinks had their routine down already and brought it to a national television audience following Spinks's one-punch knockout of Marvin Johnson in March 1981 in Atlantic City. Howard Cosell called Matt over to his broadcast position at ringside while interviewing Spinks for ABC.

MATT: "Michael *Stinks*."
SPINKS: "Matthew *Sad* Muhammad. I want *you*."
"Anytime."
"Sign the contract!"
"Give me a pen!"

The two jawed playfully at each other until Spinks brought up a sparring session that had taken place four years prior. Matt appeared surprised. Afterward, a writer asked Spinks what he was referring to. "I was letting Saad Muhammad know that we sparred in '77. He had the nerve to ask for me when I first got to town, said he wanted to work out with me," Spinks said. "He went to Hollywood, started playing with me in the gym. I jumped on Saad Muhammad, had him bleeding so bad they had to almost stop the workout. I told [my promoter] to get his name on a contract. I want Saad Muhammad next."[3]

The scene was more or less repeated in the ring and for the benefit of a TV audience following Spinks's successful title defense against Vonzell Johnson in November. "Michael *Stinks* did a very good job, he only beat a man that I knocked out before," Matt said as Spinks stood next to him. Spinks's excitable promoter, Butch Lewis, told Matt to bring his people to the table so they could unify the title. Matt nodded in agreement. Later, Lewis confirmed, "Matt agreed to have his manager, Bilal Muhammad, come and talk. He said he'd come to the table before the week's end to talk and discuss the unification."[4]

Later that week, Bilal and Mustafa Ameen met Lewis at the Playboy Club in Atlantic City. Lewis told them he had a solid vetted offer for $5 million for a unification fight. He laid out all the details and closed with, "Let's chop it up: $2.5 apiece."

Ameen spoke up first. He addressed Bilal.

"You know Bilal, everything Butch just said makes a whole lot of sense."

Bilal replied, "You know Butch, one thing I can say about you and Mustafa is neither one of you know what the *fuck* you're talking about."[5]

This concluded their meeting with Lewis and any chance that existed for a unification fight, though neither Ameen nor Bilal knew it at the time. Plans had been in place even before the Martin fight for Matt to face Camden's Dwight Braxton in his next title defense. Bilal had conferred with Angelo Dundee and legendary trainer Ray Arcel about Braxton, and both of them told him that he would be a tough opponent, but Matt would beat him. Why pass up the chance to make an extra two or three hundred thousand? After he beat Braxton, the Spinks fight would be even bigger.[6] From a manager's perspective, it made sense. To Tony Green and most others on Matt's team, it did not.

"We didn't want Braxton, we wanted Spinks," Tony Green said in 2021. "We were pushing for the Spinks fight. That was the money fight. But Bilal, he was like come on, we get the Braxton fight, beat him, and then we get the Spinks fight. We were like, 'What the fuck, Bilal? Get the Spinks fight.'"

Butch Lewis was of the same mind. "I told Saad's people they were crazy to take that fight. I kept looking at Bilal Muhammad, Saad's manager, the whole time. They kept talking about Saad's $200,000. If he'd met Michael and beat him, he could have fought Dwight for half a million."[7]

Chapter 11. The End of Miracles

They made the deal for Braxton, who would get $50,000. Matt would pull in four times that plus a $150,000 bonus from Don King in exchange for promotional rights to Matt's next defense, plus refusal rights on two more.[8]

At the press conferences and in front of reporters, Matt seemed as confident as ever. "I don't see any problem," he said the day before the fight. "He's a lot like Joe Frazier in style. I expect a lot of pressure. I have to adapt to his style. I'm just in there with a tough kid."[9]

But he knew. He knew things about himself and about Braxton that were concerning and that couldn't be fixed or changed. Matt wasn't really a fighter anymore so much as he was a businessman whose job was boxing. It wasn't life and death for him anymore. He knew this.

Braxton? The man had been out of lockup just a few years. Everything was life and death.

"Matt had real doubts about whether he could beat Qawi," Green said, referring to Braxton by the Muslim name he would adopt later. "Qawi just had his number. He was hungrier. And he had come up the same way Matt had, on the streets, in prison. So he was as tough as Matt was, and he was still hungry. Matt wasn't hungry like that anymore, he was out buying houses and limos. He wasn't hungry like Qawi. And Qawi got in his head. I could tell."[10]

Braxton was born in Baltimore and moved to Camden, New Jersey, when he was 11, and he and his brother Tony—2 of 11 boys in the family—fought on the streets for survival and for the rep. The move was his mother, Alice's, idea. His father was against it and instead of joining them went south looking for work as a lumberjack. Young Braxton was full of rage and, at 5'7", had little man's complex. "Any big guy that looked at me funny I'd say 'What the fuck are you looking at?' I did a lot of street fighting when I was young, so boxing was in my blood. I was just a natural."[11]

Alice first called the authorities on Braxton when he was 14. He was cutting school and getting into fights. Before long, he was shipped off to the State Home for Boys in Jamesburg. Later, he did time in Bordentown and Annandale, two other reform schools, and from there, it was a short trip to Rahway for armed robbery of a liquor store. He served five and a half years of an 11- to 15-year sentence. There, he honed the fighting style he'd learned in the streets. He was paroled in early 1978 after deciding enough was enough.

"I knew I was finished with that stuff [crime]. I outgrew it. I wanted something different and it wasn't there," he told a writer in 1983. "It [being in jail] holds you up. You can't do nothing except get old. It kills your spirit." He said boxing was his way out—out of poverty, out of the "social hells" he was in. "From a survival standpoint, it was something I could do."[12] He was sitting in his prison cell in Rahway watching a Víctor Galíndez fight on TV when he first knew he could win the title. "I thought he was made to order for me. I couldn't wait to get out to see what I could do."[13]

Without a single sanctioned amateur fight, Braxton turned pro in 1978. After three fights, he was 1–1–1, but an assault-and-battery charge from the prior year resulted in a conviction and threatened to end his career and any chance he had at a life outside prison. ("It was a vendetta thing, no money was involved," Braxton said later.[14]) As a third-time offender, he could have gotten 15 years. The criminal court judge in Camden, Peter J. Coruzzi, took pity on him. "His managers begged me to give him another chance. I remember him standing in front of me, tears streaming down his cheeks, and you know how tough he is. I saw something in him. Fighters, judges, robbers, we're all human. Perhaps we should all take a deeper look at our fellow man," Coruzzi[15] said during sentencing, before handing Braxton five years' probation.[16]

Braxton won six straight and then got a break: ESPN televised the American Boxing Championship tournament, which he ended up winning by beating Mike Rossman's stablemate Tony Mesoraca in the light heavyweight final in November. He didn't look great doing it, but it got him exposure and put him in the conversation. Reporters started talking about him as a future title challenger.

Before a fight with Al Bolden in March 1981, a writer asked Braxton "which of the two Muhammads"—Saad or Eddie Mustafa—he'd rather fight. "I would love to fight Mustafa; I get no pleasure out of beating a man senseless," he said. "Saad's got the perfect style for me. He will get his head knocked off. I will beat him unmercifully. If he stands in front of me I'll break his jaw. I'll break him up. He's a slow starter. I like him, but if I come out there in that robe, it's either me or him."[17] Later, after Braxton beat Bolden but looked ordinary doing it, Matt told a reporter he wasn't impressed. Solomon called Braxton an "amateur." Braxton replied, "I'll show him *and* his monkey trainer."[18]

In May, Braxton got his first big fight—against former champ Rossman in Atlantic City on ESPN on a show run by Matt's old promoter, J Russell Peltz. Peltz and Braxton's managers knew Braxton would go right through Rossman. Rossman did too—that's why when the contracts were drawn up, Braxton's purse would be around $20,000 and Rossman's $120,000. That's what it took to get Rossman into the ring. But Braxton's people wanted the fight. Rossman was a big name and it would put Braxton over the top. They held their noses, signed the contracts, and watched Braxton butcher and stop Rossman in seven rounds.

Chapter 11. The End of Miracles

"Just between us," Braxton told a writer afterward, "I carried him a couple rounds."[19]

Four months later, Braxton was back at Rahway—not as an inmate this time but facing James Scott. By now, Scott was unranked, having been found guilty of a murder he committed between incarcerations. He still considered himself the uncrowned champion and hoped to get a shot at a title if he beat Braxton. The two shared history, which accounted for some hostility Braxton showed toward Scott during a press conference. Apparently, some years before, Braxton gave Scott two days of sparring sessions for which Scott never paid him. But it was more than that. Braxton was proud of having straightened out his life and resented Scott for blowing his own chance at success and refusing to take responsibility for it.

"I don't think Scott should be glorified," he said. "He had an opportunity. It wasn't easy for me. I could have taken somebody's money when I got out. I could have pimped. I could have kicked somebody's door in. But I don't want to go back in." Braxton spoke about what it would be like to go into Rahway for the fight. "In a way, it will not be strange. And in a way, I will have a funny feeling. I'll go in saying it's only a matter of an hour. I'll do it and get out. I don't really want to stay an hour at Rahway. I'm not going around shaking people's hands. I'm not politicking for nothing."

"I've had time to prepare for it," he said. "I don't have fond memories of it, but I don't have fond memories of the ghetto, either, and I go back there after every fight."[20]

Braxton decisioned Scott over 10 rounds, ending Scott's boxing career and setting himself up for the shot at Matt's title. When Bilal passed on the Spinks fight, Braxton, who had signed a promotional agreement with Murad and was ranked fifth by the WBC, was ready.

Matt set up camp in Jacksonville, Florida, on November 11. He weighed 181 pounds and sparred in a ring set up at the Sheraton Hotel. "After I beat Braxton I want to unify the light heavyweight title by beating Michael Spinks," he said. "After unification I will look around and see if there are some things I want to accomplish but I don't plan on fighting much longer after I do that."

He already had a foot out the door.

At Matt's insistence, Bilal agreed to pay Solomon what he'd asked for, and Solomon was there when camp opened. One of the first things he said was he didn't want Michelle and her mother in camp. Matt brought them anyway and they stayed for nearly the entire camp. Everyone noticed the difference. "They threw him off his feed," Trace, Matt's photographer, said in 2021. "Eating wrong, shopping with them in stores, over-eating. We all pretty much knew he was in trouble because he wasn't in shape for a guy like Braxton. There was some grumbling going on but it was always taken on the side and not done in front of everybody."[21]

It wasn't just that. In camp, Matt always ran between five and eight miles a day. In Jacksonville, he was doing two or three. Trace, who often ran with Matt, was logging more miles.

A couple of weeks into camp, Matt and Mustafa Ameen went for a ride after dinner. Along the way, they passed a car dealership. Matt told Mustafa to pull in. They walked around looking at cars, talking to salesmen. They left. Later at the hotel, Matt told Mustafa he needed him to go back down to the dealership and put some money down on a car he'd just bought.

Ameen was confused. "What car, champ?"

"The car down at that dealer. The Rolls. The convertible."

Matt had called the salesman and told him he wanted the convertible Rolls Royce he'd been eyeing. Sticker price: $180,000 before taxes. He had them ship it up to Philadelphia so he could drive around Atlantic City with the top down.

A rich bored guy blows a small fortune on a top-of-the-line luxury car. The other can still smell the prison soap in his nose.

Who would *you* bet on?

In the final week of training camp, after dinner, Matt and Ameen took a walk. It was a ritual. Helps the digestion. Matt was quieter than usual. Then:

"Mustafa I don't want to fight this guy. It doesn't make any sense."

Ameen considered it. "Okay. Well, don't fight him then."

Matt looked at him. "What are we gonna do then?"

Ameen thought about it.

"I'll call Bilal. Tell him you slipped and fell in the shower. Your back is hurting."

Matt nodded. "Okay."

Back at the hotel, Ameen got Bilal on the phone and broke the news. Bilal said he would call Murad and let him know. A short while later, the phone rang in Matt's room. It was Murad. He told Matt he had never had to cancel a big fight like this. His reputation was at stake. And before he let everyone know it was off, he wanted Matt to consider all the people the two of them had working for them who had families to feed and bills to pay and how screwed they'd be if the fight didn't go off.

A lot of fighters would have told Murad to go fuck himself. Contractually, Matt was done with him. They were moving to Don King. It was over with Murad. He could have just hung up the phone, wrapped camp, and taken Michelle home. He didn't. He wasn't that guy. He let Murad talk him down. And by the time they hung up, the fight was back on. "Murad played him," Ameen said.[22]

* * *

At 6:00 a.m. the day of the fight, a security guard let Matt into the room where the official weigh-in was scheduled to take place two hours later. At 181, he was six pounds over, the same weight at which he'd started camp. He returned to his room, dressed in layers, and started running on the boardwalk. Then he hit the sauna. At 8:20 a.m., he was down to 177. He jumped rope in his room. Solomon gave him a rubdown.

At one point, he told Bilal, "Man, I can't do it no more."

Bilal: "We gotta do it."[23]

At 9:55 a.m., five minutes before he would have had to forfeit the title, Matt weighed in at 174¼. He went and had some beef broth and a steak. Before he knew it, it was 3:00 p.m. and they wanted him in the dressing room even though the fight wasn't supposed to start until 5:15 p.m. He had to start warming up before he'd recovered from the morning workout. Braxton, for his part, had weighed in at 174¾ at 8:00 a.m. and gone back to bed.

Solomon was livid. "The official scale was way off," he said. "We had one in our room that was certified and sealed and he was okay on that one, and on the two scales in the hotel health center. But they wouldn't let us use any of those."[24]

Later, a small crowd sat through the shallow, untelevised undercard. Joe Gramby, Richie Kates's manager, ran into Butch Lewis and Spinks while milling around between bouts. Kates had been sparring with Braxton. Gramby knew Lewis was hoping Matt would win, as it would all but assure the big-money unification fight.

Gramby said to Lewis, "You're gonna have to get your unification fight someplace else. You're gonna have to wait."

Lewis groaned. "Don't tell me that, Joe."[25]

Lewis and Spinks watched together from ringside. For a round and a half, Matt was still Matt. He still owned the ring. The big-money fight with Spinks was still in front of him. He was still Matthew Saad Muhammad. He could still move. He could still punch. He could see everything he needed to see. It was still there. He moved in a tight circle around the ring, and his jab, looking longer and straighter than ever because of the height disparity, bounced off Braxton's enormous forehead, and even when it missed, it kept Braxton busy and too far away to land anything. A couple of times, Braxton swung from too far out and Matt just missed with counterpunches, but that was okay—they would start landing soon enough and until they did, he just had to keep this guy outside. If he did that, he'd be all right.

"Good job—keep that jab in his face," Solomon said after the first round.

Matt landed a good straight right and then an uppercut in the closing moments of the second when, in an instant, everything went to hell. Braxton landed his first good punch, a hard overhand right, and followed it with a series of hard, chopping punches. Each one landed flush. Matt froze.

When the attack stopped, Matt came up for air and tried to get the jab going again, but Braxton walked through it, around it, under it, and came up with another storm of punches that sent Matt's head rocking this way and that, and then we knew the terrible truth: Matt wasn't keeping Braxton outside. Braxton could get inside anytime he wanted to. And when he did, Matt couldn't do a thing to stop him.

Braxton went back to stalking in the third, gifting Matt the illusion, again, that he was in control. Eddie Mustafa Muhammad, for so long Matt's rival and the pot of gold at the end of his rainbow but in reality his friend, yelled from ringside for Matt to keep his hands up. Matt listened, and then halfway through the round, he brought a left uppercut all the way up from Juniper Street, that knocked Braxton off stride. But Braxton got inside again and started churning those arms, and Matt, at this early stage still possessed of a little of the old arrogance, let him stay there, and they traded thumping body shots and hooks while Solomon screamed from the corner, "Get outta there!"

Matt chose to go on the inside again in the fourth, and although he landed, Braxton's sharper, harder punches ricocheted off his head and face, and soon his nose was pouring blood. Howard Cosell, calling the fight for ABC, asked the only question there was to ask:

"We've seen this so many times before. When will it become once too many?"

Matt tried to turn on the old firepower in the fifth while Braxton caught a breather, and if you didn't know better, you'd have thought he was still in it. He was not. Braxton opened up again near the end of the sixth, and the blood rushed anew from Matt's shattered nose. In the corner, Ritacco used a giant beige bath towel to wipe it away. Solomon demanded to know what Matt was waiting for. Bilal crept over to the broadcast table to steal a worried peek at Cosell's scorecard.

Matt forged a last stand in the seventh, puffing up Braxton's eye with hooks and jabs. But near the end of the round, he stopped moving and Braxton opened up again, working him over like a man working over a stubborn branch with a hatchet. After the round, Solomon told

Chapter 11. The End of Miracles

Matt, "You're blowing the title, man." He knew as well as anyone that if there was a thing in hell Matt could do about it, he would, but you can't tell a man in the corner there's no hope, especially not a man like Matt. You had to try to trick him into lying to himself, just in case he's got one more good one left in him.

But whatever was left in Matt, he bled all over the ring in the eighth, and when he laid inside with Braxton then, it wasn't because he wanted to; it was because his legs were deader than midnight in Camp Hill, deader than the futures of South Philly gang kids busting car windows and skulls with homemade clubs. Bilal, from his ringside seat, shook his head.

The butchering continued into the ninth. Cosell shared with viewers that Matt's blood was all over the broadcast table. After the round, Bilal went to Matt's corner. "You're losin' this fight. You're four rounds down. You gotta pull out these rounds. Punch with him. Punch with him!" Referee Arthur Mercante visited the corner too and stayed a long time.[26]

When the 10th started, Matt went straight back to the ropes. He knew he shouldn't be there, but his legs didn't work anymore. It was all he could do. He did all right there, all things considered, even as every member of his team screamed at him to move. The crowd, always in his corner when they knew there was even the tiniest bit of hope that he would turn things around, now turned on him:

"Braxton! Braxton! Braxton!"

Even they knew he'd run out of miracles.

Matt landed two hard punches. Braxton punished him for it, landing four brain-rattling blows, and then an innocent-looking jab that landed high on the head, behind the ear, sent Matt sprawling onto his back, his legs flailing high overhead, useless. No one would have blamed him for staying there, but a man has to be able to live with himself, and he dragged himself up at three, as sure as anyone has ever been what would come next. Mercante wiped Matt's gloves and waved Braxton in to do his work. Braxton obliged, and after a few more blows slammed home, someone from Matt's corner climbed into the ring to stop it.

It wasn't Solomon.

It wasn't Bilal.

It was Ritacco, the cutman.

Another man on Matt's team had a hold of Ritacco's shirt from outside the ring apron, trying to stop him. It was Trace, the photographer, who had seen Matt come back so many times that he couldn't imagine he wouldn't do it again, that it was really over this time. Thirty years later, he still regretted it. "I was wrong. It was a reaction."[27]

In the Bedford-Stuyvesant section of Brooklyn, a 15-year-old amateur heavyweight watched in horror as Matt took his beating. He cried and snapped off the TV. A little while later, he caught a ride to the Bronx, where he was scheduled to fight in a smoker. He cried the whole way. When his bout came up, he went in and stopped his man in the first round. As soon as he got back to the locker room, Mike Tyson started crying again.[28]

Chapter 12

The Big Lie

*This is a guy who had it all—an absolutely
beautiful new wife, a gorgeous home, a few bucks.
He had everything going for him.*
—Steve Farhood

"First, we take a few months off. He's not hurt bad at all. Then, in say, March, we take an easy fight, nothing too tough."

Matt was being held overnight at Atlantic City Medical Center. He was hungry but didn't like the hospital food. He asked Bilal to go retrieve him something. The manager complied. A reporter rode along.

"We can make a quarter of a million dollars in March, yes we can. And after that fight, we're right back in it. Matthew Saad Muhammad is still the hottest commodity in the division."[1]

What really hurt: Two days before Braxton stopped Matt, Butch Lewis and Don King had worked out a deal for a unification fight between Matt and Spinks for $2 million against 25 percent of the profit—essentially the same deal Lewis had offered Bilal before the Qawi fight.

"And for about 10 percent of that he takes this fight and loses the title," Lewis said. "I begged him not to fight Braxton. We just watched $2-million going down the drain."[2]

No one wants to admit it when a man has simply overstayed his time at the top of a business he has outgrown and had his talents dissipated through money, domestication, and overuse. Matt was a young man still, just 27—a year younger than Braxton! How could he be finished? He should have had a couple more good years left in him. He lived a clean life, never drank or took drugs. His conditioning was always superior to that of his opponent. It had to be something else. The end is always disguised as something else. So what was it?

The weight loss. Yes, that had to be it.

And when a fighter comes in as overweight as Matt did, the blame falls on his trainer. Solomon, knowing his ass was on the line, tried to deflect.

"Matt wasn't blowing. He wasn't tired. He was just weak," he said afterward. "He just didn't have anything."[3] Solomon never said a thing to the press about Michelle and her mother being in camp or about Matt slacking off and overeating in training. That would have violated the fight camp code. He fell on the sword.

Bilal hadn't been in camp with the others to see exactly why Matt wasn't in condition. But he found out, and it was his job to point the blame anywhere but at Matt. "Three other scales differed with the official scales," he said. "Our own scales, which we just had calibrated, had him at 173. The ones in the health spa said 174 and the ones in the nurse's office at the hotel said 176. But the official scales had him at 179 or something."[4] He accused Murad of tampering with the official scale. Why this would have thrown off Matt's weight but not Braxton's was anyone's guess.

"What am I, a genius?" Murad responded. "'That's what I'd have to be to fix scales in front of the New Jersey State Athletic Commission and the World Boxing Council."[5]

Either way, Solomon was gone. There would be no coming back from this. Even before the fight, Bilal had been negotiating with Richie Giachetti, who trained heavyweight champ Larry Holmes. (It made sense: Giachetti was one of King's guys and Matt was about to align with King.) Solomon's failure strengthened Giachetti's position.

"Now they really need somebody," Giachetti said after the fight. "There's no excuse for a guy to weigh that much. That really affected him. He's still got courage."[6]

"I won't lay the responsibility for what happened on any individual," Bilal told the press. "I'll just say the whole camp was at fault. But after running the entire boardwalk at 6:00 AM, skipping rope in the sauna and more running, Saad was dead tired when he stepped into the ring. Maybe his true mark as a champion was that he never complained to us that he felt so bad. Whenever we asked how he was feeling he just said 'fine.'"[7]

Several weeks later, Matt came clean, more or less, about why he had missed weight: "Champions have a tendency to lie back. Maybe I just laid back. I had eight defenses, more than anyone except Bob Foster. I was the highest-paid light heavyweight of the decade. It's my fault, I relaxed, got too heavy and got beat." He still looked for an alibi. "There was a rug in the bathroom underneath the scale we used [at the hotel]. That can make you [appear] lighter than you really are," he said.[8]

Richie Giachetti did not get the job. It went to Steve Traitz, whose

Chapter 12. The Big Lie

Montgomery Boys Club in Eagleville, Pennsylvania, Matt had used as his home training base since leaving Juniper (and when he wasn't at Deer Lake). Traitz was a local celebrity. Born in the Kensington section of Philadelphia, he fought as an amateur and then briefly as a pro into the mid–1950s before quitting and then founding the gym in 1976 in an old barn on his property. His sons, Joe and Steve III, fought as amateurs. The gym did great business; there could be 40–60 kids training there at any time, alongside local pros like Matt, Bennie Briscoe, and others. The site included running trails that encircled the seven-acre property.

Matt loved training at the Boys Club. Traitz treated all the fighters with respect and a strong hand. Matt was particularly close to the old man's sons, and it kind of made sense that when he wanted to turn the clock backward after the loss to Braxton, he would pick as his trainer a man he'd known for a long time but who was not known in the business as a professional coach of any note.

There was a dark side to the Boys Club. Traitz was the "business manager" for the Roofers Union Local 30 and later its president and was reputed to have strong ties to Philadelphia mob members including then–Philadelphia mafia don Nicodemo "Little Nicky" Scarfo. He was implicated in a long string of violence and intimidation in the '70s against non-union roofing competitors, and when longtime Philadelphia mob lieutenant and disgraced fight-fixer Blinky Palermo (who famously arranged Jake LaMotta's dive against Billy Fox in 1947, among others) attempted to get relicensed as a manager in 1978, Traitz enthusiastically testified on his behalf.[9] In 1987, Traitz and 11 codefendants, including sons Steve III and Joe, were convicted on federal racketeering charges and sent to prison.[10] One of the FBI agents assigned to the case told the press after Traitz's conviction, "We are all especially gratified because the Roofer's Union is really the living definition of a labor racketeering organization and Stephen Traitz is the most complete labor racketeer we've ever investigated."[11] Steve III and Joe were also implicated in and stood trial for the murder of a drug dealer who was their partner in a crystal meth ring being operated out of Joe's farm property. They were acquitted of the murder but pleaded guilty to federal narcotics charges and served nearly a decade in prison.

What the Traitz family did outside the gym was an open secret among the Philadelphia-area boxing community, but as far as Matt was concerned, it wasn't his business. Traitz had always let Matt use his facility free of charge, was generous and helpful to fighters and ex-fighters down on their luck, and had decades in the business. In February 1982, he hired Traitz and explained the move by saying, "My whole career I had been trained like a Trojan horse: Beat up and break up the man. And I didn't think I always had to fight that way. I decided I wanted more out of a trainer than just a guy to yell, 'Charge.'"[12]

The truth was, trainers had been trying to get Matt to adopt a more scientific approach for nearly as long as he'd been fighting. It was Matt who decided to be a puncher. Belfiore tried to refine his style. So did Solomon. His assistant trainer and childhood friend Saleem El-Amin did too. They all did. "I could have taught him things but Saad didn't want it," Saleem said in 2021. "He just fought the way he wanted to fight. He was a boxer but didn't have to be because he realized he was a hitter. That's the way he wanted to fight."[13]

Bilal had some reservations about Traitz. Big-time fighters don't have small-time coaches in their corner and Traitz was definitely small-time. "I didn't know Steve that well. I knew Matt needed a technician, a guy capable of telling him what to do and how to do it," Bilal said. "I wasn't too sure if Steve was the right guy but after the first two weeks I could see a bit of improvement. A trainer has to be like a second set of eyes and ears for a fighter. Steve has shown he's that."[14]

In March 1982, two months after the loss to Braxton, Matt told writer Steve Farhood, "I woke up the next day and said to myself, 'That little short-to-the-ground crab beat me.' Then I told some other people and they said, 'You beat yourself. You didn't want to go out and lose the title on the scales.' If I was right, I would've stopped Braxton in five rounds. I can't sleep at night sometimes. I know he's happy because he beat the best man in the division. But I'm gonna destroy everything he thinks he built up."[15]

And there was no talk of getting out, no talk of managing Michelle's singing career or how smartly he'd invested his money. Matt wasn't crying about being bored or not getting a better suite or a bigger purse. He was no longer the businessman whose commodity was his blood and sweat. He was a fighter again. Braxton beating him up and taking the title stripped him of his identity as a fighter, and not of one near the end of his career but, in his mind, of one the best in the world. He still had his cars and his disco lights in the basement. He still had his beautiful wife—now with a son on the way—the fans, the big bank account, and the celebrity, but none of it mattered if, when he looked in the mirror, he no longer saw a prizefighter looking back at him. He had to fix that.

"I know I'm not through. C'mon, who are they kidding?" he said to Farhood. "Fighters come back. If they don't, either the other fighter is better, or he doesn't have it anymore. Right now, I'm not thinking about retirement, it's not in my mind. I'll stop at nothing to get my title back. I'll know in myself when it's time to get out. The people know I'm still the light heavyweight champion. I feel as though I am. I've only vacated

Chapter 12. The Big Lie

the title. I wasn't hurt; I just got beat up. Next time they'll pick *him* up."[16]

Murad was back in the picture, as Don King had no interest in a losing fighter, and he and Bilal looked around for an opponent for Matt to come back against in April, giving Matt a nice four-month rest. It couldn't be anyone too difficult and had to be someone against whom Matt could look like his old self—or, as he said, a new and improved version of the old Matt, one who would jab more and throw combinations and not just look to load up on the right hand. He'd be better than ever, he promised.

"All I know is that it won't happen again," Matt said. "I was too cocky and took Braxton too lightly. People still call me champion. They want to know how I could lose seven pounds in one day. The other day a fat woman came up to me and said she would love to know how I did it."[17]

For the comeback fight, the team arrived on San Diego's Pete McIntyre, whose unimposing record of 16–10–1 (7) wasn't as bad as it looked. He'd lost four of his first five after turning pro in 1973 and had lost to most of the division's bigger names—Yaqui López (twice), Marvin Camel, Tony Mundine—but he'd won seven straight leading up to the fight with Matt, including a kayo of tough Eddie Davis. Matt knew him well; he'd worked in Matt's camp as a sparring partner for the Vonzell Johnson fight.

The WBC, somewhat generously, rated McIntyre the sixth-best light heavyweight in the world. He was just what the doctor ordered: not a serious threat but not so inept that a victory over him would be meaningless. They would meet at Harrah's Hotel & Casino on April 16, and if Matt won, Murad assured him, he'd get a return shot at Braxton, so long as Braxton disposed of Jerry Martin in his first title defense.

On March 21, Braxton chopped up and stopped Martin in six rounds. Afterward, he talked of unifying with Spinks next. A reporter asked him about Matt lobbying for a rematch. He smiled. "Saad is kidding himself. He thinks he's Superman. He says when he lost to me, someone hit him with kryptonite. Tell him it wasn't kryptonite. It was Dwight-onite."[18] Braxton was in good spirits. He'd recently added a member to his team—a Washington, D.C., sports-talk radio announcer named Rock Newman. Before the fight with Matt, Newman proclaimed on his show that Matt would "destroy" Braxton. After the fight, Braxton went on his show and they hit it off. Later, they went to a basketball game at the University of the District of Columbia, where Newman did the radio play-by-play. Newman noticed Braxton's car was "a bomb" and suggested he look into a promotional deal with an auto dealer whereby in exchange for a few appearances, he could get some nice new wheels.

Braxton said, "Do you think you can do that?"[19] Newman started as Braxton's publicist almost immediately. Within a year, he was negotiating his purses.

While Matt was in training for McIntyre, Michelle went into labor. Matt was at her side when she gave birth to Matthew Jr. at 11:11 p.m. on April 9 at Hahnemann Hospital in Philadelphia. When he wasn't at the Boys Club training with Traitz, he was at the hospital with Michelle and Matt Jr., but it didn't distract him from his work. He got into superb shape and weighed in for McIntyre at 174 pounds without incident.

There's nothing a fight crowd loves more than an old champion trying to make his way back into it, and the small crowd at Harrah's greeted Matt warmly. He rewarded them by opening the fight more or less as he said he would, spiriting around the ring and jabbing, crossing, and hooking in earnest. He wasn't the Matt who made ringsiders gasp against Kates, López, and Marvin Johnson, but neither was he the bored, listless version he looked against Sutherland, Vonzell Johnson, and Martin. He looked fresh, motivated. McIntyre, who appeared to be giving it the best effort he could, proved himself at the very least competent, landing his share of jabs and body shots and occasionally walking headlong into Matt's best bombs and remaining upright.

With about a minute left in the second, Matt unloaded a one-two. McIntyre took it, wobbled on his feet, then turned his back to Matt and walked over to the ropes, where he leaned over the top strand and stared out at the audience. Matt followed him there and would have been within his rights to clobber him—"protect yourself at all times" and all that—but he held back until referee Tony Perez came over, determined McIntyre wanted to continue, and waved them back together.

"Oh, I was thinking of Dwight Braxton at that point," Matt said later. "When I didn't hit him I think it showed my gentlemanship. But if it had been Braxton I'm not sure I would have been able to help myself."[20]

A few moments later, another straight right spun poor McIntyre around and bent him over, from which position he slowly toppled to the canvas. In a stupor, he beat Perez's count but was judged unable to continue. The time was 2:28 of the second round.

"This fight alone does nothing to satisfy me," Matt said afterward. "What you saw today was only a small portion of what you'll see in the future. And I won't stop until I unify the title."[21] The fight had done exactly what Matt and his team had hoped it would: gotten him an easy win in front of a television audience, thereby restoring confidence in both he and the boxing public that a rematch against Braxton wouldn't be a complete bloodletting. To many, it went some way toward substantiating the view that his problem in the Braxton fight was not Braxton per se, nor the result of a lifetime of hard fights but merely the temporary dissipation that was the result of having lost so much weight the day of the fight. And that was fixable. All he had to do was train right and he could make everything better again. He could make it almost like the Braxton fight had never happened.

Not everyone was convinced.

"The promoters needed a warm and willing body whom Saad Muhammad could pummel convincingly, and then they would be able to rush him back in against Braxton and feel justified because Saad Muhammad had proven he was not finished," one Philadelphia writer observed. "In truth, there is no way of knowing if Saad Muhammad has been reformed and restyled, because yesterday's labors were hardly a sweat-breaker for him; there was barely time to discern whether he had anything more than two legs and two arms with fists attached."[22]

Nevertheless, it was good enough for the only two people that mattered: Murad Muhammad, who would put together the rematch, and Matt himself, who needed desperately to believe that the disaster in the first fight was an aberration. Prizefighters are expert at deluding themselves, but in the entirety of the history of fighting men, there had never been one so eager to believe in a fiction as Matt was to believe this one. Of all the pugs and heroes and working men who had slung leather for money and fallen short of their aspirations, there were but a relative few who had gone as far as Matt had and from a longer distance—in his life and in so many fights. But his brief success wasn't enough; chances are, it never would be. And the realization that what he had was meaningful had come too late, as realizations so often do.

Quenzell McCall, a Philadelphia legend and Braxton's trainer, summed up the sense among many in the game as to what Matt had left. "Power is the last thing that goes. But I've seen the signs all along, the past five or six fights, that he's been slipping. Years ago, I took him to Europe with me as a sparring partner when I was training Bennie Briscoe. He was a young kid then, but I always liked his potential. There's no telling what he could have been. He should never have been beaten up so many times and have to come back from the brink of defeat."[23]

Matt's gradual physical ruin was only part of the problem. Braxton's style and stature were another. The new champion was masterful at slipping the overhand right, which was Matt's best punch. It was hard to picture him beating anyone he couldn't reliably find with the right hand. Also, Matt was just not great at fighting short guys. Wayne McGee retired in 1977 with a record of 4–5–1 (3), but one of those wins was against Matt. So was the draw. And McGee was built just like

Braxton: short, stubby, and powerful. In fight game parlance, Braxton was all wrong for him.

Nevertheless, the rematch—coined "The Liberty Brawl"—was set for August 7, 1982, and not in an Atlantic City casino but at the Spectrum in Philadelphia. At the kickoff press conference near the end of June, Braxton, tired of Matt's incessant excusing-making since the first fight, presented him a monogrammed "crying towel" and a bathroom scale (Newman's idea). The combined purses were around $700,000 with Braxton, as the champion, getting a larger amount, though not significantly so, one of several complaints his camp registered later.

Matt took no chances in training, sending Michelle to stay with her family in Alaska until the week of the fight. He shook up his group of sparring partners, adding into the rotation light heavyweights Lee Roy Murphy and Ed Smith and middleweight Al Little. He trained for five weeks with a fervor that recalled his younger days, and except for when a knee injury sustained early in camp forced him into taking a couple of days off, he was as consistent, disciplined, and dedicated as he'd ever been. Two weeks before the fight, he was already down to 171 pounds. Traitz had him scale back to keep him from getting "too fine."[24]

Another good sign: Matt was markedly grumpy in the final days before the fight—seen usually as a sign that an athlete has tortured himor herself into prime condition—skipping a press conference on August 6 and telling his team, "All I want to do is go in the ring and fight. I don't want to do no talking."[25] If he didn't win this time, there could be no excuses.

Meanwhile, Braxton's camp felt that the promotion was undermining them. First, the fight landed in Matt's hometown. Then, according to Newman, Braxton's team was told there would be transportation from the Barclay Hotel to the Spectrum on fight night when in fact no provision for it had been made. They were told also that Patti LaBelle would sing the national anthem. Imagine their shock to find it was not LaBelle walking up to microphone at fight time but Matt's wife, Michelle! There were other complaints, all centered on the promotion's apparent bias against the defending champion.

"Braxton has been treated rotten," Newman told a writer the day before the fight. "He just wants to get this fight and his next fight out of the way so he can get away from Murad." Wesley Mouzon, another of Braxton's managers, added, "I don't like the way the outcome has been treated like a foregone conclusion by this promotion."[26]

Braxton used all of this as a sort of emotional ammunition, although it was clear to anyone who knew him that he hardly needed any. Winning the title and defending it once already had done nothing to satiate him. He was as hungry for success and everything that comes with it as he was the day he walked out of prison. It was unfortunate for Matt that he would suffer the terrible brunt of Braxton's ambitions, just as Marvin Johnson, Kates, and the others had suffered his. That was the game.

On fight day, a mere 6,781 fans showed up at the Spectrum. Local writers blamed ticket prices, but the fact a big title fight rematch between local-area fighters drew less than 7,000 in a 17,000-seat arena was disappointing in any event. It was some consolation that the fans who did show up were lively and raucous, and they cheered Matt enthusiastically as he made his way to the ring flanked by Eddie Mustafa Muhammad and the rest of his entourage, some of whom had to suspect it was their last time at the big show.

Not everyone saw the event as a happy spectacle celebrating the return of a deposed king. Matt had rubbed at least some of the local media the wrong way over the years. Philadelphia journalist-turned-broadcaster Larry Merchant, commentating on the fight for HBO, said about Matt in his introduction, "Although he has the preening ego of a master boxer, he fights much like Braxton does—as if to prove over and over again that he can take a punch. He has a wife who was a beauty queen, a Rolls Royce, and a $23,000 piano that he hasn't learned to play yet."[27]

Nevertheless, Matt looked relaxed and happy climbing into the ring and acknowledging the cheers, even jawing with Braxton before the introductions, as if to assure his opponent he would do his best to knock him out quickly so as to keep his suffering to a minimum. Braxton, by comparison, appeared on the verge of bursting into flames if delayed from his duties much longer.

They were only 30 seconds in when Braxton, already raging and with a murderous smile on his face, scored with an overhand right that was as clean as anything he'd landed in the first fight. Matt responded well enough, adopting a defensive posture near the ropes and showing off some of the moves he'd worked on the previous weeks in camp. But Braxton was not the kind of fighter one defeated with mere defense, and a few moments later, he scored again. The crowd exploded, and the men taunted each other—Braxton smiling again, Matt smiling back. The referee, Carlos Padilla, separated the fighters with 23 seconds remaining, apparently under the impression the bell had rung. They resumed and finished out the round as they had started it and smiled at each other at the bell.

Halfway through the second, a right hand knocked Matt off balance, and the crowd roared yet again, demonstrating that it doesn't matter who's getting rocked; even if it's their guy, a crowd will cheer. They're getting what they paid for after all. Matt replied with a solid left uppercut, but Braxton smiled, taunted him, and then battered him on the ropes for a full 30 seconds, during which he found himself wondering, "Am I really doing all this to Saad Muhammad in the second round?"[28] A couple of rows from the ring, Michelle, sitting next to Mustafa Muhammad, put her hands over her mouth and looked away.

It was this torrent of blows while Matt was trapped on the ropes that one suspects must have produced in Matt the terrible sense that he had been here before, in this very position, in this very space in time against this very man and there was no way out of it save for defeat, slow and brutal. To a fighter, every exchange of blows within a contest has a feel, a taste, a smell unique to that fight and that opponent—his essence, his presence, and it can never be exactly replicated against another opponent. It is an entity reproducible only by that man. It may be nothing more than the rattling of the squishy insides of a man's skull that produces this déjà vu, but it is real enough to the fighter on the wrong end, and Matt had to know in that instant that all his proclamations and excuses were in the end empty, hollow fiction.

Traitz admonished Matt after the round. "I told you to hold him when he gets inside, didn't I? Didn't I?"

Ritacco joined in, trying a different tact. "It don't mean you're a coward if you grab!"

Traitz to Ritacco: "Let 'em alone. Let 'em alone."

Then to Matt: "You gotta put 'em together, Matthew. Then hold 'im on the inside."

It was easier said than done. A man in a fight has to consent to some degree to being clinched, and there wasn't a bone in Braxton's body that consented to being held by Matt. Everything that was in him told him to keep churning those arms until Matt was again a bloody, defeated mess.

Matt hadn't even made it to ring center following the bell for the third round when Braxton was all over him again, smashing him against the ropes. After another prolonged beating there, Matt finally escaped and then hit Braxton low. He extended a glove in apology. Braxton ignored the gesture and tore into him, landing a left hook that put Matt down in a corner. He rose quickly, the smashed vessels in his nose producing a waterfall of blood, just as they had in the first fight. Braxton battered him for the rest of the round while the crowd stood and cheered him on.

In the corner after the third, Traitz held up a towel to Matt's nose. "Breathe that in. Breathe it in," and if Matt had won, Braxton's corner would have done well to get that towel and hand it over to the local commission. But they had little to worry about it. They knew it. Matt knew it. Traitz knew it, but a cornerman's job is to advise. He handed off the towel and turned back to Matt.

"How do you feel?"

Matt replied, "Okay."

"Are you sure you're all right?"

"I'm all right."

"Will you hold him on the inside? And you've gotta fight him now. You're waiting too long and he's hitting you with the overhand right. You've gotta fight him now, Matthew. You gotta fight him. Hands high, you hear me? And Matthew: Punches *up*. Turn the punches *up*. And hands up!"

In the fourth, Matt did not turn his punches up or keep his hands high. He didn't jab, move, or hold on the inside. He barely moved his head out of the way. He stood and took his beating. A combination sent him reeling into the ropes. The blood from his nose splashed onto the canvas.

The fifth opened the same way. Halfway through, Braxton stopped punching. Matt took the opportunity to try to get something going. Nothing got going, and the round ended as it had begun. "I wanted to see what he had for me. When I saw that he didn't have nothing, I went back at him," Braxton said later. In the corner, Quenzell McCall gave Braxton hell for playing around. "I'll finish him," Braxton said.[29]

The champion was true to his word. He trapped Matt on the ropes and was pounding him yet again when Padilla stepped in finally and called it off at 1:23 of the sixth round. Braxton's corner and supporters swarmed into the ring to celebrate with him. Traitz walked Matt back to his corner and sponged the blood off his puffy face.

It was bad enough that Matt had lost again. It was worse that Braxton had beaten him even easier the second time, when Matt didn't have the weight loss as an excuse. Even Braxton was surprised.

"He was sharper the last time. He moved more, punched more the last time. That's why it makes me wonder if he went into the sauna last time or this time. He fought like he had to lose eight pounds this time instead of seven. He wasn't doing nothing but taking punches. He was just there. Nothing new. In fact, he was kind of raggedy. I had him going quite a few times."[30]

"There's no way I can see him coming back this way," Braxton said. "I think the way I beat him took something out of him. He wasn't the old Saad. He wasn't Superman anymore. This time, when I got to him early, I knew he wasn't coming back. By the third round I knew I had him and by the fifth he had nothing. I think younger guys will be jumping all over him with a fury now. I'd hate to see something like that happen to him. Saad doesn't need that."[31]

There was sympathy to go around. Tony Castellano, one of the judges, told a reporter, "I felt sorry for the kid." Another, Tony Perez, said, "He's showing the signs: no timing, no defense whatsoever."[32]

Matt was gracious. "He beat me fair and square," he said. "If I had listened to Steve I might've won. My plan was to box him and wait until he got tired. I tried to use the jab. It was working early. But I didn't follow the plan. Steve wanted me to use the jab and use more uppercuts. Steve told me to clinch the guy and pull out once he came and got me on the ropes. I didn't do that. I disobeyed him ... but I don't want to talk about what I should have done. I lost and that's it. He got the best of me. He just dominated the fight after the first or second round."[33]

A reporter asked Matt if he might retire. "I'm considering it. I don't think I'm through, I just want to leave while I'm able to talk, to walk, and looking good. I'm happy I'm not messed up. I've made a lot of friends through boxing."[34]

And for a couple of beats, the window seemed open for him to walk away. It was right there.

And then it was gone.

"I'd like to go on. I'll be back. I know I can beat every other contender but he was just better than me. He is one strong little guy."[35]

Chapter 13

What Goes Around

"You Don't Need This Shit."
—Eddie Mustafa Muhammad

Frank Sciacca, a mid-level fight manager from Brooklyn, was on the phone with Robert W. Lee, deputy athletic commissioner of New Jersey, pleading with Lee not to cancel a fight scheduled for the following night in Jersey that someone in Lee's office had approved without Lee's knowledge. Lee said it was a mismatch and Sciacca's guy, the underdog, was going to get hurt. "I got news for you," Sciacca told him. "We're going to win."[1] Sciacca's guy was Eric Winbush, a tall, gangly light heavyweight who had been fighting for only four years—not four years as a pro but four years total. He had no amateur fights and had been mostly unimpressive on the way to logging a record of 11–6 (3) since turning pro in New York in 1978. Winbush had no great talent to speak of and not much grace or style in the ring, but he did evince what appeared to most to be an unjustifiably large ego. He also had a brief encounter with Matt in his recent past that served to animate his already burgeoning determination and self-assurance.

The story went that in February 1982, Winbush had been scheduled to fight at the Playboy Club underneath Carlos De Léon against Marvin Camel in the main event. His fight was canceled when his opponent failed to make weight. Matt and his entourage attended the card, and Winbush ran into them in the lobby. Winbush sized Matt up, then opened Matt's sport jacket and said to him, "You've got enough butt for me to get in it too, you know."

"Who are you?" Matt asked.

"My name is Winbush. Who knows, we might run into each other someday."

Someone in Matt's detail replied, "How you gonna run into each other, jogging?"[2]

Everyone in Matt's entourage had a big laugh. This was after Matt's first loss to Braxton and two months prior to his win over Pete McIntyre, when they all still could laugh, having convinced themselves, more or less, that Matt was still Matt. Winbush and Matt went their separate ways that day, but the encounter and its sting remained in Winbush's memory and he hoped for the day when they would indeed run into each other, and not while doing roadwork.[3]

Matt took a long break after the second loss to Braxton. Everyone on the team pretty much knew it was over. Mustafa Ameen, Matt's right-hand man and best friend, pleaded with Matt to retire. When Matt refused, Ameen took his leave, remembering that night back in 1980 when he and Matt visited Muhammad Ali in his suite after the Holmes fight. Ameen and Matt remained close and spoke on the phone every week for the rest of Matt's life, but Mustafa never worked on a fight with Matt again.

The big entourage was gone. No more personal photographer or gaggle of regular sparring partners. Matt carried his own equipment, drove himself here and there. Bilal agreed to stay on to see if there was anything at all left. Technically, not all was lost. The WBC and WBA still rated Matt in their top five and the *Ring* magazine rated him the third-best light heavyweight in the world. The 175-pound division was no longer the murderer's row it was when Matt came up, and if he looked decent in a comeback fight, there were rumors that he would next get Peru's entirely harmless Oscar Rivadeneira, whom the WBA dubiously ranked second in the world. And if Matt got past him, a shot at Michael Spinks, who had outpointed Braxton in their unification fight in March 1983, was possible.

Matt kept on Ritacco as cutman and his friend Saleem El-Amin as the assistant coach, but he wouldn't work with Solomon again or Traitz. He needed a new trainer. There were rumors that Detroit's Emanuel Steward would land the job. He and Matt had gotten friendly when Steward had Thomas Hearns against Wilfred Benítez on Harold Smith's ill-fated "This Is It" show in 1980. They couldn't reach an agreement, however, and as late as February, one Philadelphia paper reported Matt was seen training at Marty Feldman's Gym at 63rd and Market Streets, "where he would spar as eight guys standing around yelled instructions to him."[4]

Eventually, Matt and Bilal hired Janks Morton, known primarily as Sugar Ray Leonard's first coach and later as Leonard's assistant coach after Angelo Dundee took over. Morton's success with Leonard led to assignments with myriad high-profile champions and contenders, future Hall of Famer Alexis Argüello among them. Matt went to Morton's gym in Phoenix, Arizona, where Morton had him sparring with

Robert Folley, son of 1960s heavyweight contender Zora Folley, and former victim Pete McIntyre. Morton told a writer he was amazed at how little Matt had been taught and that he accomplished everything he did on "native ability and heart."[5]

In the meantime, Bilal's search for an easy opponent led him to none other than Eric Winbush, whom Matt would face on March 23, 1983, at the Claridge Hotel and Casino in Atlantic City. Sciacca had succeeded in convincing Lee to allow the fight to proceed, and on fight night, 650 fans showed up, one imagines to see Matt look like his old self again, which he was favored to do, if only because of the perceived mediocrity of his opponent. Matt's purse: $20,000.

Things started well enough, which is to say Winbush didn't jump all over Matt and savage him the way Braxton had. Still, those loyal to Matt and to the fighter he once was had to be discouraged at the even nature of the first two rounds. Winbush, fighting far above his talent level, because that's what confidence will do for you, landed as much as he gave, and if one didn't know going in who the favorite was, one would be inclined to guess it was a pick 'em type of matchup. Although Matt was clearly the more experienced, conventional fighter, it served him almost not at all against Winbush's awkward, unpolished offense. Telegraphed looping blows from Winbush found the mark as frequently as did those Matt hid behind a jab or a feint.

In the third, Winbush followed a mid-ring volley with a graceless one-two that caught Matt on the left side of his head and sent him stumbling into the ropes. Winbush pummeled him there as Matt swayed back and forth and clutched Winbush in an attempt to stay upright. Winbush finally pushed him to the canvas. Technically, referee Zack Clayton was correct to rule that the fall was a result of a push rather than a punch, but it was clear to all when Matt regained his stance that he was concussed and barely holding it together. Winbush resumed pummeling him, prompting commissioner Jersey Joe Walcott to rise from his ringside position and yell, "Stop it!" just as Clayton was calling it off at 1:53 of the round.

If Matt thought after the Braxton rematch that it couldn't get any worse, he was wrong. This was worse. Much worse.

"I'm embarrassed. This is bad for me, very bad for me," he said in his locker room afterward. "The guy caught me with a good shot but I would've gotten myself together again. The referee didn't give me a chance. I went down but I felt my head starting to clear a little bit. But the referee stepped in after Eric hit me with another shot. Maybe they paid the guy off. I think it was a dirty deal. But I can't argue the point, he's the referee."[6]

A lifelong expert in hard truths, Matt had learned a new one: The breaks that one gets as a world champion who gets killer ratings on Saturday afternoon television are not accorded washed-up pugs. Moreover, nobody wanted a fatality or a serious injury on their watch, especially one as high profile as Matt. People loved the guy. They wanted to see him ride off into Jenkintown and live happily ever after, his marbles intact.

"But I can't let nothing like this stop me and retire me," he continued, "because I mean I would've really gotten myself together. I was very much aware of what was happening.... It was just that my eyes were glazy. But I could have gotten myself together if only I was given the opportunity to."[7]

Eddie Mustafa Muhammad and WBA bantamweight champion Jeff Chandler tried to console Matt in the locker room. Mustafa said to him, "You don't need this shit. You've got enough money." A reporter asked Matt about it.

"Eddie Mustafa sometimes has good opinions. If he feels I should get out, I don't feel that way. The best thing for me to do is to try one more time. They shouldn't have stopped it. Maybe they paid the guy off."[8]

Bilal was convinced that Matt should retire. If a loss to Eric Winbush didn't do it, nothing would. But to spare Matt the indignity of hearing his manager say it publicly, he took a diplomatic approach. "I'm going to give him a recommendation and he'll have to sleep on it. Then we'll decide what's going to happen. I see him with one eye and he sees himself with another eye. What we have to do is balance those two eyes to come to a decision. He has a dream of regaining the title but he has enough insight not to let pride get in the way and he'll make the right decision."

A writer said, "And if he wants to continue?"

"I'll cross that bridge when I come to it."[9]

Over the next six months, Matt struggled with the prospect of never fighting again. He tended to the various business interests he had hoped would obviate the need to fight solely for the money and found that they were not as profitable as he had thought because prizefighters make terrible businessmen. They trust too much and know too little, and when they finally take the time to look closely, it is too late.

The endorsement deals with Pony and Sasson had long since dried up, Michelle's singing career was going nowhere, and the other ventures he'd planned to undertake after boxing—acting, modeling, selling his life story to Hollywood—were dead ends. He and Michelle were fighting a lot, and money was going out a lot faster than it was coming in. Matt wondered how it could have gotten so bad so quickly and how it could be over when he wasn't even 30 years old yet. So of course he would

Chapter 13. What Goes Around

continue to fight. It was who he was and how he had made his way in the world.

In the meantime, he played with Matthew Jr., made appearances, and took part in road races. In April, he was the guest of honor at the Run for the Arts in Philadelphia. The following month, he ran the 10-mile "Trevira Twosome" through New York's Central Park. He competed in ABC TV's "Superstars" competition and upheld the long tradition of boxers performing dismally, scoring just three total points in the finals (good for $1,000) to place 11th out of 12 contestants. Only Aaron Pryor did worse, scoring zero points. (Track and field star and NFL wide receiver Renaldo Nehemiah took first place for the third consecutive year.)

Matt went back out to Arizona to train under Morton, then signed to face New York's Euclides Valdez on September 9, 1983, in the main event of a live card at Madison Square Garden that would precede the closed-circuit telecast of the Pryor-Argüello rematch in Las Vegas. The week of the fight, Valdez pulled out with an injury. His replacement pulled out too. On two days' notice, Larry Davis, from Plainfield, New Jersey, signed on. His record was 5–9 (4), which caused the New York commission some concern, but ultimately he was approved, and over the fight's first half, he comported himself well. Matt, who at 172½ was lighter than he'd been in years, finally got going in the seventh and, after a right to the body sent Davis careening across the ring in the 10th, referee Joe Cortez stopped it.

In Matt's mind, it was of no great concern that it took him 10 rounds to stop a sub-500 late replacement. "I know I was a little stale tonight but personal problems and a long layoff took their toll. I will improve and I am back on my way toward the light heavyweight title," he said.[10]

Three months later, shortly after Christmas, Matt left Jenkintown to train with Morton in Arizona again for a match against NABF light heavyweight champion Willie Edwards in Detroit underneath Hearns's match with Luigi Minchillo in the main event on February 11, 1984. Edwards was no Larry Davis or Eric Winbush. He was 17–1 (13) and a swarmer with good power in both fists. Matt again relied on Pete McIntyre as his main sparring partner; McIntyre had split a pair of bouts with Edwards, stopping him in five rounds in 1982 in Edwards's only loss and then losing by knockout in the ninth the following year.

Matt knew how important this fight was. It was make-or-break time. "I wouldn't call it a do-or-die fight," he told a writer after a workout at Cobo Hall in Detroit. "I don't like that kind of wording. I hope I don't die. But you can say that it is essential that I win this fight. If I win this, there are lots of good fights out there for me. I still think there's demand out there for a Matthew Saad Muhammad versus Michael Spinks fight for the title."

"When I set my mind to it, no one can defeat me but God. Once my mind is set I don't care who is in front of me, I'll stop him," Matt continued. "I give myself one year to do it. I'm 28 now. If I haven't got the title back in a year I'll retire."

As evidence of his dedication, Matt shared that he had done 14,000 repetitions of isometric exercises, 190 rounds of sparring, and run more than 200 miles in preparation for Edwards. He said distractions of the "materialistic world" sidetracked him after he and Michelle were married in August 1980. "I started enjoying life and forgot about boxing. I just settled down."[11]

Jerry Stokes, who assisted Janks Morton in the gym and worked with Matt every day, was upbeat. "Saad is coming back. He's got himself together. There are a lot of things we've changed, defense mostly. He's not going to be a punching bag anymore."[12] Of course, this is essentially what Traitz had said about Matt, and Solomon before him, and even Belfiore when he thought Matt needed to hear it.

It should have surprised no one to see Matt as exactly that from the second round on. Edwards, shorter, stronger, and with a clear strategy, bulled Matt backward and drove him to the ropes where he worked him over with his elbows, shoulders, and his head and occasionally thumping right hands and hooks. It was the Jerry Martin fight again except this time, Matt had neither the legs to get punching room nor the snap on his punches to discourage his opponent's forward motion. Edwards simply smothered him inside and beat him up. By the 10th round, Matt was hopelessly behind on points. His nose had been bleeding for seven rounds.

The crowd, who was there to see Hearns anyway, started booing the wrestling and lack of two-way action in the early rounds and didn't let up until Edwards exploded with a torrent of punches early in the 11th, sending Matt almost out of the ring. After an uninterrupted deluge of about 20 blows, referee Max Harnish leaped between the fighters and stopped it. The time was 0:34 of the 11th.

And this is when it got crazy.

Matt went berserk, first pushing Harnish, then going after Edwards. The two were quickly separated before Matt went after him again and this time got close enough to throw punches. "He fared no better in the postfight exchange than he had before the final bell," one writer observed. Another noted that Matt showed more fighting spirit in those few seconds than he had in the previous 40 minutes.[13] Peace was restored again until Edwards made his way into Matt's dressing room to shake his hand. Matt again went after him before security ushered Edwards out.

"Why would I want to shake his hand? He must be crazy," Matt said afterward. "He comes over here talking about shaking my hand. What would I look like shaking his hand?"[14] Matt complained about Edwards's dirty tactics, which included hitting on the break, for which he was warned many times but never penalized. However, the reason for his anger was, on the surface at least, the stoppage. Apparently, the standing eight-count was in effect and Bilal and Matt both understood following the rules meeting that Harnish would invoke it if one of the fighters was hurt but standing.

"We're going to protest this fight to the sanctioning body," Bilal said. "I thought the fight was stopped too soon. In the rules meeting he said that if any fighter was hurt he would step in and have a standing eight-count. But he never said a word."[15]

"Do I look knocked out?" Matt asked the reporters on hand. "I was conscious of every punch that was thrown at me. The referee should've asked me how many fingers he was holding up or to count to 10 or something. He just stopped it."[16]

"I felt the referee was wrong. I was conscious of everything that was going on and he didn't give me a chance to fight back," Matt said. "But I must admit, to win a fight you have to throw punches and I didn't. He smothered me. I couldn't get my punches off."[17] Promoter Bob Arum, on hand for Hearns, said this about Matt: "It's just not there anymore. As far as I'm concerned he's finished."[18]

And it didn't take a psychologist to know that was the real driver of Matt's post-fight tantrum. He'd poured everything he had left into preparing. He'd left his family for three months to train. And he talked himself into believing he could do it. Against all evidence to the contrary, he talked himself into believing he could will it into existence. And how could you blame him? Experience had taught him that his will was stronger than circumstance, stronger than reality. Why wouldn't he think it was stronger too than time?

He had willed himself off the streets and out of the Daniel Boone School and Camp Hill. He willed himself off the canvas against Richie Kates and Billy Douglas and through the rivers of pain and blood against Marvin Johnson, both times. Twice, his will was too much for Yaqui López, John Conteh, and all the other men who had better skills, a bigger punch, or better connections but who didn't have his will. Of course he thought he would win the title again. Isn't that why they called him "Miracle Matthew"?

CHAPTER 14

He's a Fighter

> *"I will never attempt a comeback after I retire.*
> *I won't need the money because*
> *I've invested my purses in a lot of good business."*
> —MATTHEW SAAD MUHAMMAD

After the Edwards fight, Matt told some close friends he was quitting. "I had a lot of hard fights," he said. "I could have gone on, but a smart man knows his limitations."[1] And to remove the temptation, he stopped attending local shows. He knew how he would feel if he was ringside again, hearing the crowd, watching them and the fighters and their cornermen, smelling the smoke, the sweat, and the fear. It was almost as bad as being in a gym. "I really don't like to go. It's like a fire within me [that] makes me want to do it again when I go. So I just stay away."[2] He pursued other professional interests, commuting from Jenkintown to New York three times a week to take voice therapy and acting lessons from famed acting teacher Jack Waltzer. He looked for gigs modeling clothes and landed some—he appeared in *Essence*, *Gentlemen's Quarterly*, and *Life* magazines. He invested in a seafood restaurant. When he ran into an old writer friend who asked him if he was making a comeback, Matt replied, "Yes, I'm making the biggest comeback of my life—to my senses!"[3]

Matt's buddy Mustafa Ameen moved to Seattle not long after Matt lost the title. Every week, he'd tell Matt to come up and start over fresh in Washington. Ameen had a lot of business contacts and knew if he could get Matt into something else that he could grow, he'd be less likely to return to the ring. Finally, Matt relented and agreed to stay for a week. He arrived on a Saturday, and on Wednesday morning, he got up early and told Mustafa he had to go, that he had some business in Philadelphia to take care of. Later, Mustafa found out someone had talked him into buying a fleet of limousines.[4]

By February 1985, a year after the Edwards fight, Matt was still talking like an old retired fighter. "It's funny but I look back at myself and it's like I was a different person back then," he told a writer. "I look at this guy in the movies of those fights and I say, 'How in the hell did he do that?'"[5]

It was around this time that Matt attended a fight card in Atlantic City and then the after party, where he met Elaine Taylor, a reservations manager at Trump Plaza Hotel and Casino. Taylor was born in Atlantic City, the youngest of eight children. Her parents divorced when she was very young and her stepfather, a butcher, died when Elaine was 10. Her mother worked several jobs and raised the brood on her own for the rest of Elaine's childhood.

Elaine was not especially aware of Matt's celebrity when they met; she just knew he was a fighter. "He just happened to be a nice guy and exceptionally handsome," she said in 2021. "We enjoyed each other's company. He was exceptionally kind; one of the nicest people I've ever known, and very caring." They started dating and before long, were serious, such that Matt put the brakes on his womanizing.

In May 1985, Matt agreed to take part in a four-round exhibition at Philadelphia's Mayfair Ballroom. Both he and his "opponent," a local club fighter named Jesse Goodman, would wear headgear, move around a little for the spectators. Nothing serious. Matt said it was a favor to his old friend and trainer Sam Solomon, a way to get publicity for the ballroom's monthly fight cards. He said it had nothing to do with a comeback necessarily; it was just for fun. For kicks, Solomon would work his corner, just like old times but without the blood.

In the third round, Goodman landed a hook and down went Matt. He rose quickly, embarrassed. In the dressing room afterward, Solomon, protecting him as always, said, "He got his feet tangled

Matt met the former Elaine Taylor, a reservations manager at Trump Plaza Hotel and Casino, after a fight card in Atlantic City in 1986. They were married in 1988 and moved to New Orleans together before divorcing in 1997 (photo courtesy of Elaine Austin).

up, that was no knockdown."[6] But it was. Solomon knew it and Matt knew it. So did everyone who saw it.

"Who says I'm making a comeback?" Matt said afterward, but Solomon spilled the beans, admitting Matt asked him to train him for a possible return. Solomon said he told Matt he had to get a thorough medical examination before he'd consider training him, and after Matt did with no adverse findings, Solomon was on board. "We can't bring him back fast over overnight," he said. "We have to bring him back slowly."[7]

Events the following month made a comeback a virtual certainty because old prizefighters can stay away only for as long as the money holds out. Once it's gone, and it always is sooner or later, they only know how to do one thing.

* * *

"He's a fighter. Apparently he did not prepare himself for anything other than fighting," Tim Crawford told the press.[8] Crawford was the Philadelphia attorney who'd helped Matt find his biological family in 1981. This time, he was talking to the press about something far less pleasant: Matt's bankruptcy.

It was June 1985. The 16 months that had passed since Matt's loss to Edwards had been a mixed bag. On the plus side, Matt and Michelle had a second son, Michael, born in November 1984. On the other, the couple had been fighting a lot and would soon divorce; the reasons depended on who one asked. Some said it was Matt's repeated infidelities, which were enabled by his still-large group of friends, many of whom got along well with Michelle while simultaneously helping Matt conceal his affairs.

Others, in the main comprised of those with knowledge of Matt's business dealings, saw his bankruptcy and divorce as the predictable results of his wife and in-laws having taken over his finances. They found many things curious, chief among them that at around the same time Matt was declaring bankruptcy, Michelle's parents in Alaska were forming a partnership to develop a $2.1 million office building in Anchorage.[9]

Whatever the case, the numbers were grim. The bankruptcy petition was necessary so Matt could negotiate a schedule with the IRS to pay $239,076 for taxes unpaid from 1980, the same year he made $650,000 for beating Lottie Mwale. His bankruptcy forms listed projected income at $8,400 a month, but another attorney said that was based on "some ventures" that had not panned out. He listed no current income but said he was training for future fights. All that was left of his many business ventures and investments was the small limousine company he owned.[10]

Chapter 14. He's a Fighter

"I'm not going to stand here and say I have all this money I don't have," Matt told the press. He said it was his fault, but he "had people who basically did work my work for me, because I did not have the knowledge to go about paying taxes."[11]

Bilal said he had set Matt up with an account that was supposed to be used only to pay taxes but that Matt raided it for other things. "After each fight we would put tax money in that account and he was the only one who had access to it," Bilal said in 2021. "A year after he got married, he would be in New Jersey a lot because the account was in New Jersey at Fidelity. He was taking the money out of that account. There was over $100,000 in there."[12]

Bilal also said that an investment in an equipment leasing company that he arranged for Matt would have shielded him from any tax burdens if he had claimed it as a deduction the way he was supposed to, but when Michelle's family took over Matt's finances, they didn't know about it and efforts to tell them about it failed. Eventually, he gave up.[13]

When the divorce was finalized, Michelle took the house in Jenkintown and the kids. The couple remained on good terms and agreed to never talk badly about each other to the kids. "We still loved each other," Michelle said in 2021. "We were both young—too young and dumb to fight for what we had." Down the road when Matt would visit the boys and see Michelle with another man, he would mutter to Michael and Matthew Jr., "I gotta get myself together and get my woman back." On one occasion, he nearly got into a fistfight with one man after he thought he saw Michelle being disrespected.[14]

Things got worse. Not long after the bankruptcy news, Matt was pulled over in Linden, New Jersey, on the Garden State Parkway for going 85 mph in a 55 mph zone. (Then he went through a red light while exiting the highway.) When Matt opened his glove compartment to retrieve his paperwork, the state trooper saw a .25 caliber handgun. Matt had a Pennsylvania permit to carry but not one for New Jersey.

He was charged with possession of a concealed dangerous weapon without a permit to carry, arrested, and released on $1,000 bail later that day.[15] He was then placed on probation and admitted to a pretrial intervention program. The weapons violation charge would have been dropped if he served a supervised probation period and performed 60 hours of community service. He did neither, and when he skipped a hearing the following April, the judge removed him from the program and issued a bench warrant for his arrest.[16]

Two weeks later, Matt was indicted on new charges after it was learned he had been convicted of aggravated assault and battery and aggravated robbery back in 1973 when he was still an amateur, which should have precluded him from owning a weapon in the first place.

Matt had to do something. He was broke. He was bored. He had no direction. His marriage had fallen apart. What could he do? It wasn't like he could go be an accountant somewhere, a business executive, or a basketball coach. Fighters who become world champions do so at the exclusion of everything else. As young kids, they are told that the only way they can succeed is to dedicate themselves to it fully. There can be no backup plan. Then when it ends and the money is gone—and it is always gone—they are asked, "Why didn't you learn how to do something else?"

Not long after the exhibition in Philadelphia with Solomon, Matt was at a card on the East Coast when he ran into Randy Gordon, who was providing commentary for the USA network's boxing series. He told Gordon he was making another comeback.

"Why, Matthew?" Gordon asked. "You're one of the greatest light heavyweight champions of all time. You'll never be able to duplicate that."

Matt responded, "But I can still be a piece of that fighter."[17]

He was a fighter. He was going to fight. Later, he explained it this way.

"My self-worth was hurting something fierce. So I wanted to be successful again. But I thought the only way I could do it was through boxing. After all, I was once a great warrior and a great champion, all of which made me a wealthy man. And I wanted to be all those things one more time. So once again, I put on the gloves."[18]

In late 1985, Matt relocated to south Florida and signed a three-year deal with promoter Stu Kauffman, who, along with partner Phil Vasta,[19] agreed to finance Matt's comeback. Matt moved into an apartment behind the Beau Jack Gym in Hallandale, which Kauffman owned, and Kauffman and Vasta paid his living expenses. Matt said the personal (marital) problems that had hampered previous comebacks were behind him and he was ready to make another title run.

The reaction to Matt's comeback among most boxing media was summed up by one influential New York columnist: "Matthew Saad Muhammad, beaten into retirement two years ago, has lost his wife, house, and money, and is going to Miami to train for a comeback. There was never a more gallant fighter than the former light heavyweight champ and any commission that allows him to fight should itself be banned."[20]

Matt was resolute.

"I know what I want to do. I still feel strong, and my mind is relieved

Chapter 14. He's a Fighter

of all the problems," he said. "I'm not ready for Marvin Johnson or Leslie Stewart yet. That may take six months."[21] He said the bankruptcy was the result of some "bad business decisions" and that "a lot of it had to do with mismanagement and being misled. I'm not making this comeback because of financial reasons," he said. "I still have enough money." Then why the comeback?

"A man has to do what a man has to do," he said.[22] Matt had only been training for about a month when Kauffman asked him to fill in for Dexter Smith, who pulled out of a fight with journeyman Chris Wells in a show Kauffman was promoting on January 10 at the Diplomat Hotel in Hollywood. Although he weighed 187 pounds, Matt obliged and floored Wells four times on the way to a sloppy sixth-round stoppage win. The 1,200 fans in attendance cheered his every move.

"I helped this guy out, I took the fight on four days' notice," Matt said afterward. "If I'm going to get into it, why not get into it now? Boxing's a gamble. I could've gotten my head knocked off in there."[23]

Kauffman quickly set up a fight the following month with Uriah Grant at the Gault Ocean Mile Hotel in Fort Lauderdale. Matt, at 31 years old now, an age at which most fighters were washed up even if they hadn't been through the wars he had, was nevertheless as confident as ever.

"I don't care about what happened in the past. I don't care about Grant. I know what I can do and he's the one who has to prove something to me. These fights are steppingstones to the championship."[24] The plan was to put Matt in with Bridgeport's Mike Costello on March 25 in Atlantic City if he beat Grant and then a fight for the vacant Continental America's light heavyweight title later in the year. Grant ruined those plans, mauling and outworking Matt over the second half of the fight and winning a unanimous decision in front of 1,500 spectators.

"Physically he was stronger than I was," Matt said. "He hurt me several times but I was conscious. I knew what I had to do but his style was confusing to me."[25] The loss to Grant ended Matt's association with Kauffman, and he returned to the Philadelphia area and to the familiar confines of Champs Gym, where he sparred with up-and-comer Henry Milligan, Leslie Stewart, and others, while he and Solomon plotted their next move. Somehow, Matt's loss to Grant propelled him to what would have been a fight against future long-reigning light heavyweight title holder Virgil Hill in North Dakota had Matt not injured his hand.

Matt and Hill were scheduled to meet in a 10-rounder at the Civic Center in Bismarck on October 17. On October 9, Matt's camp notified Hill's attorney that he had injured his right hand while sparring at Pleasantville Recreation Center in Pleasantville, New Jersey. Hill's camp moved quickly to find a replacement and landed on none other than Eric Winbush, who had stopped Matt three years earlier. (Hill floored Winbush twice and outpointed him.)

In the early morning hours of Halloween in 1987, Matt was visiting a cousin at a bar the cousin owned in Atlantic City when someone ran into the bar yelling that the apartment building next door was on fire. Matt and another man, one Arthur Johnson, ran into the building and helped its residents, many of whom were frightened children, escape before the fire spread. No one was injured.[26]

"This is normal for me," Matt said. "It's as natural as being human to help another person. Maybe someday someone will save my life."[27] A month later, Matt was in Weirton, West Virginia, to face 13–13 (6) Bobby Thomas. Joining Solomon as Matt's assistant trainer was Cash White. White fought out of Philadelphia in the 1960s, losing to Bennie Briscoe and Joey Giardello, among others. Cash joined Matt and Solomon on a local radio show to promote the bout with Thomas. Soon, he would take over Matt's training entirely at the Pleasantville Rec Center as Solomon moved on. "I've been with him the last four weeks," White said. "He's starting to peak now and he's ready to fight. We're doing a lot of running and a lot of soul searching and we're ready to rumble."

Matt won a 10-round decision over Thomas, who the local promoter billed as the "light heavyweight champion of West Virginia," then got a call he wasn't expecting: He was invited to help Thomas Hearns prepare for his title defense against Iran Barkley, which was scheduled for June. It wasn't the first time the two would spar; they worked together in 1979 when Hearns was in Philadelphia to fight Alfonso Hayman. Matt jumped at the chance, and after a rough start in camp, he did well enough to impress Kronk maven Emanuel Steward—though it's possible too that Steward knew Matt was in dire straits and wanted to talk him up to get him more work.

"The guy looks good, damn good," Steward said. "I was shocked by how good he looks. When he first came to camp he didn't look that sharp. He was slow, awkward, insecure. But after eight or nine days he really got into it. He started looking like the old Matthew Saad Muhammad."[28] Matt enjoyed being in camp with championship-level fighters again but was careful to remind everyone who he was. "I appreciate the job but I want to say that I am not a punching bag and I am not a sparring partner, at least on a regular basis. I am a past and future world champion," he said.[29]

As well as Matt was doing, his stay at camp was short-lived. Steward had him spar with his latest find, a young power puncher from Monessen, Pennsylvania, who would soon turn pro. Michael Moorer fractured one of Matt's ribs, thereby ending his employment. Steward took Matt to the hospital, where a doctor told him it looked like Matt had been hit with a hammer.[30] Two months later, in April, Matt's rib was well enough for him to stop Lee Harris in the first round in Mechanicsville. It was Harris's second pro fight and his second loss.

Matt and Elaine had been growing closer during the preceding period, and on June 3, 1988, they were married in Las Vegas. Both had children from previous marriages who had to get used to having a stepparent. Matt had Matthew Jr. and Michael, who were six and four, respectively. Elaine had a 12-year-old daughter of whom Matt was supportive, but out of respect for the girl's father, to whom Elaine was not married, Matt was careful not to overstep boundaries they had established.

Matt saw Matthew Jr. and Michael as much as his schedule would allow. According to Michelle, for the first four or five years after the divorce, it was quite a lot, then less so as Matt's circumstances changed and became more desperate, requiring him to travel frequently. As is often the case with small children and stepparents, the dynamic between Matt Jr. and Michael and Elaine was not always ideal, and Matt struggled trying to find a balance that would make everyone happy.

In the meantime, Matt's comeback continued. He took his three-fight winning streak—the most consecutive wins he'd strung together since 1981—to Newark, New Jersey's Quality Inn to face Atlanta's Harry Daniels on October 21, 1988. It would be a reunion of sorts; on the same card, his old nemesis-turned-friend Eddie Mustafa Muhammad, now 36 years old and three fights into a comeback of his own, would face journeyman Arthel Lawhorn.

Daniels's record was reported to be 16–7 (10), but when the New Jersey State Athletic Control Board couldn't find anyone to verify it, they refused to sanction the bout. Daniels was out, and puncher Frankie Swindell, the International Boxing Federation's third-ranked light heavyweight contender and the United States Boxing Association champ, stepped in on 24 hours' notice. That was terrible news for Matt. Any other fighter in his position would have backed out. He did not.

"Don't get caught on the ropes," Cash White told him right before the opening bell. Seconds later, Matt was on the canvas courtesy of a right hand. Where did he go when he got up? Right to the ropes, which is where he was when referee Randy Neumann stopped it moments later to save him from having his head knocked into the fourth row. Swindell could punch. Unsurprisingly, Matt complained that the stoppage was too quick.

Later, in the main event, Lawhorn stopped Mustafa Muhammad in the third round.

Matt's reputation and sheer likability worked to his benefit (as it had when he was called to help prepare Tommy Hearns) when Jeff Harding, who had recently won the WBC light heavyweight title by beating Dennis Andries, asked Matt to come to Brisbane to help him prepare for his maiden title defense against Tom Collins. Matt would face Australia's Kevin Wagstaff on the undercard. Matt jumped at the chance for the salary, the purse, and the chance to fight in front of 8,000 fans at the Boondall Entertainment Centre. He hadn't fought in front of a crowd that big in a decade. On fight night, he and Wagstaff fought to a dreary eight-round draw. In the main event, Harding stopped Collins in two. Matt flew back to Pleasantville.

Between fights, Matt was helping to train fighters at Joe Mari's Boxing Gym on Atlantic Avenue, two blocks from the Atlantic City boardwalk. That, the occasional fights, his small limousine service, and the sparring gigs kept him busy. Like everyone else, Elaine wanted him to retire from fighting altogether.

"I happen to love him and I want to grow old with him. I don't want him taking any more punches than he has up to now. I worry every time he steps in the ring. Will it be the last time I see him? Or will he survive today and be punch-drunk tomorrow? I've said this all to him but he says 'A man must do what a man must do.' But to me he is endangering his health and tarnishing the championship he once held."[31]

In February 1990, Matt was off to Hamburg, Germany, where four-fight pro Markus Bott stopped him in three rounds. Matt blamed it on not being able to get up for the fight and on Bott being bigger. "He was a cruiserweight and he wore me down," he said.[32] Back home, he met with a writer and talked about his heyday, about owning a Mercedes, a BMW, and a Rolls all at the same time, about his house and bank account, how he paid a 17-man entourage $500 a week every time they were in camp for the duration of his title reign, and how quickly it all fell apart.

"All that is gone now," he said. "But I block it out because if I thought about what I've lost, I just might start crying. Can't think negative. Got to think positive and never give up on myself and the title shot."[33]

For a full year after the Bott debacle, Matt didn't fight. He said he was "semi-retired" and occasionally hung around the Police Athletic League Gym in Atlantic City. Pat Doran, who ran a civil engineering consulting firm in nearby Brigantine, managed a couple of the young pros at the gym and told Matt he'd pay him a salary to train them. Matt accepted the offer and that was all it took; being back in the gym all the time was more than Matt could resist. Soon, Doran agreed to manage him in a comeback, and Matt was going to war in the gym with young Atlantic City heavyweight Bruce Seldon. This time, Matt made it clear that he was in it for one thing: the money.

"I don't want to talk about my problems—they're in the past," he said. "But if I win the world championship, I'm going to retire." Asked how his wife felt about him making another comeback, at age 36, he said, "She supports me but she knows about all the hardships I went through before and she doesn't want me to go through them again."[34] Doran lined up a comeback fight against journeyman Randy Rivers on December 11 in Philadelphia, but it was pushed back to January 15 because of competing bouts in nearby Atlantic City. Even that date was tentative, as the Pennsylvania athletic commission dragged its feet issuing Matt a license—a move clearly designed to both cover its ass and discourage him from fighting again. "We still need a couple more medical reports," commission chairman Howard McCall said in December.[35] In January 1991, the commission finally approved Matt's license. They didn't have a choice. There was no provision for denying a fighter a license so long as he passed the physical. "He passed every medical test we threw at him," said Greg Sirb, the commission's executive director.[36]

Across the river, Larry Hazzard, who in another lifetime it seemed had stopped Matt's bout with Jerry Martin, had a different take. He was now the New Jersey State Athletic Commission chairman, and although he acknowledged Matt as "one of the greatest warriors who ever lived," he said he would not grant him a license.[37]

Naturally, Matt failed to see what all the fuss was about.

"I still have a lot of fans, people who don't want to see me box again," he said in February. "They say, 'Saad Muhammad is a nice guy. We don't want to see him hurt.' But they don't really know me. People are not going to see a sad Matthew Saad Muhammad. Sure, I want to win the title and make some money. But it's more than that. I have this ability. God gave it to me. And as long as I have the talent—and I'm not getting hurt—let me use it."[38]

You had to give Matt credit. If he was going to keep losing, it wouldn't be because he didn't work hard enough in the gym. Every time the Rivers fight was canceled and pushed back, he just kept training, logging more than 300 rounds of sparring since November. Then in February, Rivers dropped out and Matt agreed to face up-and-coming Ed Mack in an eight-rounder on February 26 in the National Guard Armory in Philadelphia. His purse: $1,800.

Unsurprisingly, Matt lost an eight-round decision, though it might have been his best showing in several years. He moved and boxed and showed some defense, and every once in a while, one could catch a glimpse of what he was back when he was still Matt. The problem was that at the end, he knew he had looked better than people expected him to, and this served only to encourage him.

"I'm not going to stop. I felt I had outpointed him, but I knew I was rusty. I was inactive for so long. My timing was off, but I was still in the fight."[39]

In the audience with about 600 other spectators with Dwight Muhammad Qawi. After watching Matt lose, he told a reporter, "If I don't look any better than Matthew in my next fight, I'm going to quit. Looking at him, it made me realize how good he once was. For someone who has no legs at all, he put up a hell of a fight. He did some nice things. Matthew still has the heart of a lion. But in my opinion, he should walk away."[40]

The smart observers knew Mack laid back the first few rounds to see what Matt had left. He said as much afterward, admitting that he gave Matt too much respect early. Recent history had demonstrated that the best way to get rid of this version of Matt was to blitz him early. Mack had let the old car warm up. Either way, Matt was so encouraged by his performance that he was back in the gym the following day.[41]

Two months later, Matt was in Novi Sad, Serbia, of all places, getting outpointed by undefeated novice Anton Josipović. Then it was onto a bullring in Marbella, the very south of Spain, to fight on the undercard of featherweight champion Marcos Villasana's defense against Ricardo Cepeda on August 15, 1991. Cepeda was a Madison Square Garden fighter, so a contingent of American media were there to record a broadcast of the fight, including Bobby Goodman, the vice president and matchmaker for Madison Square Garden.

What most of the fighters and their teams and even some of the visiting media didn't know was that the card wouldn't start until 11:00 p.m. at the earliest, as dinner time in Spain is generally between 9:00 p.m. and midnight. There were five scheduled bouts. Matt's fight against once-beaten Govoner Chavers was scheduled to go on last. Two of the fights went 12 rounds and there were the usual delays between bouts. Just before 3:00 a.m., with Matt's bout yet to start, rumors circulated on press row that it would be canceled. This was fine with visiting media, who all had booked flights that were scheduled to depart at 6:00 a.m.

Just as the next-to-final bout was wrapping up, Goodman went to Matt's locker room and told him that since it was so late, they were just going to cancel his fight. They would pay him the purse they agreed to and maybe some more for his trouble, but this way, Matt and his guys could get ready to head back to the hotel and get a couple hours' sleep before the flight home.

Matt responded: "Nah, I came here to fight. I'm gonna fight."[42] The lights went down in the bullring, Matt came out, Chavers came out, and in the first round, Matt, looking every bit his 37 years, nevertheless landed a left-hook, right-cross combination. Chavers went down like he'd been deboned and stayed down for the referee's full 10-count. It was over that quick.

Matt never won another prizefight.

He tried. Two months after the Chavers fight, he lost to 2–1 Michael Green. Then he got an offer to step in against once-beaten Olympian Andrew Maynard in Washington, D.C., on the undercard of top heavyweight contender Riddick Bowe's fight against Elijah Tillery. Two weeks' notice. He took it for probably about $3,500.

Maynard brutalized him from the opening bell. After the second round, a member of the local commission went to Matt's corner to assess his ability to continue.

COMMISSIONER: "Where are you?"
MATT: "Maryland!"

They let him come out for the third anyway. Twenty seconds in, referee Sylvester Stevens stopped it.[43]

The next day, a New York sportswriter observed that the ugliest sight of an evening that included a shooting outside the arena, a disqualification in the main event, and Bowe's manager getting Tillery in a choke hold was the sight of Rock Newman cheering Maynard on as he butchered what was left of Matthew Saad Muhammad.

Matt offered his usual objections and then this: "What else can I do? People say I should retire. And do what? I ain't goin' to shoot people, or sell no nickel coke. They ain't givin' me no work."[44] It came to an end, finally, in the Colonial Theater in Fredericksburg, Virginia, on March 21, 1992, when Jason Waller, a pudgy, stubby-armed journeyman from nearby Stafford, stopped Matt in the second round.

He had reached rock bottom as a fighter.

Or had he?

A few weeks after the loss to Waller, Matt got a call from Gene Pelc, who, working under the auspices of the Union of Wrestling Forces International, was producing a series of pay-per-view specials featuring "shoot matches"—matches between fighters of different fighting disciplines. He asked Matt if he would be willing to travel to Japan to face one of their top wrestlers, Kiyoshi Tamura.

"I get paid?" Matt asked.

"Of course."

"When do you want me there?"

On May 5, 1992, in front of a huge and enthusiastic crowd, Tamura swept Matt's legs out from underneath him, climbed on his back, and choked him from behind until Matt "tapped out" 32 seconds into the first round.

Looking back on it years later, Matt assessed the end of his boxing career.

"Toward the end I started losing my power. You can't fight the way I did unless you can back it up. I couldn't back it up anymore. But you know what? I have no regrets. I was like Frank Sinatra: I did it my way."[45]

Chapter 15

A Reckoning

*"You have to understand,
a fight wouldn't start for Matthew until he got hurt.
And he was hurt a lot."*
—J Russell Peltz[1]

Over the last decade, Matt had developed a fondness for marijuana and was a frequent smoker; this bothered Elaine, who felt that with all the punches he had taken over the course of his life he shouldn't further risk his cognitive health smoking weed. It was worrying enough that although she never noticed any slurred speech, there were times when it would take him longer than she felt was normal to answer a question, gather his thoughts, or find the word he wanted to use. She didn't want his smoking to make it worse.

It bothered Matt still that he had lost the fancy cars, big houses, and the adoration and attention, but according to Elaine, his disposition the majority of the time was one of contentment, even if not far below the welcoming smile and big handshake there lived a boatload of regret and shame.

"Matthew is a person you want to take care of from the very first," she told a reporter after they were married. "He's sort of a sad person, in a way, because he's so trusting. When I met him he was very carefree. He could make me smile, and I'm not a person prone to smile a lot."[2]

He particularly disliked not having spending money and working in manual labor for the little he had; his old friend Steve Traitz, president of the roofers' union, had gotten him some work in that field—as he had Tony Green, Mike Rossman, Rochelle Norris, and other former fighters—but Matt saw everyday work as something he would do just temporarily until he struck it rich again.

In the mid–1990s, he was working on roofs in Atlantic City on a crew that included Rossman, Norris, and some other guys who had never boxed but knew their way around roofs better than Matt did. He did mainly grunt work—pitch pockets, spreading tar, the things that were physical but didn't require a lot of skill. He, Rossman, and Norris would talk boxing all day, with Matt going on and on about how he was going to get that big fight again and win the title and get back his cars and riches.

Rossman, an infamous ballbuster, would laugh and remind Matt how easily Braxton had beaten him (as though Braxton hadn't beaten *him* just as easily), and Matt would shadowbox on the roof to remind everyone he could still do it. Some of the kids on the crew would hear the boxing talk and ask Matt questions. "Meet me at the gym tonight and I'll show you some pointers," he'd tell them, but he rarely followed through. It got to be a running gag; every time Rossman and the other guys in the boxing clique heard Matt tell someone to meet him at the gym, they'd all bust out laughing, knowing he wasn't going to show up.[3]

He hadn't fought in years and would never fight again, but boxing was still everything to Matt. It was all he knew. It was all he wanted to know. The life of an ordinary man was not the life for him. Not after what he had. Tarring some God-forsaken casino roof in August in Atlantic City was okay for some guys if they'd never had anything else, if they never really tasted life the way he had. But he knew what it was like to live the life of a king. And it hurt him so much to have lost it.

"I'm living a normal life now but I'm just so spoiled, man," he said in 1995. "I know that somewhere I have lump sums of money. I just don't know what damn banks I put it in. This is some of the things that's gotten to me. I'm going through frustration and confusion and just agony."[4]

Some years later, after being asked for probably the thousandth time where all his money went, Matt responded, "Money was flying everywhere. Friends, friends of friends, their mothers, their fathers, their brothers. They were all happy to be around me, eating me alive, taking money from me, rob me, steal from me, and I'd always say: 'That's all right, buddy!' I was always so happy. Matthew Saad Muhammad was always up for it, with everybody."[5]

In mid–1995, Elaine received a job offer from Harrah's Casino in New Orleans. She accepted it, and she and Matt moved from their home in Egg Harbor Township, New Jersey, to Louisiana. After they settled in, Matt looked for work that suited him. But old prizefighters can do only one thing, and after about six months, Matt landed at John Carmody's Neutral Corner Gym, earning $20 a lesson teaching kids how to jab or roll under and come up with the hook. Matt was happy enough to do it, but the idea of fighting again was never completely off the table. "I'm not the man I was before but I could be," he told a visiting writer.

Carmody pulled the writer aside.

Chapter 15. A Reckoning

"He must never, ever fight again," Carmody said, detailing for him all the small ways in which he believed Matt showed the effects of having taken too many punches. Above all, Matt needed to be recognized. "When he first came here we went to a little fight in Mobile and we asked that Matthew be called up into the ring before the first bout. He stepped up and there was this sense of him once again being recognized, being somebody. I could see the strength and the dignity of the man. Honestly, I just cried."[6]

Matt attended other cards in the area, one of them comebacking Larry Holmes's fight against Anthony Willis at a casino in Mississippi in June 1996. From his seat at ringside, he kept coaching Holmes, "Use the left hook! Use the hook!" In the middle of the seventh round, Holmes finally turned and glared at him at ringside as if to say, "Shut up!" Questioned about it later, Holmes said, "I never had a left hook. I throw one every Christmas. I'm afraid to do it. My left hook is awful."[7]

Although he was finally officially retired, Matt drew the attention of fans, even those who weren't exactly sure who he was. At the Holmes fight, Matt was ringside waiting for the main event to start when he was approached by an attractive young woman in a short blue dress. She kneeled in front of him.

"You're Riddick Bowe, aren't you?" she asked.

"No, I'm not," Matt said.

"Well, I know you're somebody. Can I have your autograph? I'm a huge boxing fan."

Matt signed her fight program. She looked at the signature.

"When will I get to see you fight again?" she asked.

Matt looked at the media guys in the rows next to his and shook his head. "Wow."[8]

Matt and Elaine were in New Orleans for 16 months when Elaine got word that Harrah's was closing its site there. She received an offer to relocate again, this time to the company's home office in Fort Lauderdale, Florida. She accepted the offer and moved. Matt wasn't able to find a gym he wanted to work at in Fort Lauderdale, so he stayed in New Orleans during the week and flew to Fort Lauderdale on the weekends.

In late 1996, Elaine drove to the airport to pick Matt up. His luggage had arrived, but he hadn't. When she inquired, an airline employee told her he'd been detained at a stopover in Tampa; he'd smoked pot in the airplane bathroom during the flight and been arrested.

Matt got lucky; the authorities in Tampa knew who he was and didn't charge him. Elaine was not as forgiving. She told him to stay in New Orleans. Shortly afterward, in early 1997, they divorced. "I felt if he didn't care enough about himself to not put himself in a predicament like that, how much did he really care about me?" she said in 2021. Elaine ended up moving again to work at the Ritz Carlton in Puerto Rico. After a while, Matt went back to the only place he could: Philadelphia.

Matt's return to the Philadelphia area initiated a period of transience, of sleeping on this friend's couch or in that one's basement, of visiting different gyms looking for work, of periods of depression and desperation, and of feeding addictions that had come to grip him over the years. He would drop out of sight for days or weeks. After a time, he'd resurface and then disappear again.

In 1998, things started looking up. Matt was inducted into the International Boxing Hall of Fame in Canastota, New York, and for five glorious days drank in the love and attention of fans, media, and fellow fighters. He hired a business manager named Polly Wilkinson who told him they would finally sell his life story to a movie studio, something he'd been talking about doing since the early 1980s. The New Jersey Hall of Fame also inducted him, and not long after, there was talk about Matt getting his own gym in Philly where he could train local kids and draw a salary from the city. Someone was donating equipment. There was going to be a segment on the local news. It was all coming together, finally.

Two weeks before the gym was set to open, there was a problem.

Matt had disappeared.

* * *

Shawn Darling was working the late shift at the Atlantic County jail in 1999 when a couple of uniforms brought in a guy who looked familiar. Darling, a 30-year-old correctional officer, was an amateur boxer and lifelong fight fan. He recognized the guy almost immediately: Matthew Saad Muhammad. Darling found out Matt had caught a possession charge with intent to distribute. Matt looked friendly enough, smiling and chatting with the officers and other inmates, being Matt. On his second day in, Darling approached him and they started talking. They clicked.

Darling picked Matt's brain for training methods and fighting techniques. Matt was happy to share. He told Darling he didn't smoke weed that much and he hadn't been looking to sell. It was a small amount he'd been caught with, but the way the seller had bagged it, they were able to get him for intent. Even with that, he did only a couple of weeks. Back on the outside, he and Darling kept in touch. When Darling had a couple amateur fights in South Jersey, Matt worked his corner.

Matt was living in a trailer park in Egg Harbor Township near Pleasantville. Joe Johnson, one of the boys the Santos family had taken in around the same time they adopted Matt, owned a trailer there and rented it to a friend. He let Matt stay rent-free. It was sparsely furnished: a white plastic chair, the kind one commonly finds in a backyard, and a cinderblock, presumably used as a kind of end table. No television.

Matt's old beat-up Cadillac was parked outside the trailer. One day when Darling stopped by to pick him up, he pointed to it and said, "Hey, I didn't know they made purple Cadillacs back in the day, Matt." Matt replied, "No, no, it was black, it just faded in the sun from sitting out there." People in town told Darling they often saw Matt sleeping in it.[9]

It was better for everyone when the old Caddy was parked rather than on the road. Matt

Matt poses with Mustafa Ameen after being inducted into the Pennsylvania Boxing Hall of Fame in 2008. Ameen was the best man at Matt's first wedding, ran the training camp during his championship run, and remained his close friend for the rest of Matt's life (photo courtesy of Paul Trace).

drove the same way he fought: 100 mph with no regard for safety. Delaware-area ring announcer Larry Tornambe was friends with Matt through the early 2000s, and whenever they went out to various shows or boxing events, he drove because Matt's license was suspended. Tornambe once talked to a cop he knew to try to get Matt's license reinstated. He was told it would never happen, that Matt would be in driver education classes for the next five years. His record was just a list of violation after violation.[10]

In 2000, Darling opened the Gladiator Gym and hired Matt as a trainer. They developed a close friendship and a mutually beneficial professional relationship. Matt trained the kids at the gym and accompanied Darling and the boxers whenever they traveled to meets or to other gyms. Matt's presence and association with the gym gave Darling instant credibility. Plus, Matt's personality made him a favorite among the kids. They loved him. In return, Darling helped Matt find a small apartment in nearby Lacey Township and paid his rent, about $500 a month. He helped Matt get some government assistance, and members of his church donated furniture.

Darling also served as a kind of business manager, helping Matt benefit from being Matthew Saad Muhammad: he'd arrange interviews, autograph signings, personal appearances. Matt kept whatever he was paid. It was never all that much, but he would take whatever he could get.

Matt was still a member of the roofers' union, but the work was sporadic. He didn't get called much because he wasn't particularly good at it and, more than anything, was a liability up on roofs, as his balance was poor. There were times when he was sent to a jobsite with instructions to move this or that pile of supplies to a location in the morning and then in the afternoon was told to move it back, just to get him some hours and a paycheck.

This was generally a relatively good period for Matt. He was upbeat and gracious to everyone he met and his character was evident. Whenever Darling would have him over to his home, Matt would ask if there was anything he could do, if he needed help with anything. Darling told him to just enjoy himself. "He was just that much of a gentleman. Like, he wanted to help me in the yard, but all I wanted him to do was what I paid him to do at the gym," Darling said.

Darling repaid Matt's kindness with kindness of his own. When a newspaper reported that Matt's championship belts were seen at a pawnshop, Darling took up a collection, bought them, and presented them to Matt at the gym.

Everyone in the community got to know Matt and called him "Champ." He got along with everyone. When he went out to eat, he almost never had to pay the check; there was always some-

Matt works with aspiring boxers at Shawn Darling's Gladiator Gym in New Jersey, ca. early 2000s (photo courtesy of Shawn Darling).

Chapter 15. A Reckoning

one picking it up for him. And he was still a ladies' man. He rarely spent a night alone in his apartment, partaking of the many pleasures afforded by willing women in the community.

On occasion, Matt had to remind those in his company of his roots.

Two or three times, Darling took Matt to the Gleason's Fantasy Boxing Camp in New York, where fans would sign up and pay a fee to spend a weekend with their favorite fighters. One year, they took along another ex-fighter, a very well-known guy from New Jersey who had won a light heavyweight world title. At the time, Darling was driving a small green Toyota Echo, a two-door. On the ride up, Matt sat in the front and this other fighter, who was shorter than Matt, squeezed into the back. When they left camp for the long ride back to Jersey, the other fighter said, "I'm not getting in that back seat again."

Matt said no problem; he'd ride in the back for the ride home. They'd been on the road for about five minutes when Darling pulled into a gas station to fill up. The other fighter ran into the station to use the bathroom, and Matt said to Darling, "Shawn, I'm too tall, I can't sit in that back seat again." He waited for the other fighter to come back out so he could let him climb into the back. When this other fighter returned to the car, he and Matt started arguing about who was going to get in the back. Matt told the other passenger, "Look man, I'm too tall to sit in that back seat." They went nose to nose, arguing over who would get in the back. Eventually, the other fighter stepped back, sized Matt up, and climbed into the back seat. He didn't say a word the whole ride home.[11]

One day, Darling asked Matt where all his money went. "The money was going here, there and everywhere," Matt told him. "When you're poor and you come up with nothing and then you get all this money you go back and help all your friends in the neighborhood. When you get money there's a million right behind that million and then one day there is no more million and you're left with nothing."[12]

Matt maintained too that his management had proved untrustworthy and not paid him money he was owed. He blamed Bilal in particular, who was a frequent subject of conversation with old friends who were there during Matt's championship days. The two were on bad terms over the last 20 years at least of Matt's life and saw each other just once during this period, in 1995.

Mike Tyson's jail stay following a rape conviction was nearing its end in '95, and he was preparing to announce who would manage and promote his fights upon his release. He had converted to Islam while incarcerated at the Indiana Youth Center in 1992, and this was seen by many as a sign that he would not resume his long business relationship with Don King when released. Enter Akbar Muhammad, who was a member of Cornerstone Enterprises way back in the early 1970s along with Bilal. When Cornerstone dissolved, Akbar joined Bob Arum's Top Rank Promotions and worked on several of Matt's fights when they had Matt under contract. Akbar, like most other promoters, hoped to handle Tyson's career, a dividend of which would be access to the tens of millions of dollars the cable TV networks would throw at him.

Tyson held a press conference in Cleveland on March 30 to announce the identity of his promoter. Akbar attended, along with Bilal. Both were dressed in Muslim garb. Matt was there too, one must assume at the behest of Bilal and Akbar, who had to know of Tyson's long affection for Matt and hoped to use it to influence Tyson in their favor. It didn't work. Before Tyson came out to address the audience, handlers were dispersed with orders to remove everyone dressed like a Muslim, and Akbar, Bilal, and Matt were ushered out of the building. (So too was Harold Smith, who had claimed to represent Indonesian interests that were prepared to pay Tyson $45 million for a return bout.[13])

It was during this period when Matt was training kids at Darling's gym that his younger son, Michael, would join them. He was around 17 at the time and was filling out like his father, except shorter—strong, athletic, intense. With Matt showing him the basics, Michael picked up fighting right away. Once he got his legs under him, Matt would take him around to fight gyms in Jersey and around Philadelphia, and the kid would hold his own and then some with any kid of comparable size and experience.

There was a problem and it was this: Matt had not been a consistent presence in his boys' lives. Indeed, there were years-long spans when they didn't see each other at all, and much of the time, such distance between a man and his sons breeds in the young men a storm of fury and resentment that can only be cured by time, maturity, and when possible, forgiveness.

It doesn't matter if, as was largely the case here, the absences are a by-product of the father's pride, which tells him he can't let his sons see him in such a state, living hand to mouth, sleeping on friends' couches or in a car, scrambling this way or that to earn mere gas or food money, especially when he was once a rich man.

Too embarrassing.

What son wants to see his father like that?

Answer: They all do. A father merely has to be there for his boy, to show him how to be a man. That is all a son requires, all he wants.

But the further down the hole Matt slipped, the harder it was to get out, and the harder it was to get out, the less inclined he was to show his boys how far he'd fallen.

Chapter 15. A Reckoning

When Michael started coming to the gym, Matt was more stable than he'd been for a while, but a son doesn't forget, so when Michael sparred with other boys, and especially with Matt, everything that raged within him came out.

"He had a lot of pent up anger," Darling said. "He would go very hard in sparring. Matthew would try to de-escalate the situation."[14]

Matt's relationship with his older son, Matt Jr., was not dissimilar. They fought, seethed, went silent, and fought again, and Matt Jr., while striving to emulate his father and meet his standards of toughness and resilience, did it on his own terms, becoming renowned in extreme sports circles for his fearlessness in freestyle BMX competition.

Michael's immersion in boxing was short-lived and, as it turned out, so too was his father's job at Darling's gym. After about two years of working together at the gym, at shows, at appearances, at boxing events, and at fundraisers, Darling noticed that whenever Matt came around, he smelled strongly of marijuana.

He'd pick Matt up at his apartment and drive him to the gym for work, and as soon as Matt opened the door, Darling would smell weed. On one level, it didn't matter to Darling; if that's what Matt wanted to do on his free time, that was his choice. But at the gym, it was another matter. He couldn't have Matt around kids reeking of weed any more than he could if he reeked of alcohol. And when he was high, it affected his job performance. Moreover, Darling was still a cop. Marijuana was illegal.

Finally, Darling had to call him out on it. You couldn't blame him.

Matt blamed it on his neighbors, but it was clear it wasn't just his neighbors, and it continued. No one wants an employee who shows up high to work every day. It doesn't work that way. Darling had to let him go.

They ran into each other at a fundraiser four or five years later, and there were no hard feelings, just smiles and hugs. That was Matt.

* * *

"I just kind of put my head down sometimes. It's almost like I don't want people to see me," Matt told a writer in July 2010. "There are times when I can't believe I'm here." He was talking about being in the RHD Ridge Center, the largest homeless shelter in Philadelphia. He'd walked in one day in May. He had to. He didn't know what else to do.[15]

"I was in a state of shock. I thought, 'Am I going to go in this shelter?' I had to go somewhere. My money ran out. I was going from hotel to hotel, [bills] piling up," he said.[16] The RHD Ridge Center was run and funded by the Resources for Human Development, a Philadelphia-based nonprofit. When Matt first arrived, he asked other residents and the shelter's organizers to keep his identity secret. He was embarrassed. Eventually, another resident, Jose Espinosa, convinced Matt to share his story. The result was an article titled "Fighting Back" in *One Step Away*, the shelter's newspaper. The article won an International Network of Street Papers award for Best Interview. More importantly, Matt was sharing his story as a way to help others.

"It was very hard. My name is Matthew Saad Muhammad. I've been a big celebrity. But I needed some support. I didn't want to sleep on the streets and I wasn't going to sleep on the streets. So this is what I did," he said.[17]

"When you've got nothing, that's when you can really start over," Matt said. "I will start from the ground up again. I know I will be successful again. I thank God for this chance, actually. I'm not mad. I'm delighted. Even if it kills me, I'm willing to make a change in my life."

"I'm not going to say I was a drug user. I'm better than that. But I did things that were not productive, that held me back. When I say to people, I'm trying to change, I mean I'll start over again from the bottom. I'm willing to do that. I'm ready for a change," he said.[18] "I needed a rest when I first got here. I needed it to make decisions. I needed a place to nod my head and think about what's my next move—and this move has to be a good move. I'm hoping this is the beginning of a new thing."[19]

It was.

Some of Matt's friends from the old days rallied around him and started a collection. There was a fundraiser. Some roofing jobs came through. He got a small place in North Philadelphia and moved out of the shelter. Soon, Matt, working with Kevin Roberts, was the spokesman for *One Step Away*'s "Knock Out Homelessness" campaign. He spoke at their fundraisers and reconnected with Tornambe and other friends with whom he had lost touch during the bad years.

Working for charities didn't pay the bills, however, and soon Matt was doing the only thing he could do to make money, and that was training fighters in and around Philadelphia. He hustled here and there like he always had, scrambling for a buck and working to keep his head above water.

Matt repaired his relationships with Matt Jr. and Michael and spoke frequently with Zakiyyah. He started telling them more, sometimes over games of chess, about their siblings and their shared histories, as if letting them know the time was coming, sooner or later, when they would have to know and rely on their family more than they had, that he wouldn't be there to bring them together. If you didn't know better, you'd have thought he was planning for a graceful exit, the way one does who knows the end is coming and is not fearful of it and wants to know that he is leaving things as well as he can.

In February 2014, Zakiyyah made a mental note that she hadn't heard from her dad in about a month. It was unusual but not worrying, as he was forever losing phones and changing his mobile number. She was working in an administrative capacity at Pennsylvania Hospital at 8th and Spruce Streets in Philadelphia when she received a call from a coworker in the admissions department.

"You know your dad's here?"

Zakiyyah rushed to the hospital and found Matt being admitted to the floor on which she worked. He was happy to see her, explained that he'd lost his phone and wasn't feeling well so he had a friend drop him off and got admitted. He'd been in a lot of pain. Zakiyyah spoke to his doctors and was told they were trying to get information from another hospital about a prior admission but not making much headway.[20] More troubling was Matt's recollection of the prior month contradicted what the doctors were saying. They suspected he'd had a stroke and subsequently transferred him to the nearby rehab facility to work on restoring some lost function.

While Matt was in rehab, Zakiyyah assumed caretaking duties full time and did everything for him, including making sure he got haircuts—he had to "look good for the ladies," he told her. After several weeks, she returned to work part time at the hospital while a friend of Matt's sat with him at rehab. His conditioned worsened. The therapy sessions seemed to drain him.

Several weeks passed. While she was at work, Zakiyyah received a call from the rehab facility. Something was wrong with Matt; he was incoherent. They rushed him back to the hospital, and she went to his room. He was more unconscious than not but perked up when he saw her.

"Dad, are you okay? Are you okay?"

He looked up at her, laboring to breathe. "Baby girl," he said. "Do you have my wallet?" And if only the circumstances weren't so dire, Zakiyyah would have laughed; it was so much like him to ask her that.

"Yes, Dad, I have it," she said.[21]

Matt lost consciousness. The attending doctor intubated him.

* * *

A couple of weeks before the fourth annual "Knock Out Homelessness" fundraiser event, Tornambe, who played emcee and host at the events, talked to Kevin Roberts, one of the organizers. Roberts told him Matt was in the hospital and probably wouldn't make it. On the night of the event, Roberts took Tornambe aside and again told him Matt wasn't going to make it. Tornambe nodded, assuming Roberts meant the event. Roberts clarified, "No, not the event; he's not gonna *make* it, he's in really bad shape."[22]

Dwight Muhammad Qawi, standing nearby, heard the conversation and left early to see Matt. Over the next week, scores of others did as well—managers and trainers, spit-bucket men from Atlantic City and Pleasantville, from Philly and Jersey, roofers, pugs and ex-pugs, homeless advocates, girlfriends, newspaper types. Matt had touched a lot of people. They wanted to say goodbye.

Tony Green called Paul Trace and Mustafa Ameen. They were there the next day.

"Hey champ. Champ, come on we got work to do," Ameen whispered at Matt's bedside.

Matt's eyelids fluttered.

"Come on champ, you been resting too long."[23]

Someone had to decide when to remove Matt's life support. Michael was getting married at the end of the week. They decided to wait until after the wedding. Michelle visited him a final time, singing softly in his ear. The kids said their goodbyes.

Matt died at Chestnut Hill Hospital at around 1:00 a.m. on May 25, 2014. He was 59 years old. Doctors attributed his death to complications of ALS, or Lou Gehrig's disease, and this was a surprise, since Matt exhibited none of the classic symptoms, such as paralysis. But dead is dead. In early June, there was a service at a local mosque and then a funeral at Enon Tabernacle Baptist Church in Germantown. Mike Rossman was there. J Russell Peltz too. Yaqui López flew in from California. Philadelphia middleweight Buster Drayton, whom Matt mentored early in Drayton's career, was there. Tim Witherspoon too. So too Bobby "Boogaloo" Watts and Cyclone Hart. All the Philly legends, large and small. Several members of the Loach family showed up, as did most of the old friends who were there with Matt during the good days. The line stretched out into the parking lot.

And after all the times that Matt had come back, there wasn't a mourner among them who'd have been surprised to see him sit up in the casket and start swinging.

Chapter Notes

Chapter 1

1. Steve Farhood, *KO*, 1981.
2. https://blog.phillyhistory.org/index.php/2016/02/roots-of-hyper segregation-in-philadelphia-1920-1930
3. Chuck Slater, *New York Daily News*, April 19, 1981, 234.
4. Norman O. Unger, *Jet*, August 28, 1980, 28.
5. https://jdc.jefferson.edu/cgi/viewcontent.cgi?article=1001&context=ascps_fellowship
6. UPI, *Detroit Free Press*, November 24, 1980, 50.
7. Tom Cushman, *Philadelphia Daily News*, June 6, 1979, 71.
8. UPI, *The Times Argus*, July 12, 1980, 9.
9. Edgar Williams, *Philadelphia Inquirer*, May 26, 1979, 29C.
10. Stan Hochman, *Philadelphia Daily News*, January 10, 1980, 52.
11. Saleem El-Amin, 2020.
12. Stan Hochman, *Philadelphia Daily News*, January 10, 1980, 52.
13. Skip Myslenski, *Philadelphia Inquirer*, March 6, 1977, 110.

Chapter 2

1. Nigel Collins, 2020.
2. Stan Hochman, *Philadelphia Daily News*, March 13, 1981, 43.
3. *Ibid.*
4. *Ibid.*
5. *Ibid.*
6. Cy Peterman, *Philadelphia Inquirer*, January 13, 1941, 19.
7. *Ibid.*
8. Nick Belfiore, Jr., 2021.
9. *Ibid.*
10. https://www.facebook.com/watch/?v=1527113514109819
11. Jack McKinney, *Philadelphia Daily News*, March 24, 1973, 32.
12. Nick Belfiore, Jr., 2021
13. Stan Hochman, *Philadelphia Daily News*, January 10, 1980, 52.

Chapter 3

1. Gary Smith, *Philadelphia Daily News*, April 19, 1977, 56.
2. Ron Avery, *Philadelphia Daily News*, December 27, 1993, 8.
3. *Ibid.*
4. Larry McMullen, *Philadelphia Daily News*, November 27, 1972, 32.
5. Larry McMullen, *Philadelphia Daily News*, July 20, 1976, 6.
6. *Ibid.*
7. Tom Cushman, *Philadelphia Daily News*, March 20, 1980, 71.
8. *Ibid.*
9. J Russell Peltz, 2020.
10. Gene Courtney, *Philadelphia Inquirer*, August 15, 1974, 24.
11. Gene Courtney, *Philadelphia Inquirer*, November 13, 1974, 42.
12. Tom Cushman, *Philadelphia Daily News*, March 20, 1980, 71.
13. John Blanchette, *Missoulian*, October 20, 1976, 13.
14. *Ibid.*
15. Ben Swesey, *Sacramento Bee*, July 18, 1976, 76.
16. UPI, *Tribune*, May 15, 1976, 14.
17. Bill Mang, *Times Tribune*, September 16, 1976, 31.
18. Frank Gelb, 2020.

19. John Blanchette, *Missoulian*, October 20, 1976, 13.
20. *Ibid.*
21. *Ibid.*
22. John Blanchette, *Missoulian*, October 27, 1976, 13.
23. *Ibid.*
24. Gene Courtney, *Philadelphia Inquirer*, October 28, 1976, 34.
25. Tom Cushman, *Philadelphia Daily News*, December 1, 1976, 79.
26. Tom Cushman, *Philadelphia Daily News*, December 2, 1976, 76.
27. Dick Young, *New York Daily News*, March 28, 1980, 288.
28. *Ibid.*
29. *Ibid.*
30. Bill Verigan, *New York Daily News*, March 21, 1980, 310.
31. Jack Smith, *New York Daily News*, January 22, 1972, 181.
32. Jack Smith, *New York Daily News*, March 19, 1971, 76.
33. Jack Smith, *New York Daily News*, January 22, 1972, 28.
34. *Ibid.*, 82.
35. Bill Verigan, *New York Daily News*, December 4, 1973, 100.
36. Bill Verigan, *New York Daily News*, November 16, 1977, 91.
37. Gene Courtney, *Philadelphia Inquirer*, March 12, 1977, 21.
38. Gary Smith, *Philadelphia Daily News*, March 12, 1977, 34.
39. *Ibid.*, 36.
40. *Ibid.*
41. Gary Smith, *Philadelphia Daily News*, April 19, 1977, 56.

Chapter 4

1. AP, *News Journal*, April 20, 1977, 22.
2. Tom Cobourn, *Morning News*, April 22, 1977, 29.
3. Tom Cushman, *Philadelphia Daily News*, May 27, 1977, 22.
4. *Ibid.*
5. *Ibid.*
6. *Ibid.*
7. Tom Cushman, *Philadelphia Daily News*, June 11, 1977, 34.
8. *Ibid.*
9. Gary Smith, *Philadelphia Daily News*, October 27, 1977, 60.
10. Gene Courtney, *Philadelphia Inquirer*, July 23, 1977, 21.
11. Russ Leonard, *Indianapolis Star*, August 1, 1976, 12.
12. *Ibid.*
13. Gene Courtney, *Philadelphia Inquirer*, July 23, 1977, 3C.
14. *Ibid.*
15. Dick Weiss, *Philadelphia Daily News*, July 22, 1977, 80.
16. *Ibid.*
17. *Ibid.*
18. Bill Livingston, *Philadelphia Inquirer*, July 27, 1977, 35.
19. *Crowley Post-Signal*, July 29, 1977, 5.
20. Tom Cushman, *Philadelphia Daily News*, April 21, 1979, 35.
21. Bill Livingston, *Philadelphia Inquirer*, July 27, 1977, 35.
22. *Ibid.*
23. Stan Hochman, *Philadelphia Daily News*, July 27, 1977, 87.
24. *Ibid.*
25. J Russell Peltz, 2021, 159.
26. Gary Smith, *Philadelphia Daily News*, September 14, 1977, 82.
27. Stan Hochman, *Philadelphia Daily News*, July 27, 1977, 87.
28. Bill Livingston, *Philadelphia Inquirer*, July 27, 1977, 31.
29. Nigel Collins, 2021.
30. Gary Smith, *Philadelphia Daily News*, September 14, 1977, 82.
31. Gene Courtney, *Philadelphia Inquirer*, October 27, 1977, 31.
32. Tom Cushman, *Philadelphia Daily News*, May 10, 1973, 48.
33. *Ibid.*
34. Tom Cushman, *Philadelphia Daily News*, March 21, 1972, 63.
35. *Ibid.*
36. *Ibid.*
37. *Ibid.*
38. Tom Cushman, *Philadelphia Daily News*, February 7, 1972, 53.
39. *Ibid.*
40. *Ibid.*
41. Tom Cushman, *Philadelphia Daily News*, February 7, 1972, 52.
42. Gary Smith, *Philadelphia Daily News*, September 14, 1977, 83.
43. *Ibid.*
44. Gary Smith, *Philadelphia Daily News*, September 14, 1977, 82.
45. Tom Cushman, *Philadelphia Daily News*, September 19, 1977, 59.

46. *Ibid.*
47. J Russell Peltz, 2021, 162.
48. Stan Hochman, *Philadelphia Daily News*, December 2, 1982, 79.
49. Gene Courtney, *Philadelphia Inquirer*, October 27, 1977, 31.

Chapter 5

1. Gary Smith, *Philadelphia Daily News*, October 27, 1977, 58.
2. *Ibid.*, 60.
3. Gene Courtney, *Philadelphia Inquirer*, October 27, 1977, 31.
4. Gary Smith, *Philadelphia Daily News*, November 1, 1977, 68.
5. *Ibid.*
6. Gary Smith, *Philadelphia Daily News*, November 2, 1977, 97.
7. *Ibid.*
8. *Ibid.*
9. *Ibid.*
10. Tom Cushman, *Philadelphia Daily News*, May 18, 1971, 64.
11. Art Ogden, *Daily Journal*, June 1, 1971, 7.
12. https://www.youtube.com/watch?v=OHmy2LuieWE
13. *Ibid.*
14. Leroy Samuels, *Courier Post*, May 23, 1974, 68.
15. Tom Cushman, *Philadelphia Daily News*, May 18, 1971, 64.
16. https://www.youtube.com/watch?v=OHmy2LuieWE
17. Don McDermott, *News Journal*, January 8, 1975, 12.
18. Don Benevenyo, *Courier Post*, November 2, 1977, 63.
19. Tom Cushman, *Philadelphia Daily News*, February 10, 1978, 79.
20. Michael Smith *Millville Daily*, January 31, 1978, 7.
21. Thom Greer, *Philadelphia Daily News*, February 2, 1978, 54.
22. Gene Courtney, *Philadelphia Inquirer*, February 10, 1978, 30.
23. Tom Cushman, *Philadelphia Daily News*, February 10, 1978, 79.
24. *Ibid.*
25. Michael Smith, *Millville Daily*, January 30, 1978, 5.
26. Gene Courtney, *Philadelphia Inquirer*, February 11, 1978, 25.
27. Tom Cushman, *Philadelphia Daily News*, February 11, 1978, 35.
28. *Ibid.*
29. https://www.youtube.com/watch?v=mEri81t9Taw
30. Michael Smith, *Millville Daily*, February 6, 1978, 7.
31. Michael Smith, *Millville Daily*, February 13, 1978, 9.
32. Tom Cushman, *Philadelphia Daily News*, February 11, 1978, 36.
33. Gene Courtney, *Philadelphia Inquirer*, February 11, 1978, 21.
34. Gene Courtney, *Philadelphia Inquirer*, November 2, 1977, 37.
35. Tom Cushman, *Philadelphia Daily News*, February 10, 1978, 79.
36. *Ibid.*
37. Gene Courtney, *Philadelphia Inquirer*, June 16, 1978, 23.
38. Frank Gelb, 2021.
39. Stan Hochman, *Philadelphia Daily News*, January 10, 1980, 52.
40. Bob Davis, *Times-Tribune*, June 25, 1978, 48.
41. Tom Cushman, *Philadelphia Daily News*, October 19, 1978, 67.
42. Gene Courtney, *Philadelphia Inquirer*, June 16, 1978, 23.
43. *Ibid.*
44. Thom Greer, *Philadelphia Daily News*, June 20, 1978, 69.
45. *Ibid.*
46. *Ibid.*, 71.
47. Tom Cushman, *Philadelphia Daily News*, October 19, 1978, 67.
48. *Ibid.*
49. Tony Green, 2021.
50. Bilal Muhammad, 2021.
51. Tom Cushman, *Philadelphia Daily News*, October 19, 1978, 67.
52. J Russell Peltz, 2020.
53. Tom Cushman, *Philadelphia Daily News*, October 9, 1978, 67.
54. *Ibid.*
55. *Ibid.*
56. *Ibid.*
57. Tom Cushman, *Philadelphia Daily News*, October 29, 1978, 91.
58. *Ibid.*

Chapter 6

1. Tom Cushman, *Philadelphia Daily News*, October 19, 1978, 67.

2. Gene Courtney, *Philadelphia Inquirer*, October 19, 1978, 29.
3. Gene Courtney, *Philadelphia Inquirer*, October 21, 1978, 23.
4. Gene Courtney, *Philadelphia Inquirer*, October 19, 1978, 29.
5. Stan Hochman, *Philadelphia Daily News*, October 25, 1978, 76.
6. https://www.youtube.com/watch?v=7qp_J3qAWok
7. Stan Hochman, *Philadelphia Daily News*, October 25, 1978, 76.
8. *Ibid.*
9. *Ibid.*
10. Gene Courtney, *Philadelphia Inquirer*, October 25, 1978, 23.
11. Don Benevento, *Courier Post*, October 25, 1978, 61.
12. *Ibid.*
13. UPI, *Tribune*, October 25, 1978, 32.
14. Stan Hochman, *Philadelphia Daily News*, October 25, 1978, 76.
15. John Bansch, *Indianapolis Star*, January 5, 1979, 27.
16. *Ibid.*
17. Tom Cushman, *Philadelphia Daily News*, April 18, 1979, 71.
18. UPI, *Indianapolis News*, January 6, 1979, 13.
19. Tom Cushman, *Philadelphia Daily News*, April 18, 1979, 71.
20. *Ibid.*
21. *Ibid.*
22. John Bansch, *Indianapolis Star*, April 21, 1979, 29.
23. Tom Cushman, *Philadelphia Daily News*, April 23, 1979, 66.
24. John Bansch, *Indianapolis Star*, April 19, 1979, 33.
25. https://www.youtube.com/watch?v=pnq13fuxJp0&t=2960s
26. Tom Cushman, *Philadelphia Daily News*, April 23, 1979, 66.
27. *Ibid.*
28. *Ibid.*
29. *Ibid.*
30. https://www.youtube.com/watch?v=pnq13fuxJp0&t=2960s
31. https://www.youtube.com/watch?v=pnq13fuxJp0&t=2960s
32. Tom Cushman, *Philadelphia Daily News*, April 22, 1979, 66.
33. *Ibid.*
34. AP, *Home News*, April 23, 1979, 11.
35. AP, *Daily American*, April 23, 1979, 15.
36. Tom Cushman, *Philadelphia Daily News*, April 23, 1979, 66.

Chapter 7

1. John Bansch, *Indianapolis Star*, April 26, 1979, 40.
2. *Ibid.*
3. *Ibid.*
4. Tom Cushman, *Philadelphia Daily News*, June 6, 1979, 71.
5. Clive Gammon, *Sports Illustrated*, August 27, 1979.
6. Tom Cushman, *Philadelphia Daily News*, August 20, 1979, 62.
7. Ralph Cipriano, *Philadelphia Inquirer*, March 29, 1994, 29.
8. *Ibid.*
9. Tom Cushman, *Philadelphia Daily News*, June 6, 1979, 71.
10. Clive Gammon, *Sports Illustrated*, August 27, 1979.
11. Jay Greenberg, *Philadelphia Daily News*, August 16, 1979, 64.
12. *Ibid.*
13. Nigel Collins, 2021.
14. Jay Greenberg, *Philadelphia Daily News*, August 16, 1979, 64.
15. Jeff Jacobs, *Courier-Post*, August 10, 1979, 21.
16. *Ibid.*
17. Dick Weiss, *Philadelphia Daily News*, August 17, 1979, 76.
18. https://www.youtube.com/watch?v=ULDb_t_mXVY
19. Danny Robbins, *Philadelphia Inquirer*, August 19, 1979, 124.
20. *Ibid.*
21. AP, *Chicago Tribune*, August 19, 1979, 65.
22. Tom Cushman, *Philadelphia Daily News*, August 20, 1979, 62.
23. *The Guardian* (London), August 21, 1979, 23.
24. Tom Cushman, *Philadelphia Daily News*, August 20, 1979, 62.
25. *Ibid.*
26. *Ibid.*
27. Stan Hochman, *Philadelphia Daily News*, January 10, 1980, 52.
28. *Ibid.*
29. *Philadelphia Inquirer*, September 13, 1979, 22.
30. Stan Hochman, *Philadelphia Daily News*, January 10, 1980, 53.

31. *Ibid.*
32. *Ibid.*
33. Lewis Freedman, *Philadelphia Inquirer*, September 9, 1981, 30.
34. Pat Putnam, *Sports Illustrated*, March 13, 1978.
35. *New York Times*, December 1, 1988.
36. AP, *The Record*, June 25, 1973, 27.
37. Pat Putnam, *Sports Illustrated*, March 13, 1978.
38. *Ibid.*
39. *Ibid.*
40. Pat Putnam, *Sports Illustrated*, September 25, 1978.
41. *Ibid.*
42. Mustafa Ameen, 2021

Chapter 8

1. Lewis Freedman, *Philadelphia Inquirer*, March 24, 1980, 22.
2. Tony Green, 2021.
3. Lewis Freedman, *Philadelphia Inquirer*, March 24, 1980, 22.
4. *Ibid.*
5. AP, *Evening Sun*, March 15, 1980, 12.
6. Larry Fields, *Philadelphia Daily News*, March 26, 1980, 31.
7. Lewis Freedman, *Philadelphia Inquirer*, March 26, 1980, 27.
8. AP, *El Paso Times*, March 29, 1980, 48.
9. https://www.youtube.com/watch?v=93rN1bM0xBs&t=790s
10. https://www.youtube.com/watch?v=93rN1bM0xBs&t=790s
11. Lewis Freedman, *Philadelphia Inquirer*, March 28, 1990, 95.
12. Greg Logan, *The Record*, March 30, 1980, 38.
13. Lewis Freedman, *Philadelphia Inquirer*, May 9, 1980, 29.
14. *Philadelphia Daily News*, May 12, 1980, 66.
15. https://www.youtube.com/watch?v=_Y2xWjfMDDk&t=1080s
16. Steve Farhood, *KO*, December 1980, 24.
17. Mustafa Ameen, 2021.
18. *New York Daily News*, November 1, 1981, 145.
19. Mustafa Ameen, 2021.
20. Norman O. Unger, *Jet*, August 28, 1980, 28.
21. Mustafa Ameen, 2021.
22. Steve Farhood, *KO*, December 1980, 27.
23. Norman O. Unger, *Jet*, August 28, 1980, 28.
24. UPI, *Philadelphia Daily News*, July 10, 1980, 54.
25. Dick Young, *New York Daily News*, April 2, 1980, 68.
26. Dick Weiss, *Philadelphia Daily News*, July 11, 1980, 90.
27. Lewis Freedman, *Philadelphia Inquirer*, July 19, 1980, 19.
28. Dick Weiss, *Philadelphia Daily News*, July 11, 1980, 90.
29. Steve Farhood, *KO*, December 1980, 27.
30. *Ibid.*
31. Tom Cushman, *Philadelphia Daily News*, July 14, 1980, 67.
32. Rich Wallace, *Herald News*, July 14, 1980, 18.
33. Bill Verigan, *New York Daily News*, July 14, 1980, 56.
34. Lewis Freedman, *Philadelphia Inquirer*, July 14, 1980, 17.
35. Mark DiIonno, *Daily Record*, July 14, 1980, 15.
36. Tom Cushman, *Philadelphia Daily News*, July 14, 1980, 67.
37. Gary Smith, *Philadelphia Daily News*, July 16, 1980, 63.
38. Mark Heisler, *Los Angeles Times*, November 23, 1980, 48.
39. *Los Angeles Times*, November 28, 1980, 65.
40. Steve Farhood, *KO*, December 1980, 27.
41. Tom Cushman, *Philadelphia Daily News*, July 14, 1980, 67.
42. Mustafa Ameen, 2020.
43. Rich Hoffman, *Philadelphia Daily News*, October 2, 1980, 78.
44. Mustafa Ameen, 2020.

Chapter 9

1. Tom Cushman, *Philadelphia Daily News*, April 18, 1979, 71.
2. Bilal Muhammad, 2021.
3. *Jet*, December 25, 1980, 50.
4. Bilal Muhammad, 2021.
5. Mustafa Ameen, 2020.
6. Jimmie Angelopolous, *Indianapolis News*, July 12, 1978, 34.

7. Steve Farhood, *KO*, December 1980, 27.
8. Lewis Freedman, *Philadelphia Inquirer*, November 28, 1980, 25.
9. Dave Distel, *Los Angeles Times*, November 28, 1980, 11.
10. Lewis Freedman, *Philadelphia Inquirer*, November 29, 1980, 21.
11. Pat Putnam, *Sports Illustrated*, February 9, 1981.
12. *Ibid.*
13. Thom Greer, *New York Daily News*, February 28, 1981, 284.
14. *Jet*, February 26, 1981, 13.
15. Tom Cushman, *Philadelphia Daily News*, February 20, 1981, 87.
16. Vic Ziegel, *New York Magazine*, March 2, 1981, 48.
17. George Govlik, *The Courier News*, February 27, 1981, 28.
18. Tris Dixon, *RingTV.com*, January 23, 2020.
19. AP, *Clarion-Ledger*, February 28, 1981, 23.
20. Ruth Bonapace, *Courier News*, February 27, 1981, 28.
21. Rich Hofmann, *Philadelphia Daily News*, February 26, 1981, 53.
22. Lewis Freedman, *Philadelphia Inquirer*, February 28, 1991, 21.
23. Tom Cushman, *Philadelphia Daily News*, February 20, 1981, 87.
24. *Ibid.*
25. *Ibid.*
26. *Ibid.*
27. Rich Hoffman, *Philadelphia Daily News*, March 27, 1981, 83.
28. Lewis Freedman, *Philadelphia Inquirer*, March 1, 1981, 1D.
29. https://www.youtube.com/watch?v=r1zGrwcvgMc&t=2080s
30. Rich Hofmann, *Philadelphia Daily News*, March 2, 1981, 56.
31. *Ibid.*
32. *Ibid.*
33. *Ibid.*

Chapter 10

1. Chuck Slater, *New York Daily News*, April 19, 1981, 234.
2. Tom Cushman, *Philadelphia Daily News*, April 22, 1981, 71.
3. Chuck Slater, *New York Daily News*, April 19, 1981, 234.
4. Paul Domowitch, *Philadelphia Daily News*, August 6, 1982, 92.
5. Nigel Collins, *Ring*, July 1981, 20.
6. Tom Cushman, *Philadelphia Daily News*, April 22, 1981, 71.
7. Nigel Collins, *Ring*, July 1981, 20.
8. Like Matthew, Rodney was in trouble with the law in his youth. He and three other boys were charged with burglary, vandalism, conspiracy, and violation of curfew and remanded to the Youth Study Center in August 1965, about two years before Matt was there. Jim Cartin and Tom Fox, *Philadelphia Daily News*, August 18, 1965, 4.
9. Mustafa Ameen, 2021.
10. Rich Hofmann, *Philadelphia Daily News*, April 15, 1981, 62.
11. Rich Hofmann, *Philadelphia Daily News*, April 24, 1981, 85.
12. *Ibid.*
13. *Ibid.*
14. Tom Cushman, *Philadelphia Daily News*, April 22, 1981, 71.
15. Danny Robbins, *Philadelphia Inquirer*, April 26, 1981, 45.
16. Rich Hofmann, *Philadelphia Daily News*, April 24, 1981, 85.
17. Phill Marder, *Courier Post*, April 26, 1981, 17.
18. https://www.youtube.com/watch?v=leNsp43bYVU
19. Phill Marder, *Courier Post*, April 26, 1981, 17.
20. Danny Robbins, *Philadelphia Inquirer*, April 26, 1981, 52.
21. Phill Marder, *Courier Post*, April 26, 1981, 17.
22. Michael Katz, *New York Times*, September 26, 1981, 18.
23. AP, *Poughkeepsie Journal*, May 1, 1981, 42.
24. Members of the Loach family declined to be interviewed for this book.
25. Michelle LeViege, October 2020.
26. *Ibid.*
27. Paul Trace, 2020.
28. Bilal Muhammad, 2022.
29. Paul Trace, 2020.
30. Ellen Kaye, *Philadelphia Inquirer*, February 14, 1982, 23, 24.
31. *Ibid.*
32. Zakiyyah Mitchell, 2021.
33. Stan Hochman, *Philadelphia Daily News*, September 22, 1981, 67.

34. Lewis Freedman, *Philadelphia Inquirer*, September 9, 1981, 30.
35. *Ibid.*
36. Stan Hochman, *Philadelphia Daily News*, September 22, 1981, 67.
37. *Ibid.*
38. Stan Hochman, *Philadelphia Daily News*, September 16, 1981, 69.
39. Bilal Muhammad, 2022.
40. Stan Hochman, *Philadelphia Daily News*, September 22, 1981, 67.
41. Tom Cushman, *Philadelphia Daily News*, July 21, 1980, 68.
42. Lewis Freedman, *Philadelphia Inquirer*, September 24, 1981, 68.
43. *Ibid.*
44. Lewis Freedman, *Philadelphia Inquirer*, September 25, 1981, 29.
45. *Ibid.*
46. Lewis Freedman, *Philadelphia Inquirer*, September 27, 1981, 11-D.
47. Rich Hofmann, *Philadelphia Daily News*, September 28, 1981, 60.
48. Lewis Freedman, *Philadelphia Inquirer*, November 28, 1981, 28.
49. https://www.youtube.com/watch?v=AqPGHQnA4QA&t=11s
50. Bill Lyon, *Philadelphia Inquirer*, September 27, 1981, 43.
51. Lewis Freedman, *Philadelphia Inquirer*, September 27, 1981, 11-D.
52. Rich Hofmann, *Philadelphia Daily News*, September 28, 1981, 60.

Chapter 11

1. Stan Hochman, *Philadelphia Daily News*, September 22, 1981, 67.
2. Lewis Freedman, *Philadelphia Inquirer*, September 25, 1981, 29.
3. Rich Hofmann, *Philadelphia Daily News*, March 30, 1981, 50.
4. Rich Hofmann, *Philadelphia Daily News*, November 9, 1981, 60.
5. Mustafa Ameen, 2021.
6. Bilal Muhammad said in 2021 that he turned down Lewis because he was offering just $1 million for Matt to Spinks's $4 million. This seems unlikely given that Spinks and Braxton later fought for a 50-50 split of a $4 million, essentially the same deal Ameen confirmed.
7. Mark Whicker, *Philadelphia Daily News*, March 3, 1983, 75.
8. Pat Putnam, *Sports Illustrated*, December 28, 1991.
9. *Ibid.*
10. Tony Green, 2021.
11. Gary Smith, *Philadelphia Daily News*, June 6, 1980, 99.
12. *Vancouver Sun*, February 10, 1983, 67.
13. Mark Whicker, *Philadelphia Daily News*, March 3, 1983, 75.
14. Jack McCallum, *Sports Illustrated*, August 8, 1992.
15. In November 1981, Coruzzi was arrested on the steps of the Camden County Courthouse carrying $12,000 in marked bills. He was charged with bribery and conspiracy and, in March 1982, was convicted and sentenced to five years in prison for accepting $47,000 in bribes in exchange for handing out lenient sentences.
16. Pat Putnam, *Sports Illustrated*, December 28, 1991.
17. Lewis Freedman, *Philadelphia Inquirer*, March 5, 1981, 5.
18. Rich Hofmann, *Philadelphia Daily News*, March 6, 1981, 79.
19. Lewis Freedman, *Philadelphia Inquirer*, June 1, 1981, 17.
20. Lewis Freedman, *Philadelphia Inquirer*, September 5, 1981, 27.
21. Paul Trace, *KO Magazine*, 2021.
22. Mustafa Ameen, 2021.
23. Steve Farhood, *KO*, June 1982, 58.
24. Pat Putnam, *Sports Illustrated*, December 28, 1991.
25. Mark Whicker, *Philadelphia Daily News*, March 3, 1983, 75.
26. https://www.youtube.com/watch?v=f0tXbPTV7cM&t=13s
27. Paul Trace, 2021.
28. Michael Katz, *New York Daily News*, November 16, 1986, 156.

Chapter 12

1. Rich Hofmann, *Philadelphia Daily News*, December 21, 1981, 71.
2. *Ibid.*
3. *Ibid.*
4. Michael Katz, *New York Times*, April 11, 1982, section 5, 8.
5. *Ibid.*
6. Lewis Freedman, *Philadelphia Inquirer*, December 21, 1981, 33.

7. Thom Greer, *Philadelphia Inquirer*, April 15, 1982, 49.
8. *Ibid.*
9. Tom Cushman, *Philadelphia Daily News*, February 10, 1978, 84.
10. Emilie Lounsberry, *Philadelphia Inquirer*, November 24, 1987, 13.
11. Dan Meyers and Edward Power, *Philadelphia Inquirer*, November 24, 1987, 12.
12. Paul Domowitch, *Philadelphia Daily News*, August 4, 1982, 66.
13. Saleem El-Amin, 2021.
14. Paul Domowitch, *Philadelphia Daily News*, August 4, 1982, 66.
15. Steve Farhood, *KO*, June 1982, 59.
16. *Ibid.*
17. Michael Katz, *New York Times*, April 11, 1982, section 5, 8.
18. Ray Didinger, *Philadelphia Daily News*, March 22, 1982, 75.
19. Rich Hofmann, *Philadelphia Daily News*, March 17, 1983, 86.
20. Rich Hofmann, *Philadelphia Daily News*, April 19, 1982, 74.
21. Thom Greer, *Philadelphia Inquirer*, April 18, 1982, 8E.
22. Bill Lyon, *Philadelphia Inquirer*, April 18, 1982, 62.
23. Michael Katz, *New York Times*, August 6, 1982, 27.
24. Bill Lyon, *Philadelphia Daily News*, August 7, 1982, 43.
25. AP, *Courier News*, August 7, 1982, 34.
26. Bill Verigan, *New York Daily News*, August 8, 1982, 79.
27. https://www.youtube.com/watch?v=SvMz8DWCxyg
28. Thom Greer, *Philadelphia Inquirer*, August 9, 1982, 28.
29. Thom Greer, *Philadelphia Inquirer*, August 8, 1982, 62.
30. Paul Domowitch, *Philadelphia Daily News*, August 9, 1982, 60.
31. Thom Greer, *Philadelphia Inquirer*, August 9, 1982, 28.
32. Marc Markowitz, *Morning Call*, August 9, 1982, 21.
33. Paul Domowitch, *Philadelphia Daily News*, August 9, 1982, 60.
34. Marc Markowitz, *Morning Call*, August 9, 1982, 21.
35. *Ibid.*

Chapter 13

1. Wes Moon, *Asbury Park Press*, March 24, 1983, 41.
2. https://www.youtube.com/watch?v=vVQyalXZ7jg&t=9s
3. https://www.youtube.com/watch?v=vVQyalXZ7jg
4. Tom Mahon, *Philadelphia Daily News*, March 24, 1983, 74.
5. Dick Young, *Asbury Park Press*, August 27, 1983, 23.
6. Tom Mahon, *Philadelphia Daily News*, March 24, 1983, 74.
7. *Ibid.*
8. Phill Marder, *Courier Post*, March 24, 1983, 32.
9. *Ibid.*
10. Charles Seaton, *New York Daily News*, September 10, 1983, 145.
11. Mike Bruton, *Philadelphia Inquirer*, February 11, 1984, 43.
12. *Ibid.*
13. *Ibid.*
14. *Ibid.*
15. Elmer Smith, *Philadelphia Daily News*, February 13, 1984, 78.
16. Mike Bruton, *Philadelphia Inquirer*, February 12, 1984, 61.
17. Clifton Brown, *Detroit Free Press*, February 12, 1984, 48.
18. Elmer Smith, *Philadelphia Daily News*, February 13, 1984, 78.

Chapter 14

1. UPI, *Atlanta Constitution*, November 26, 1981, 141.
2. *St. Louis Dispatch*, September 18, 1988, 30.
3. Dick Young, *Burlington Free Press*, October 20, 1984, 18.
4. Mustafa Ameen, 2021.
5. John Schulian, *Philadelphia Daily News*, February 21, 1985, 74.
6. Ira Winderman, *Sun Sentinel*, January 8, 1986.
7. Mike Bruton, *Philadelphia Inquirer*, May 7, 1985, 37.
8. Stuart Ditzen, *Philadelphia Inquirer*, June 14, 1985, 33.
9. *Jet*, August 12, 1985, 16.
10. Stuart Ditzen, *Philadelphia Inquirer*, June 14, 1985, 33.
11. AP, *Post-Crescent*, June 16, 1985, 48.

12. Several sources told me that Bilal borrowed a large sum of money from Matt during the title reign and never paid it back. Matt told me this himself as well during an interview I conducted with him in 2004. Bilal denied owing Matt anything.
13. Bilal Muhammad, 2021.
14. Michelle LeViege-Cortija, 2021.
15. AP, *Asbury Park Press*, June 3, 1986, 63.
16. Derrick Hinmon, *Courier News*, May 6, 1987, 27.
17. Tony DeMarco, *Miami Herald*, January 8, 1986, 160.
18. Joseph Tintle, *Ring*, August 1990, 25.
19. In 1986, Vasta was arrested and charged as the kingpin of a narcotics ring after authorities found $5.6 million in cash in a house he owned in Mineola. They also found 13 pounds of heroin, 14 pounds of cocaine, 7 weapons, and various narcotics paraphernalia including an elaborate heroin-cutting mill.
20. Michael Katz, *New York Daily News*, December 15, 1985, 92.
21. Tony DeMarco, *Miami Herald*, January 8, 1986, 160.
22. Ira Winderman, *Sun Sentinel*, January 8, 1986, 25.
23. Tribune Wires, *Tampa Tribune*, January 12, 1986, 63.
24. *Fort Lauderdale News*, February 21, 1986, 28.
25. *Fort Lauderdale News*, February 22, 1986, 38.
26. Elaine Austin, *Philadelphia Daily News*, 2021.
27. AP, *New York Daily News*, November 1, 1987, 2.
28. Bernard Fernandez, *Philadelphia Daily News*, August 16, 1988, 74.
29. *Ibid.*, 75.
30. Bruce Keidan, *Pittsburgh Post-Gazette*, February 14, 1989, 8.
31. Joseph Tintle, *Ring*, August 1990, 25.
32. Robert Seltzer, *Philadelphia Inquirer*, November 28, 1990, 38.
33. Joseph Tintle, *Ring*, August 1990, 25.
34. Robert Seltzer, *Philadelphia Inquirer*, November 28, 1990, 38.
35. Robert Seltzer, *Philadelphia Inquirer*, December 5, 1990, 41.
36. Robert Seltzer, *Philadelphia Inquirer*, February 20, 1991, 7C.
37. *Ibid.*
38. *Ibid.*
39. Robert Seltzer, *Philadelphia Inquirer*, February 27, 1991, 39.
40. Bernard Fernandez, *Philadelphia Daily News*, February 27, 1991, 66.
41. Robert Seltzer, *Philadelphia Inquirer*, March 6, 1991, 43.
42. Tokyo Rosenthal, *New York Daily News*, 2021.
43. Ron Borges, *Boston Globe*, November 3, 1991, 54.
44. Michael Katz, *New York Daily News*, October 31, 1991, 90.
45. Bernard Fernandez, *Philadelphia Daily News*, June 11, 1998, 68.

Chapter 15

1. Tim Whitaker, *Philadelphia Magazine*, July 26, 2011.
2. Bill Grady, *Daily World*, November 24, 1995, 23.
3. Ray Chmelowitz, 2021.
4. AP, *The Times*, November 23, 1995, 27.
5. Jose Espinosa, *One Step Away*, July 2010.
6. AP, *The Times*, November 23, 1995, 27.
7. Michael Katz, *New York Daily News*, 335.
8. Mike Hall, *Albuquerque Journal*, June 18, 1996, 27.
9. *Ibid.*
10. Shawn Darling, 2021.
11. Larry Tornambe, 2021.
12. Shawn Darling, 2021.
13. *Ibid.*
14. *Tampa Bay Times*, March 31, 1995, 43.
15. Shawn Darling, 2021.
16. Rich Hofmann, *New York Daily News*, July 9, 2010, 85.
17. Phil Sheridan, *Philadelphia Inquirer*, July 9, 2010, C01.
18. Rich Hofmann, July 9, 2010, 85.
19. Jose Espinosa, *One Step Away*, July 2010.
20. Larry Tornambe knew Matt had been in the hospital in 2013, but "no one would tell me why and Matt wouldn't go into it," Tornambe said in 2021.
21. Zakiyyah Mitchell, 2020.
22. Larry Tornambe, 2021.
23. Mustafa Ameen, 2021.

Bibliography

Books

Collins, Nigel. *Boxing Babylon: Behind the Shadowy World of the Prize Ring.* Secaucus, NJ: Carol, 1990.

DiSanto, John, and Matthew Ward. *Boxing in Atlantic City.* Charleston, SC: Arcadia, 2021.

Mullan, Harry. *The Illustrated History of Boxing.* New York: Hamlyn, 1997.

Peltz, J Russell. *Thirty Dollars and a Cut Eye: 50 Years in Boxing.* Philadelphia: New Book Authors, 2021.

Weston, Stanley, ed. *Ring: Boxing in the 20th Century.* Illus. by Steve Farhood. New York: BDD Illustrated Books, 1993.

Interviews

Mustafa Ameen
Elaine Austin
Nick Belfiore Jr.
Ray Chmelowitz
Nigel Collins
Shawn Darling
Saleem El-Amin
Eddie Everett
Steve Farhood
Frank Gelb
Tony Green
Steven C. Gurley
Matthew LeViege
Michael LeViege
Michelle LeViege-Cortijo
Zakiyyah Mitchell
Bilal Muhammad
J Russell Peltz
Zac Pomillo
Tokyo Rosenthal
Aaron Snowell
Larry Tornambe
Paul Trace
Rose Trentman

Magazines

Jet
KO
New York Magazine
One Step Away
Philadelphia Magazine
The Ring
Sports Illustrated

Newspapers

Albuquerque Journal
Asbury Park Press
Atlanta Constitution
Boston Globe
Burlington Free Press
Chicago Tribune
Clarion-Ledger
Courier News
Courier Post
Crowley Post-Signal
Daily American
Daily Journal
Daily Record
Daily World
Detroit Free Press
El Paso Times
Evening Sun
Fort Lauderdale News
The Guardian
Herald News
Home News
Indianapolis News

Indianapolis Star
Los Angeles Times
Miami Herald
Millville Daily
Missoulian
Morning Call
Morning News
New York Daily News
New York Times
News Journal
One Step Away
Philadelphia Daily News
Philadelphia Inquirer
Pittsburgh Post-Gazette
Post-Crescent
Poughkeepise Journal
The Record
Sacramento Bee
St. Louis Dispatch
Sun Sentinel
Tampa Bay Times
Tampa Tribune
The Times
Times Tribune
Tribune
Vancouver Sun

Index

Abner, Perry 27
Adams, Robert 21
Ahumada, Jorge 86
Alexader, Sandra 87
Alexandria, Virginia 51
Ali, Muhammad 67, 69, 70, 78, 82, 83, 86, 92, 93, 95, 96, 99, 102, 103, 109, 110, 112–115, 120, 125, 131, 162
Ali, Veronica 69, 102, 112
Aliano, Eddie 14, 98
Ameen, Mustafa 94, 101–103, 110, 111, 118, 123, 124, 131, 133, 140, 144, 145, 162, 168, 185, 192
Andries, Dennis 176
Annunciation Boys Club 21
Antonetti, Joe 33
Antuofermo, Vito 35, 36
Apolosa, Mukeba 27, 28
Arcadia Gym 21
Arum, Bob 67, 69, 90, 99, 108, 109, 110, 111, 167, 188,
Ayella, Alfred 54, 55

Bailey, Milt 27, 94, 136,
Ballard, Jody 95, 117, 132
Ballard PAL 21
Barr, Johnny 23
Barr, Sammy 44
Basilio, Carmen 26
Belfiore, Joe 16–18, 21, 23
Belfiore, Nick 15–23, 26, 27, 29, 30, 32–34, 38, 43, 46, 48, 49, 55–57, 62, 63, 66, 68, 76, 78, 80, 83, 84, 86–88, 90–92, 94, 98, 99, 152, 166
Belfiore, Nick, Jr. 16, 19,
Bennett, Lonnie 65, 73, 85
Benton, George 92, 93, 94
Beresin Gym 21
Bernadine, Sister 10
Berry, William "Red" 39
Bethea, Bob 29

Blackburn, Jack 92
Blome, Bob 33
Blue Horizon 22, 26, 29, 39
Bok Vocational Technical High School 42
Bonavena, Oscar 85
Bossung, Richard 83
Bott, Markus 176
Bowman, Fred 127
Boyce, Elmer 30, 31, 33, 34
Braxton, Dwight (aka Dwight Muhammad Qawi) 135, 139, 140, 153, 154, 178, 192
Bright, Freddie 69
Briscoe, Bennie 26–28, 37, 44, 45, 48, 51, 84, 92, 93, 151, 155, 174
Brown, Harry "Kid" 24
Brown, Roosevelt 30
Brownsville, Brooklyn 35
Brownsville Community Center 35
Bryan, James 7
Bucceroni Gym 21
Burnett, Jesse 73, 74, 86, 112, 134

Camel, Marvin 30–34, 37, 153, 161
Camp Hill 13, 14, 20, 80, 147, 167
Campbell, Ray 59
Canada, Nova Scotia 5
Cappuccino, Frank 67, 76
Carbrera, Radames 36
Carlis, Edgar 12, 14
Carmody, John 182
Carter, Harold 30
Carter, Pres. Jimmy 76
Carter, Rubin 14
Cassidy, Bobby 51
Catholic Social Services 10
Celestine, Jerry 101, 116, 134
Chavers, Govoner 178
Chisholm, Larry 23
Christodolou, Stanley 60

205

Cisco, Hank 31, 54, 55
Clancy, Gil 112, 119, 126
Clark, Jimmy 22
Clayton, Zach 163
Cline, Chris 50
Cloverlay Gym 21
Cobbs Creek PAL 21
Coccaro, Bonnie 59
Coccaro, Tony 59, 60
Cohen, Nessim 36
Cokes, Curtis 50, 51
Collins, Joe 27
Collins, Nigel 40, 48, 87
Collins, Tom 176
Columbus, Ohio 50
Conteh, John 31, 65, 73, 77, 78, 84–91, 96–100, 105, 125, 127, 131, 167
Coruzzi, Peter J. 142
Cosell, Howard 52, 53
Costi, Jimmy 16
Crawford, Mary Lou 33
Crawford, Tim 103, 170
Cruz, Jack 73
Cuello, Miguel 86
Curley, Angelo 50
Cutler, Marilyn 131

Daniel Boone School 12, 13, 80, 167
Daniels Athletic Club 23
Darling, Shawn 184–189
Davis, Chuck 21, 22
DeFabis, George 81
Din Ali, Imam Shamsud 95
DiPiano, Jimmy 64, 65, 68, 71, 75
DiSanto, John 53
Doran, Pat 176
Dore, Art 127
Douglas, Billy 29, 49, 50–58, 61, 62, 74, 75, 108, 121, 134, 167
Duff, Mickey 99, 112
Duffy, Pat 24–27, 29, 44
Duncan, Eddie 98
Dundee, Angelo 51, 84, 91, 96, 116, 117, 119, 132, 140, 163
Dundee, Chris 24
Dupree, Rodell 127
Duran, Roberto 52, 97
Durham, Yank 14, 49–51

Eastside Gym 21
Edwards, Marvin 23
Edwards, Willie 165–168, 170
El-Amin, Saleem 13, 14, 94, 136, 152, 162
Elbaum, Don 35
Ellis, Jimmy 97
English, Obie 45

Escalera, Alfredo 34, 41
Evans, Alfonso 11, 14, 21, 29, 39, 40, 41
Evans, Peter G. 6, 7
Everett, Mike 21, 26, 42
Everett, Tyrone 26, 29, 34, 40, 42, 52

Farhood, Steve 101, 149, 152
Father Brown 12
Feldman, Marty 25
Ferrera, Chickie 36
Ferriola, Nick 17
Fifth Street Gym 96
Finnegan, Chris 85
Fischetti, Al 36
Flathead Indian Reservation 30
Folsom Street 8
Foreman, George 24
Foster, Bob 33, 34, 150
Francis, George 88, 89, 98, 112
Francisville, Philadelphia 7, 12
Frankford PAL 21
Franklin, Rashida 23
Franklin, Sheena 23
Frazier, Joe 14, 49, 78, 85, 103, 109, 141
Free, Lloyd 36
Freeman, Billy 29
Fullmer, Don 50
Fullmer, Gene 26
Futch, Eddie 49

Gagliardi, Joe 31
Galíndez, Victor 31, 44, 45, 48, 57, 60–64, 66, 67, 70 73, 74, 76, 78, 87, 99, 106, 142
Gavilan, Kid 14
Gelb, Frank 29–35, 40–43, 49, 52, 56, 58, 60, 63, 64, 66, 67, 69, 83, 84, 86, 90, 91, 99
Gholston, Joe 45
Giardello, Joey 14, 65, 84, 85, 174
Gibbs, Harry 89
Goodman, Bobby 178
Goodman, Eddie 27
Goodman, Jesse 169
Goss, Sammy 25
Gramby, Joe 59, 60, 145
Grant, Dale 56, 67, 68
Grant, Uriah 173
Graziano, Gino 21
Great Migration 7
Gregory, Eddie (aka Mustafa Muhammad) 35–40, 42, 43, 45, 69, 70, 74, 76, 99, 100, 101, 104, 105, 108, 109, 111, 113–115, 117, 120, 134, 139, 142, 146, 157, 158, 161, 164, 175, 176
Gunner, Roberta 5, 7–9, 12

Index

Hahnemann Hospital 12
Hall, Ray 29
Harding, Jeff 176
Hardney, "Wild" Bill 40
Harnish, Max 166, 167
Hart, Eugene "Cyclone" 35, 36, 92, 192
Hartman, David 128
Hayes, Jimmy 52, 63, 75, 79, 86, 88, 91
Haynes, Bobby 59
Hayward, Kitten 85
Hazzard, Larry 136–138, 177
Hearns, Thomas 114, 162, 165–167, 174, 176
Hennelly Boys Club 21
Hill, Virgil 173
Holmes, Larry 102, 110, 117, 150, 162, 183
Hutchins, Len 85

Ingram, Roy 27

Jackson, Harold 77
James, the Rev. Horace 6
James City 5–7, 12
Jenkintown, Pennsylvania 97, 102, 129, 131, 164, 165, 168, 171
Johnson, Vonzell 30, 115, 118, 121, 122, 126, 127, 140, 153, 154
Johnson, Willie 96
Jones, Anthony 78
Jones, Joe 27
Judge, Jerry 30
Juniper Gym 14, 15, 17, 19–22, 49, 66, 68, 86, 90, 146, 151

Kane, Bob 52
Kates, Richie 31, 58, 59–66, 74, 75, 101, 108, 121, 124, 145, 154, 157, 167
Kenville, Tommy 66
Kid, Virgil 21
King, Carl 83
King, Don 35, 40, 50, 52, 83, 110, 115, 133, 141, 144, 149, 153, 187
Knoxville, Tennessee 99
Koopmans, Rudi 111, 113, 114

Lambast Athletic Club 17
Laurel Athletic Club 21
Lee, Robert W. 161
LeViege, Michelle 112, 118, 129, 130
LeViege, Sam 129
Lewis, Benjamin 114
Lewis, Butch 92, 93, 140, 145, 149
Liston, Sonny 14, 21, 92
Lloyd, Bill 51
Loach, Andrea 128, 129
Loach, Bessie 8

Loach, Daniel 8
Loach, Desiree 128, 129
Loach, Frances 128, 129
Loach, Helen 8 9, 12
Loach, Henrietta (2) 8, 9, 12
Loach, Henrietta 5, 8–9
Loach, Henry 8
Loach, Nathaniel 5, 7
Loach, Rodney 123, 124, 128, 129
Loach, Rosa 5
Loach, Shade 5
Loach, Willie 5, 7–8, 12
Lopez, Alvaro "Yaqui" 31, 65, 69, 70–76, 79, 101, 104–108, 111, 121, 153, 154, 167, 192
Luca, Frank 126, 127

Mack, Ed 177
Major, David 12
Mangone, Pete 23
MAPS 110, 111, 114, 115
Marciano, Rocky 85
Martin, Jerry 104, 105, 108, 109, 115, 132–140, 153, 154, 166, 177
Martin, Leotis 25
Martini, Tony 17
Matthews, Len 26
Maye, Joe 40
Maynard, Andrew 179
McCall, Howard 83
McCall, Quenzell 27, 155, 159
McClain, Bernard 78
McClure, Kelsey 48
McFarland, Billy 33
McGarvey, Ronnie 29
McGee, Wayne 28–30, 44, 56, 155
McIntyre, Pete 117, 153, 154, 162, 163, 165
McKendrick, Carolyn 41
Merchant, Larry 157
Meyran, Octavio 98
Miami Beach 51
Micelli, Joe 17
Mid-Atlantic Gym 21
Middleton, Joe 27
Millville Athletic Club 21
Milton, Chuck 66
Mitchell, Shirley 69, 131
Moncrief, James 22
Monroe, Willie "The Worm" 29
Montana 30
Missoula, Montana 31
Montana, University of 32
Montgomery, Mike 21
Moorer, Michael 174
Morgano, Tony 15–17

Morton, Janks 91, 162, 163, 165, 166
Mouzon, Wesley 156
Moyer, Denny 51
Mtume, James 131
Muhammad, Akbar 69, 87, 187, 188,
Muhammad, Bilal Sayyid 69, 81, 84, 86, 87, 90, 91, 94, 95, 97, 98, 104, 111, 114, 115, 118, 124, 130–133, 140, 143–147, 149, 150, 152, 153, 162–164, 167, 171, 187, 188
Muhammad, Murad 69, 70, 115, 116, 131, 133, 143, 144, 145, 150, 153, 155, 156
Mundine, Tony 27, 56, 153
Murphey, Matilda 5
Mwale, Lottie 111–114, 119, 130, 132, 170

Negro, Jennie (Belfiore) 16, 19, 22
Nelson, Lloyd 29
Neuse River 6
New Bern 6
Newark, New Jersey 50, 69
Newman, Rock 153, 154, 156, 179
North Carolina 6
Norton, Ken 69, 114, 115, 125

Ocean City Boxing Club 21
Ocean City Boys Club 21
O'Day, Sonny 33
Olive Street 8
Olympia Gym 21
Orange, Texas 50
Owens, Eddie 60

Padilla, Carlos 88, 89, 157
Parker, Danny 21
Parlov, Mate 30, 31, 34, 37, 63, 64, 65, 76, 77, 86
Parodi, Gus 40
Passyunk Gym 14, 21, 26, 68, 70, 85
Patrick, Clinton 35
Pelc, Gene 179
Peltz, J Russell 26–30, 42, 44, 45, 48, 49, 51–54, 57, 61, 64, 65, 67–69, 71, 77, 142, 181, 192
Perez, Isidro 127
Pergaud, Louis 99, 100, 104, 105, 112, 119
Petway, Letty 59, 61
Price, Tyrone 41

Quarry, Mike 65, 96

Rahway State Prison 70, 101, 115, 134, 141, 142, 143
Ramon, Rocky 42
Randolph, Willie 36
Red Summer 8

Reddish, Willie Jr. 21
Reid, Tommy 37, 38
Rhodes, Herb 38
Riggio, Jimmy 14
Righetti, Alfio 93
Ringo, Ken 117
Ritacco, Adolph 84, 85, 88–90, 97, 98, 105, 126, 132, 136, 146, 147, 158, 162
Rizzo PAL 21
Roanoke Island 6
Roberts, Leroy 29
Robinson, Leon 22
Robinson, Luke 21
Robinson, Sugar Ray 25
Robles, Rudy 31
Rodriguez, Luis 51
Rosa, Mario 36
Ross, Tom 38
Rossman, Mike 64, 65, 68, 69–72, 74, 76, 78, 84, 96, 97, 99, 125, 134, 142, 181, 182, 192
Royster, Lee "Junior" 56–58
Rubin, Harry 66, 67, 69, 83, 91

Sabbatini, Rodolfo 44
Saddler, Ozzie 47
Saint Gabriel's Hall 11
St. Luke's Hospital 12
Sams, Tim 95, 118
Samson, Kid 78
San Antonio, Texas 40
Santos, Bertha 10, 97
Santos, John (Pop) 10–11, 23, 95, 97, 184
Saxton, Johnny 14
Schafer, Pinny 24–27, 29
Schenkel, Chris 100
Schmidt, Waldemar 108
Schwartz, Hank 35
Sciacca, Frank 161
Scorcia, Joe 36, 37
Scott, James 56, 70, 101, 104, 115, 134, 143
Scranton, Pennsylvania 31
Scranton Youth Center 31
Seales, "Sugar" Ray 67
Seldon, Bruce 177
Seven Champs Gym 21
Sgrillo, Charlie 62, 63, 64
Shabazz, Lana 95, 123, 131
Shah, Yusef 95
Sharif, Wayne 95, 118
Shea, Jimmy 33
Singer, Jack 36
Singleton, Charlie 96
Sirb, Greg 177
Smith, Bob 68, 69

Smith, Harold (aka Ross Fields) 109, 114, 162, 188
Smith, Red 85
Snider, Eddie 53
Solomon, Sam 91–94, 96–98, 100, 103, 105, 107, 111, 112, 115, 117–120, 126, 132, 142, 143, 145–147, 150, 152, 162, 166, 169, 170, 172–174
Soo, Jimmy 25
South Africa, Johannesburg 31
Southside Boys Club 16, 21
Spina, Charlie 89, 127
Spinks, Leon 67, 69, 92, 103, 139
Stanley, Jack 16
Steward, Emanuel 162, 174, 175
Stockton, California 30
Sulaiman, Jose 98
Swain Street 8
Swindell, Frankie 175
Sydenham Street 12

Tabbs, Leon 134, 135, 137
Taylor, Elaine 169, 175, 176, 181, 182, 183, 184
Temple, Steve 23
Terrell, Ernie 14, 92
Tiger, Dick 36, 84
Tillis, James "Quick" 97
Tornambe, Larry 185, 190–192
Trace, Paul 95, 120, 129, 130, 135, 136, 143, 144, 147, 185, 192
Traitz, Steve 77, 150, 151, 152, 154, 156, 158, 159, 162, 166, 181
Trampler, Bruce 50, 51
Traversaro, Aldo 76
Tree, Lou 34
Trent River 6
Tureaud, Lawrence 93, 103
Turner, Ed "Savage" 42
Turner, Gil 21, 25
Turnersville, New Jersey 64
23rd Street PAL 21
Tyrone Everett Memorial Scholarship Fund 42

Upper Darby Junior High 22
Upper Darby PYA 21

Valan, Harold 92
Vaughn, Loach Tondylea 128
Venti, Paul 127
Vinson, Karl 30, 31
Viruet, Edwin 52

Walcott, "Jersey Joe" 89, 90, 108, 127, 163
Walker, Bobby 31
Walker, Matt 83
Warfield, Chuck 69
Watts, Bobby "Boogaloo" 25, 51, 84, 192
Weichers, Ed 22
Weiss, Arnold 27, 29, 44, 45
Wepner, Chuck 92
White, Cash 174, 175
White, John Harold 9
Williams, Dell 116
Williams, Fly 36
Williams, James 21
Williamson, J.B. 77
Willingboro, New Jersey 22
Wilmington, Delaware 40
Winbush, Eric 161–165, 174
Witherspoon, Tim 95, 192
Wolgast, Midget 24
Woods, Vandell 29
World War I 7

Young, Ann 122
Young, Jimmy 25, 29

www.ingramcontent.com/pod-product-compliance
Lightning Source LLC
Chambersburg PA
CBHW030622230426
43661CB00053B/2111